The

ARE YOU AFRAID OF THE DARK?

Campfire Companion

by Jose Prendes

Published in the USA by:
BearManor Media
P O Box 71426
Albany, Georgia 31708
www.bearmanormedia.com

Printed in the United States of America

ISBN   978-1-59393-989-2 (paperback)

Book & cover design and layout by Darlene Swanson • www.van-garde.com
Photo on cover by Jonathan Wenk

For Abby & Remy, two new members to the Midnight Society, who plan to keep the campfire burning.

"We're called the Midnight Society. Separately, we're very different, we like different things. We go to different schools, and we have different friends. But one thing draws us together . . . the dark. Each week, we gather around this fire to share our fears and our strange and scary tales. It's what got us together and it's what keeps bringing us back. This is a warning to all who join us. You're going to leave the comfort of the light and step into the world of the supernatural."

~ Gary's introduction for Episode 1.

CONTENTS

ACKNOWLEDGMENTS

This book was a labor of love, but a monumental challenge, and one that would not have been possible without the support and assistance of the following amazing individuals, which I thank from the bottom of my scare-loving heart:

D. J. MacHale, for the support, openness, and his kindness to a fan. His involvement opened doors for me, and frankly this whole thing would not have been possible if he hadn't have thought of the show.

Ross Hull and Jason Alisharan, for caring about the fans who remember them as kids, and for their willingness to share their time with me for the book.

Ron Oliver and David Winning, two directors who defined the look of the series and were nothing but gracious, lovely people who were so thrilled to be a part of this.

Jeff Fisher, a composer like no other, who shared his time with me during a very busy schedule to expound on the musicality of the series.

Ned Kandel and Paul Doyle Jr., two men responsible for steering the *AYAOTD?* ship, who were very open and willing to share their memories.

Richard Dumont, a magnificent actor who will live on in my memories, and in almost everyone else's, as the incomparable Sardo, who made certain we never lost out on a deal.

Jessica Prendes, my wife, who is my first line of defense again typos and grammatical gobbledygook, and reminds me how lucky I am.

Graham Denman, a fellow *AYAOTD?* fan, who helped me decide to really pursue a project based on our fondly remembered show.

Ben Ohmart, my publisher, who said yes immediately to my pitch for this book.

Adam Lima, an amazing artist who whipped together the official Midnight Society certificate.

To my kids, whose love reminds me I am not a failure, and whose trust reminds me I shouldn't wear a clown mask and chase them around the house.

Finally, to all the fans on the internet who worked on the wiki pages and posted random bits of info here and there and helped me fill in the blanks. This book is for you. Please keep the campfire burning wherever you are, do your best to keep the dark at bay.

FOREWORD

By D. J. MacHale

I'm not much of a clairvoyant.

Twenty five years ago, I never would have guessed that gas prices would spike to over $4 four dollars a gallon,; everyone would have a personal communicator that rivals Captain Kirk's,; or that I'd have no way of playing back my vast collection of VHS tapes.

Nor did I predict that I'd still be talking about *Are You Afraid of the Dark?*

However, one strangely accurate prediction was made back then. Before we began filming our first season, one of the creative consultants on the show, Bill Bonecutter, and I were in the wardrobe workshop staring up at a hideous seven- foot- tall carnival-clown mannequin that would be featured in one of the very first episodes. After a long moment of introspection, Bill said,: "Do you worry that twenty years from now somebody will come up to you and ask if you're D. J. MacHale, and when you say you are, he'll pull out a gun and say,: "Well I'm Zeebo the Clown! Thanks for warping my childhood!" BOOM!"

I wasn't worried at all. Not really. But a few years ago while in a restaurant a waiter asked me if I was D. J. MacHale, and when I said yes, his eyes got wide and he screamed,: "Zeebo the Clown!" Seriously. No joke. I was ready to dive under the table, fearing the second half of Bill's prophesy was about to come true.

But there was no need. The waiter simply wanted to share with me how much the show meant to him those many years ago when he had to beg his parents to let him stay up past his bedtime on Saturday nights so he could revel in the dark imaginations of a group of kids known as The Midnight Society. And he's not alone, n. Not by a long shot. I find myself answering questions about the show every day. A couple of generations have grown up with it, and new kids are finding it still. It feels like I'm talking about it more now than when we were making it. If I died tomorrow, "Are You Afraid of the Dark?" would be engraved on my tombstone—which, . Which, come to think of it, would be kind of cool.

Reading Jose Prendes' fine account of the show was like stepping into a time machine. The memories he stirred were as much about the making of the show as about the episodes themselves. Producing *Are You Afraid of the Dark?* (Or "Dark" as we called it) was the hardest I've ever worked on a project, but also the most fun and rewarding. It was a result of the combined efforts of hundreds of talented people, starting with my partner and co-creator of the show, Ned Kandel, when he asked me the fateful question: 'What Kind….'

Of course my answer was: "*Scary stories.*"

That's how it started. We didn't set out to make a "kid" show. We never talked down to our audience. As Ned once put it, our goal was to: "Write a show for adults and then cast short people." And that's pretty much how it went. We made dramas, something I feel is sorely lacking in kid's TV today. While every story had some different supernatural boogey-man to harass and confound our heroes, at the heart of every episode was a story about a young person dealing with real, relatable conflict. Their challenge was to work through their own issues, while battling frighteningly impossible supernatural situations. It's tough enough growing up; but doing it with malevolent spirits breathing down your neck makes it all a wee bit trickier.

Yes, there was humor. G, good scary stories always have comic relief, but our goal wasn't to make you laugh. It was to make you think, get you caught up in the mysteries, and creep you out a little.

Or a lot.

The beauty of making an anthology series was that we could tell all different types of stories. Some were deeply dramatic and heartfelt, others more whimsical. Some were thought-proving, others flat out scary. We worked in many genres: science fiction, fantasy, horror, supernatural, mystery, thriller, and sometimes we even went full-on monster. When you sat down at that campfire, you never knew what kind of story would be told.

And there wasn't always a happy ending.

I'm often asked what the appropriate age is for watching *Dark*. My answer is that age is irrelevant. There are seven-year-olds who aren't scared in the least . . . . . . and adults who cower behind pillows. It's all about imagination. Getting scared isn't necessarily about what you're seeing; it's about what you *think* you *might* see. If you had a rich and active imagination, we owned you, no matter what your age.

It's hard to say why *Dark* has withstood the test of time. I guess a big part of it is a feeling of nostalgia that 1990's kids have for that era. (Though to me, the 1990's were like, last week) But I believe it's more than that. A story well-told is timeless, and we had some great storytellers spinning their tales. We knew that everyone is afraid of something, whether it's an annoying sibling, a domineering teacher, an obnoxious bully, loneliness, heartbreak, alienation, or plain old injustice. We covered all the bases of tween drama . . . . . . aand then raised the stakes by throwing in supernatural villains. Our stories were about battling personal demons, as well as the ones that sprang from crypts. Ultimately, I think that's what made the show exceptional and why it's remembered so fondly . . . . . . and still watched today, all over the world.

So, we're not here to turn back the calendar. Instead, let's reach for a place that exists in the dark recesses of your mind. You know it's there. It's a place characterized by both good and evil,; by shadow and light. It's a place where ghosts, vampires, witches, aliens, and sorcerers lurk, waiting to be released. It's populated by Frozen Ghosts, Crimson Clowns, Renegade Viruses, Bookish Babysitters, Ghastly Grinners, Night Nurses, Phone Police; Silent Servants, and a Prom Queen.

You may even come across a shopkeeper named Sardo and a doctor named Vink.

There are plenty of ways to get there. You can take a Phantom Cab, ride a Shiny Red Bicycle or paddle a Dead Man's Float. You can't miss it. Take Highway 13 over Bigfoot Ridge and past Vampire Town until you enter the Watcher's Woods.

Follow the winding path through the dense forest until you come to a clearing. And a campfire. Seated around the fire, waiting for you, will be a group of familiar faces. You know them all: Andy, Betty Ann, David, Eric, Frank, Kiki, Kristen, Megan, Quinn, Samantha, Stig, Tucker, Vange, and of course . . . . . . Gary.

They're all there. Take a seat. The Midnight Society and Jose Prendes have a story for you. Let the warmth of the fire embrace you while your memory drifts toward a time and place when possibility was limited only by your imagination. It's a place where anything can happen.

Especially in the dark.

Submitted for *your* approval, I call this story: The Tale of Are You Afraid of the Dark?

D. J. MacHale,
April, 2016

OPENING CAMPFIRE: A FEAR OF THE DARK

I can remember distinctly when *Are You Afraid of the Dark?* was on my television. The eerie music from the opening sequence still shoots chills up my spine and sends me back through the years to become that teenaged boy, huddled in the dark with a bowl of popcorn and a soda by my side. These are the wonderful, candy-colored, buttered-popcorn memories I wanted to pass on to my children, and because of that need, I rediscovered the beauty of *Are You Afraid of the Dark?,* (which will be referred to as *AYAOTD?* from here on for brevity's sake).

I bought the DVDs online and watched the entire series with my six-year-old daughter. She's not a scaredy cat by nature, because growing up with a father who loves monsters and leaves the Halloween decorations up year round gets into your blood. She immediately fell in love with the series and became as big a fan as I was. I did a quick search online for details about the show and any other extra goodies, and discovered that while there was an avid fan community and a wiki page, there wasn't much written of the show beyond its years of existence.

I decided then that there was only one thing to do. I had to rectify the situation! I had to make myself an honorary member of the Midnight Society, which I felt I had earned watching the series as much as I had, and I had to put something together to reinvigorate *AYAOTD?,* to remind the fans of the wonderful, sublime pleasures of the show that taught us that a dark imagination isn't necessarily a bad thing. One thing led to another, and here we are, this book is the thing, and it's for you, the initiating Midnight Society member. Wait until you get to the end, there is a surprise waiting for you, but don't flip there just yet. Trust me. There's much to do first.

Welcome friend. Grab a seat at the campfire. It's cold out tonight.

You hold in your hands a Rosetta Stone to the mysteries of the series, a guide to its monsters and mischief, and a loving epitaph to a show that encouraged kids to find their tribe, no matter how weird. Its efforts to stimulate childhood fears in order to make kids stronger and more capable of dealing with the world at large made it not only entertaining but crucial to the creative and sociological development of most of us.

Of course, there were ups and downs in the series, as with anything long-ranging. Nothing is perfect, but nostalgia usually papers over most of the rough spots. Luckily, this show can stand on its own, and, as far as I'm concerned, still holds up today. Yeah, the 1990s wardrobe is baggy and -ridiculous looking at times. Sure, the effects can be hammy and goofball, but that doesn't take away from the impact the show had on television and its young audience, who finally got a chance to peek into the deep, dark well that Rod Serling mined and instead of being afraid of the dark, the show taught us to embrace it and understand we ultimately had the power over it.

So, come closer. Help me stoke the flames of our own campfire. It's just you and me tonight, around this crackling blaze, in the middle of the lonely woods that funnel cold breezes to raise our hairs. The clouds have parted, the rain has let up, and the ice white moon shines down on us, pushing the shadows back a few steps, giving us room to breathe in this unknown country.

Yes, hand me more of those dry leaves and those bundle of twigs there. I'll toss them into the fire to keep it fed, to keep us warm, so the shivers down our backs don't cleave us in two. Is that an owl hooting, I hear? Or a creature of the night, lurking and watching us beyond the tree line, swallowed in darkness?

It's getting late, so let's just begin, shall we?

It's my turn tonight, and boy have I got a tale to tell.

Submitted for the approval of the Midnight Society, I call this story: "The Tale of the Campfire Companion."

-Jose Prendes, August 2015

THE TALE OF SEASON ONE

Original U.S. airdate: August 15, 1992-November 14, 1992

Midnight Society Year One Roster:
Gary (Ross Hull)
Kristen (Rachel Blanchard)
Eric (Jacob Tierney)
Betty Ann (Raine Pare-Coull)
Frank (Jason Alisharan)
Kiki (Jodie Resther)
David (Nathaniel Moreau)

EPISODE 1:

"The Tale of the Phantom Cab"

U.S. Airdate: August 15, 1992

Written by: Chloe Brown

Directed by: Ron Oliver

Guest Cast: Jason Tremblay, Sean Ryan, Brian Dooley, and Aron Tager.

Favorite Line: "Nah, we didn't break the curse, you did.
Nice going. But you're still a loser."-Denny Crocker

Opening Campfire: Frank arrives blindfolded to the great and powerful campfire. He plays it cool, but he wants to join the mysterious Midnight Society. To join the group, he must tell a scary story, based upon which the group will vote to see if he's Midnight Society material.

The Tale: Denny and Buzz Crocker, two warring brothers, get lost in the woods. They soon meet the Hagrid-looking Doctor Vink, (with a va-va-va)! He can help them find their way back home, but they must first answer a riddle, failing to do so could mean their deaths.

Closing Campfire: Frank wraps up the tale by telling us that the boys brought the police back to Vink's cottage, but all they found was an old, stone foundation. Vink vanishes to fright again another day. After a brief thumbs up deliberation, Frank is officially inducted into the Midnight Society and the group is complete, at least for this freshman season. The episode wraps with the gang shaking hands with Frank, leaving the campfire conspicuously still roaring. This is, no doubt, a not-so-subtle hint that this is only the beginning.

Review: We open on a roaring campfire, the first of many. The Midnight Society is in full swing when we first meet the gang and get a Rod Serling-esque intro to not only the Midnight Society's purpose, but also the show itself. Vink's debut finds him a warlock-like hermit, who lives in the woods and has a penchant for riddles. This is a solid first episode, displaying everything the series will come to be known for, namely hapless kids and dark dilemmas that usually don't pull their punches, but offer a resolutely happy ending. Sometimes.

Series Mythology

- First appearance of Aron Tager as the memorable, recurring villain Dr. Vink.

- Frank's first and last story for Season 1.

- This episode was written by Miss Chloe Brown who, believe it or not, is actually Mister D. J. MacHale the series creator and Executive Producer.

EPISODE 2:

"The Tale of Laughing In the Dark"

U.S. Airdate: August 22, 1992

Written by: Chloe Brown

Directed by: Ron Oliver

Guest Cast: Christian Tessier, Aron Tager, Daniel Finestone, Tamar Kozlov

Favorite Line: "It's the most fun in the park, when
you're laughing in the dark!" -Carney

Opening Campfire: Only Episode 2 and the show already breaks with what will soon become tradition. The episode begins with the story already in progress. Betty Ann introduces us to the Playland carnival, which houses an infamous haunted maze known as "Laughing in the Dark", home to Zeebo the clown. We slam back to the campfire setting to discover that Kristen is not a clown fan and wants to get the heck out of there. Kiki takes a jab at her pride, and Kristen decides to face her fear and tells Betty Ann to do her worst.

The Tale: Josh wants to prove to his friends Weegee and Kathy, that there's nothing to the rumors of a ghost clown called Zeebo haunting their local fair's haunted house. He steals the big, red nose off a clown dummy in the maze and gloats that he bested Zeebo, but when the clown shows up at his house to get his nose back, Josh sings a different tune.

Closing Campfire: Kristen survived the clown story! There is some discussion on whether the Carney was Zeebo's ghost or not, but attention quickly turns to poor Kristen. Kristen sits up tall, happy to have made it to the end and not let the story scare her away. At which point, Eric dons a clown mask and chases her off into the forest. Gary adjourns the meeting with his bucket of water over the campfire and the gang follows the fleeing Kristen.

Review: This is one of those nightmare fuel episodes that are permanently ingrained in the minds of *AYAOTD?* viewers. Zeebo has become a cult figure among not only fans of this show, but those who had brief run-ins with this episode in particular. You might not remember any one episode or character, but boy you'll remember Zeebo for sure. The one moment that cracks me up about this episode the most is when Josh brings Zeebo a box of cigars. How the heck did a kid get his hands on a box of cigars? I know things aren't that lax in Canada, so this element always played funny to me.

Series Mythology

- Aron Tager, clean-shaven and with a trim haircut, appears her as the Carney. This is his one and only appearance on the show beyond the Doctor Vink character.

- Zeebo becomes a recurring character in background gags throughout the show, displaying the fact that the series as a whole existed in its own contained universe.

- Actress Tamar Kozlov will return to the series in the Season 2 episode, "The Tale of Old Man Corcoran."

EPISODE 3:

"The Tale of the Lonely Ghost"

U.S. Airdate: August 29, 1992

Written by: Naomi Janzen

Directed by: D. J. MacHale

Guest Cast: Laura Bertram, Laura Levin, Pauline Little, and Sheena Larkin

Favorite Line: "Come on, Zeeb. I'll buy you a soda to cool you off."-Frank

Opening Campfire: Kristen stumbles through the woods on her way to the campfire and runs into David. He brings her an early birthday present and they share a sweet moment. At the campfire, Eric is showing off his popcorn catching skills, but Frank douses him with water and Gary runs to the rescue to break up the fight. David and Kristen arrive and Betty Ann prompts David to start his story because the natives are getting restless.

The Tale: Amanda tries to prove to her sourpuss cousin Beth that she's not a "Zeeb" by spending a night in the abandoned house next door. Did I mention that it's haunted? Yep, the ghost of a little girl who starved in her locked bedroom resides in the house, and yes she's lonely. Thanks to a locket the ghosts hands Amanda, there might be a way for her to cure the ghost's loneliness.

Closing Campfire: Kristen wonders what became of Amanda, and David wraps it up by letting us know she had a great rest of the summer. Gary adjourns the meeting and Frank grabs his feuding buddy Eric, making a peace offering of soda to cool him off. The gang walks off into the woods, leaving Kristen to open David's present. It turns out to be a locket, like in the story, and she promises to think of him every time she wears it. He even gets a kiss on the cheek! This is the beginning of the David/Kristen affair, which is sadly not paid off.

Review: This is one of the sweeter, gentler episodes in the series. You have the mystery and the ghost, but this isn't a scary tale in the least. It's really more of a sad story with a happy, though improbable ending. Creator D. J. MacHale's first time at bat in the director's chair shows promise, and marks the start of twenty episodes he would come to direct. It's not necessarily a memorable episode and feels way too contained for its own good, but it's a solid episode with no major plot holes.

Series Mythology

- This is the first episode starring Sheena Larkin, who would go on to appear six more times in the series as various other grandmotherly types.

- The term "Zeeb," which is assumed to be synonymous with "dork," is no doubt a reference to Zeebo from the last episode.

- Actress Laura Bertram, who played Amanda, would go on to appear in the Season 5 episode: "The Tale of the Mystical Mirror".

- Actress Jennie Levesque, who played the lonely ghost, would go on to play the bratty, living sister in the best episode of Season 1, "The Tale of the Dark Music."

EPISODE 4:

"The Tale of the Twisted Claw"

U.S. Airdate: September 12, 1992

Written by: Chloe Brown

Directed by: D. J. MacHale

Guest Cast: Maxwell Medeiros, Noah Plener,
Ann Page, and Jason Tremblay

Favorite Line: "Dougie, he's dead! He may be a skeleton!"-Kevin

Opening Campfire: We join the Midnight Society, with a story already in progress, but not to worry, you didn't miss anything because Eric hasn't figured out how to finish it, so it's tossed aside. The group scrambles for a new storyteller and David steps forward once again. Frank is surprised that David has finally spoken, and Kristen says he hasn't told one in a long time, which is odd because he just went last week. But anyway, he's been working on one and he's ready to spill the beans.

The Tale: Kevin and Dougie run afoul of a witch on Halloween night and instead of candy, she gives them a wooden vulture claw with the power to grant three wishes. However, it turns out to be more trick than treat, because everything they wish turns out for the worse.

Closing Campfire: The Midnight Society sits in appreciative silence, as David brings his Halloween tale to close. Gary grabs the water bucket and wishes everyone pleasant dreams, as he douses the fire and adjourns the meeting

Review: This homage to the famous "Monkey's Paw" story by W. W. Jacobs reminds you to be careful what you wish for. I wish more episodes of *AYAOTD?* took place during Halloween, but then again monsters exist every day of the year. This fun, cautionary tale is perfect for a Halloween evening's viewing. In fact, this episode was shown on Nickelodeon on Halloween of 1990, even before the series was picked up officially by the channel, no doubt as a pilot to see if there was an audience. Obviously, there was.

Series Mythology

- Jason Tremblay, who plays Bostick the track and field star that Kevin defeats with the help of his wishing claw, appeared in the inaugural episode, "The Tale or the Phantom Cab," as big brother Denny.

- Ann Page, who plays Miss Clove the witch, is married to Aron Tager, also known as Doctor Vink.

- Noah Plener, who plays Dougie, will appear again in the Season 2 episode, "The Tale of the Magician's Assistant." His brother, Benjamin Plener, will later appear in the Season 1 episode, "The Tale of Jake and the Leprechaun"

- David's last story for Season 1.

EPISODE 5:

"The Tale of the Hungry Hounds"

U.S. Airdate: September 19, 1992

Written by: Ann Appleton

Directed by: D. J. MacHale

Guest Cast: Mia Kirshner, Jennifer Gula, David Francis, Ais Snyder

Favorite Line: ". . . don't forget to feed your dog, or
he may have a bone to pick with you."-Gary

Opening Campfire: We find the campfire non-existent as the gang piles on dry twigs to get the party started. Everyone is accounted for, except for Kristen, who arrives last with her hound dog Elvis. She promises that she has a tale that will have us shaking in our boots, and that Elvis is here for the sound effects. She has her hands full with the dog, so David helps her dish out the midnight dust onto the fire to start the tale . . . or should I say tail?

The Tale: Cousins Pam and Amy discover a trunk containing the clothes of their Aunt Dora, who died tragically, and when Pam tries it on she becomes possessed by Dora and opens a literal doorway to a long ago evening. Amy tags along and tries her best to save her possessed cousin from a ghostly caretaker and hungry hounds that are thirsting for blood, but not to worry because a fox comes to their rescue when the hounds get lose.

Closing Campfire: Kristen closes out the story by resolving a plot point that wasn't very clear in the episode. Her dog whines, prompting laughs. Gary adjourns the meeting with a terrible dog-related joke (see favorite line) and the fire is extinguished amidst eye-rolling groans.

Review: This is a multi-layered episode, and normally that's a great thing. It starts off slow with two girl cousins yet again on summer vacation, but then becomes a time-travel story, a vengeful ghost story, and a killer dog story all wrapped up into one. The problem is, there is no ending, or at the very least no clear ending. I would call this the first not-so-great episode, mainly because there is so much happening and none of it is very clear, much less the resolution involving a magic fox leading the hungry hounds away. We never really learn what happened to Dora and what the hounds had to do with anything, except for the fact that she forgotten to feed them. Beyond that, the episode is pretty confusing and doesn't really deliver the goods—especially when you see the hounds and they turn out to be cute Beagles instead of imposing bloodhounds.

Series Mythology

- The first time we see the campfire unlit, which then ignites to a full roar off camera. Nickelodeon didn't want to teach kids how to light fires, so usually the campfire is either already ablaze or happens discreetly.

- Kristen likes to make an entrance, as will be evidenced in the later Season 1 episode, "The Tale of the Prom Queen."

EPISODE 6:

"The Tale of the Super Specs"

U.S. Airdate: September 26, 1992

Written by: Chloe Brown

Directed by: Ron Oliver

Guest Cast: Eugene Byrd, Graidhne Lelieveld-Amiro,
Richard Dumont, and Rachelle Glait.

Favorite Line: "It's SarDO! No 'mister.' Accent on the 'do.'"-Sardo

Opening Campfire: We find ourselves pre-campfire in the magic shop owned by Gary's father. Gary is showing Kristen around and she mentions that the gang thinks his stories haven't been very scary lately. Seeing as Gary hasn't told a story yet, it further solidifies that the Midnight Society has been meeting without us. Gary grabs a pair of goofy-looking x-ray specs and plans to make them eat their words. That night, he arrives last at the campfire and tells them that David is sick and won't be coming tonight, then he proceeds to live up to their expectations.

The Tale: Weeds and his girlfriend Marybeth grab a pair of bewitched x-ray specs that allow them to see into an alternate dimension full of shadowy figures. They enlist the help of the not-so-professional Sardo, a magic shop owner, who pretends to know more than he does, and that may end up getting them killed.

Closing Campfire: Gary wraps up his tale and the gang appears impressed. He brings them a pair of x-ray specs as an April Fool's Day gift, and when they put them on a creepy shadow figure appears, scaring them off into the forest.

Gary high-fives Kristen and the shadowy figure joins in, having been revealed as a healthy David, who has been waiting in the wings for the right moment.

Review: This is a good episode, but mostly because it features the appearance of the man, the myth, and the legend: Sardo. The goofy, lovable owner of the Magic Mansion will become a staple of the series and a welcomed recurring character, despite his dire end in this episode. Speaking of that ending, it's one of the rare episodes that had a negative ending for the heroes, and even though the wrap up is way too quick to be satisfying, the setup and Sardo make for a watchable *Twilight Zone*-style episode.

Series Mythology

- Marks the first appearance of Sardo, who will appear a total of eight times, becoming the most recurring character in the show's history, beating out the extravagant Doctor Vink by two episodes.

- Kristen wears the same outfit that Marybeth wears in the opening of the tale. Gary has a similar shirt to Weeds, but the colors are different.

- The only episode where one of the members was missing from the campfire ring, since David was off lurking in the woods.

EPISODE 7:

"The Tale of the Captured Souls"

U.S. Airdate: October 3, 1992

Written by: Ann Appleton

Directed by: D. J. MacHale

Guest Cast: Ethan Tobman, Maria Taylor (credited as Maria King), Don Jordan, and Barbara Eve Harris.

Favorite Line: "Well, you messed with the wrong girl, Petey-boy."-Danny

Opening Campfire: Gary is figuring out how many hours Eric has lived with his calculator when Kiki arrives and starts snapping photos of the gang with her Polaroid camera, shocking the gang with the candid results. She talks about the old Indian superstition that, if you took a photo of someone, you stole their soul, and with that, she launches into her story.

The Tale: Danny and her family are spending a quiet weekend by the lake at what appears to be a quaint bed and breakfast run by a creepy kid named Peter, with a haircut straight out of the Yahoo Serious fashion guide. Of course, Peter isn't what he appears to be. He's really an old man, who stays young by stealing the life from his guests, and Danny's parents are next.

Closing Campfire: Kiki announces she has one shot left in her camera. She sets the timer and the gang gets together for a group photo. Frank gives Eric bunny ears, because someone has to give someone bunny ears. It's just something you do.

Review: Despite the fact that we never really get a good idea how Peter's stay-young machine works, this is a pretty good episode. You don't ever really know where it going, until the halfway point, and by then Peter's endgame has been in play for a while. It's not a particularly scary episode, but it's certainly intriguing, and Danny makes for a fun and sassy heroine. No doubt this episode was inspired by Oscar Wilde's *The Picture of Dorian Gray,* but told in modern-day trappings.

Series Mythology

- Kiki's first and last story for Season 1.

EPISODE 8:

"The Tale of the Nightly Neighbors"

U.S. Airdate: October 10, 1992

Written by: Chloe Brown

Directed by: Jacques Payette

Guest Cast: Suzanna Schebib, Noah A. Godfrey,
Carl Alacchi, and Françoise Robertson.

Favorite Line: "With ghosts and ghouls, there are no rules,
but a vampire's bite only comes at night."-Betty Ann

Opening Campfire: , "Why do they always tell ghost stories at night, because if they're scary, shouldn't they work during the day, too?" Kristen wonders. The rest of them assure her that it's always scarier at night, because some ghoul could sneak up on you in the dark and you wouldn't know it until it was too late. Betty Ann announces that she's going tonight and Eric expresses his disappointment because her stories are usually the same and they always end happily ever after. Betty Ann ignores him and begins to preface her story, referencing the earlier conversation. She tells us that you could be scared during the day, but we shouldn't bother because the real terror happens when night falls. She submits the following tale for the approval of the Midnight Society, except for Eric.

The Tale: Emma and her improbably named brother Dayday discover that the new neighbors across the street only come out at night. Couple that with a strange sickness that is turning the townsfolk weak, and Emma makes the leap of logic that leads her to believe the neighbors are vampires. Now she has to prove it before it's too late.

Closing Campfire: Betty Ann wraps her story up, book ending the night vs. day discussion. In between the story sections, they were passing around a thermos of what appeared to be fruit punch and when Gary adjourns the meeting they put out the campfire with their cups of the blood red stuff, allowing the dark to embrace them.

Review: Obviously a remake, or at the very least, an homage to the awesome 1985 flick, *Fright Night*, about a teenager fighting the vampire next door, who has designs on his girlfriend, and the Joe Dante directed Tom Hanks movie *The 'Burbs* (1989). This is a fun episode, very reminiscent of those films, and giving us a pretty perfect ending. The story seems to be wrapped up as far as the characters know, but we get an extra scene that reveals that there will be way more to this story and it won't go in favor of our heroes. This is the best kind of ending for the show, because it doesn't leave loose ends, but gives it an internal life beyond our scope that enriches it.

Series Mythology

• The director of this episode, Jacques Payette, only directed this one full episode, but he went on to direct four of the campfire sequences in Season 2.

• This story is one of the two that went on to be novelized, with several additional scenes, which were cut for time when airing.

EPISODE 9:

"The Tale of the Sorcerer's Apprentice"

U.S. Airdate: October 17, 1992

Written by: Stephen Zoller

Directed by: D. J. MacHale

Guest Cast: Matthew Mackay, Staci Smith,
Jane Gilchrist, and Emma Stevens.

Favorite Line: "I bet my Michael Jordan rookie
card we find a maggot-ridden corpse."-Frank

Opening Campfire: Frank leads the gang to a mound of dirt that appears to be a fresh grave. A skeleton springs from it, sending the Midnight Society running for the hills. That is except for Kiki, who triggered the plastic skeleton's rise from the grave, and Frank who was in on it all along. The gang settles by the campfire later, playing with the head of the skeleton. Betty Ann grabs it. It's her turn again and she says her story is of a head of a different sort, an ancient wizard's good luck charm that is more than is bargained for.

The Tale: Dean is a lackluster student, until he stares into the glowing eyes of golden snake head and becomes possessed by an evil force, known as Goth, that grants him good luck and a superior attitude. His best friend Alix must fight his newly converted minions and save Dean from the dark side before he can perform the ritual that will bring Goth back to our world, which he plans to devour.

Closing Campfire: David smells a sequel, what with the open-ended finale that Betty Ann signs off with, but we never get one. Maybe one was planned, but it never happened. The fire is doused with the bucket of water and the gang walks off into the woods, leaving the plastic skull behind on the storyteller chair.

Review: This is a fun episode, because the plot comes out of left field. An Egyptian-style curse spreading like an evil virus through a high school? That's a new one. The plot moves at breakneck speed and while we only get the briefest debriefing on Goth, we get the idea that he's bad news. Dean is a good guy, but Goth's power demonstrates that absolutely power corrupts absolutely. The chemistry solution at the end brings it back around to Dean's trouble with school and gives the character a small, but satisfying arc.

Series Mythology

- Michael Mackay, who plays Dean, starred in the infamously bizarre kids film *The Peanut Butter Solution* (1985). I'd tell you what it's about, but you wouldn't believe me. He will also go on to star in the Season 1 episode "The Tale of the Prom Queen."

- Jane Gilchrist, who plays Ms. Crenshaw, returns to the series in the Season 6 episode "The Tale of the Zombie Dice."

- Betty Ann's last tale for Season 1.

EPISODE 10:

"The Tale of Jake and the Leprechaun"

U.S. Airdate: October 24, 1992

Written by: Nick Webb

Directed by: D. J. MacHale

Guest Cast: Benjamin Plener, John Dunn-Hill,
David Steinberg, and Frayne McCarthy

Favorite Line: "Yours be mine and mine be yours!"-Sean O'Shaney

Opening Campfire: Gary informs us that Frank was supposed to go tonight, but something happened and he has agreed to pass the baton to Eric. Eric's Irish grandfather has just passed away, and in his honor he wants to tell his Pop Pop's favorite story.

The Tale: While rehearsing for a new play, young actor Jake becomes the target of a banshee, who not only wants his soul, but is also directing the play. Jake enlists the help of an expert on magic herbs, who turns out to be a leprechaun with a hatred for banshees.

Closing Campfire: Eric dedicates the story to his grandfather and the Midnight Society applauds. They stand and embrace him as the show fades out.

Review: Setting a leprechaun tale in the theater is an interesting idea and allows for the fantastical elements to play out somewhat realistically. David Steinberg shines as the little person that comes to the aide of our young Jake, who turns out to be a good leprechaun instead of the nasty ones we get in the movies. The banshee envisioned in this episode is very different from the one you would normally picture. Banshees conjure images of wailing woman, and not red-nosed, wrinkly old men as portrayed by actor John

Dunn-Hill, but somehow it works and the episode is another fast-paced one with a satisfying happy ending. I would've loved to see Sean O'Shaney return to the series, but alas he never did.

Series Mythology

- Lead actor Benjamin Plener, who went on to appear in three episodes of *Goosebumps,* returns in the Season 7 episode "The Tale of Highway 13." He is also the brother of Noah Plener, who appeared in the Season 1 episode, "The Tale of the Twisted Claw."

- Writer Nick Webb goes uncredited in the episode.

- The only tale that features the name of the story's heroes in the title.

- One of two episodes where a Society member gives up his turn in the storyteller chair for another member.

EPISODE 11:

"The Tale of the Dark Music"

U.S. Airdate: October 31, 1992

Written by: Chloe Brown

Directed by: Ron Oliver

Guest Cast: Graham Selkirk, Kathryn Graves,
Jennie Lévesque, and Leif Anderson.

Favorite Line: "Howdy, neighbor."-Andy

Opening Campfire: Frank arrives, breathless. He's mad at Eric, because Eric left without him, forcing Frank to walk through the dark woods alone. Betty Ann wonders what the big deal is, and Eric reveals that Frank is scared of the dark. He denies it, and proceeds to threaten Eric with a beating, but Gary steps in and prompts Eric to start his story, because it is his turn again tonight. It just so happens that his story has to do with a boy who is very much afraid of the dark, among other things.

The Tale: Andy is a scaredy cat. His bratty little sister and the neighborhood bully, a longhaired rocker kid who tucks in his shirts neatly, make life a living hell for him. But when he discovers a ghostly entity that reacts to music and resides in the root cellar of his new home, he finds not only an ally but a weapon against his tormentors.

Closing Campfire: Eric closes the story by assuring us that Andy never used his newfound powers to kill his sister, but he did make sure she never annoyed him again. Gary douses the fire, and everyone gets up to leave, but Eric stays because Frank disappeared during the middle of the tale with his flashlight. He sits and waits for Frank to return, assuring himself that he isn't afraid of the dark, and as expected Frank pops out with a scare that sends Eric hightailing it into the woods.

Review: This is my favorite episode of Season 1, and quite possibly of the entire series. It's great that the episode that actually references being afraid of the dark is a solid *scare fest* and hands down one of the most memorable from this freshman season. The combination of creepy imagery, from the beady red eyes of the entity to the freaky as hell giant doll that wants a hug, this episode knows how to push the right buttons. Taking a young character from sad sack lows to homicidal mastermind highs is not only scary in a very human sense, but also very satisfying story-wise. It's like Rocky winning the big fight, in a sense. Everything about this one works, even the simple story mechanics, which don't explain a lot, but that mystery is what makes the episode all the creepier.

Series Mythology

- Airing on Halloween night, this episode has become for many a yearly holiday staple alongside "The Tale of the Twisted Claw," and I am thoroughly in that camp.

- Eric's last story as a member of the Midnight Society (and what a way to go!)

EPISODE 12:

"The Tale of the Prom Queen"

U.S. Airdate: November 7, 1992

Written by: Chloe Brown

Directed by: Jean-Marie Comeau

Guest Cast: Katie Griffin, Graeme Millington,
André Todorovic, and Irene Kessler.

Favorite Line: "Sit down, you geek! I'm doing this for effect."-Kristen

Opening Campfire: A ghostly figure arrives at the campfire while the Midnight Society sits around waiting for Kristen. They notice the ghost and freak, but soon discover the thing underneath the white veil is the very much alive Kristen, making another grand entrance, with a true version of an oft-told tale of woe.

The Tale: Greg and his ridiculously named friend Jam, meet a girl named Dede at the cemetery. The boys are on the hunt for the grave of the prom queen who died in a tragic hit and run accident decades ago and is said to haunt the cemetery. Intrigued, Dede tags along and as they investigate they discover that Dede's boyfriend died that night too. Dede enlists the boys into helping the dearly departed boyfriend reconnect with the wandering prom queen's spirit, which may be closer to them than they think.

Closing Campfire: Kristen removes her white veil to reveal herself finally and ends her tale, no muss, no fuss. Gary declares the meeting closed, douses the fire, and the gang stands to congratulate Kristen on not only acting the part of a ghostly maiden, but telling a heck of a good tale.

Review: This re-telling of the classic urban legend of the phantom hitchhiker makes for a compelling episode and a bittersweet one, as well. The leads work well together, especially the sweet Katie Griffin as Dede, who manages to really humanize the tale. The ending that satisfyingly ties it all up is surprising without feeling like a cheat, and is well- earned, which isn't always the case. This is a feel-good ghost story, and I recommend it as a gateway into the series if you want to get someone hooked onto the show and they don't necessarily want to see creepy stuff. It reminds me of a great TV movie called *The Midnight Hour* (1985). I recommend you check that one out, also!

Series Mythology

- Kristen's last tale for Season 1.

- Cameo by Matthew Mackay, who appeared in the Season 1 episode, "The Tale of the Sorcerer's Apprentice."

EPISODE 13:

"The Tale of the Pinball Wizard"

U.S. Airdate: November 14, 1992

Written by: Louise Lamarre and Tom Rack

Directed by: D. J. MacHale

Guest Cast: Joe Posca (as Joseph Posca),
Polly Shannon, A.J. Henderson, and Tom Rack.

Favorite Line: "You are outta here."-Ross

Opening Campfire: The gang plays hot potato with David's Gameboy, discussing the pros and cons of gaming as they try to beat the game that David can't seem to conquer. Kristen questions the merits of videogames and their pointlessness, because it doesn't matter whether you win or lose. Gary arrives to snatch the Gameboy away and proclaims that his story tonight is coincidentally exactly about a game where winning is important because the stakes are life and death.

The Tale: Ross Campbell, a pinball enthusiast, plays a strange new pinball game that traps him in an alternate dimension where the mall he once knew has now become the setting of a very real game. Now he has to retrieve a tiara and a throne to save a princess, or risk being stuck in the game's world forever.

Closing Campfire: Gary ends his story with a terrifying and bleak ending, and then tosses the Gameboy back to David, who realizes he's outgrown games. He passes it to Frank, who thinks he's outgrown it as well, and passes it to Kiki, who doesn't want it either. Gary ends up with it and reminds us that "whoever's got the game, just make sure the game doesn't get you." The meeting adjourns for the first roster of the Midnight Society. Sadly, we will never see Eric again. They all walk off into the woods, leaving Gary alone to address us directly. "Till next time," he says, and douses the Season 1 campfire.

Review: This episode is a lot of fun, especially if you're into videogames. The mall at night is a great setting, as evidenced in classic horror movies, such as *Dawn of the Dead* (1978) and *Chopping Mall* (1986), and it's used to great effect here. Joseph Posca is a likable lead, and the challenges faced make the episode a breezy delight. The twist ending is a nice cherry on top, and plays to the series' strengths. Also, if you look closely, in the scene where Ross is riding the throne through the witch's spider web, you can clearly see a crew person pushing the throne from behind. It's those little imperfections that make something all the more lovable, though.

Series Mythology

• The final episode featuring Eric.

• A.J. Henderson, aka Mr. Olson, appeared in "The Tale of The Dark Music."

• Co-writer Tom Rack cameos as the security guard that chases Ross around.

THE TALE OF SEASON TWO

Original U.S. airdate: June 19, 1993-October 2, 1993

Midnight Society Year Two Roster:

Gary (Ross Hull)

Kristen (Rachel Blanchard)

Betty Ann (Raine Pare-Coull)

Frank (Jason Alisharan)

Kiki (Jodie Resther)

David (Nathaniel Moreau)

EPISODE 14:

"The Tale of the Final Wish"

U.S. Airdate: June 19, 1993

Written by: Chloe Brown

Directed by: D. J. MacHale

Guest Cast: Bobcat Goldthwait, Samantha Chemerika, Thomas Sievewright, and Jane Wheeler.

Favorite Line: "Uh, isn't it obvious? I'm the Sandman."-Sandman

Opening Campfire: Sitting around the good, old campfire, Kristen reads to David from a fairy tale book as the Midnight Society trickles in for the first of thirteen tales for Season 2. Eric is missing from the gang, departed to parts unknown, but no one mentions it because they are too busy giving Kristen grief about how fairy tales are kid's stuff. She disagrees and explains that it if you forget the difference between reality and imagination, a fairy tale can become a scary tale.

The Tale: Jill is a huge fairy tale fan, to the point that she lets it affect her everyday life, and of course everyone makes fun of her for it. One night, she wishes on a star that everyone would leave her alone, and she is suddenly spirited away by the Sandman to a fairy tale dream world where it isn't exactly rainbows and happily-ever-afters.

Closing Campfire: Kristen warns us that we must be careful, because we never know which fairy tales are fake and which aren't, changing everyone's mind about the kiddie status of fairy tales in general. Frank grabs her fairy tale book and starts digging through it for the gory bits as the gang gathers around, no doubt on a similar hunt.

Review: This a good episode from an art department standpoint, and series art director Réal Proulx does a bang up job of making the Sandman's world an expressionistic dreamscape. The lead actress, Samantha Chemerika, is a solid heroine, but the usually fun to watch Bobcat Goldthwait stumbles here with some awful line readings. It's a shame too, because this character could have been very memorable, but sadly Bobcat doesn't deliver as strong a performance as at least *I've* grown to expect. Also, why is everyone sleeping in bathrobes in the Sandman's world? Is that a Canadian thing?

Series Mythology

• First well-known guest star with comedian Bobcat Goldthwait, known for classic, goofball films and his unforgettable turn as Zed in the *Police Academy* movies.

• Kristen reads from the Grimm fairy tale "Faithful John" in the opener, and it's the only time she doesn't make her typical grand entrance to the campfire.

• Samantha Chemerika will return in Season 5's "The Tale of the Chameleons."

• Jane Wheeler, who played Jill's mom, will return in the Season 5 episode, "The Tale of C7."

EPISODE 15:

"The Tale of the Midnight Madness"

U.S. Airdate: June 26, 1993

Written by: Chloe Brown

Directed by: D. J. MacHale

Guest Cast: Eddie Robinson, Melanie Wiesenthal, Harry Standjofski, and Aron Tager.

Favorite Line: "Vink's the name, doctor Vink!"-Doctor Vink

Opening Campfire: Kiki and David are in a hurry for the campfire meeting to be done with because they got free tickets to a horror triple feature playing at their local theater. Frank says he's been to one of those and he'll never go back, not because he's scared, but because when you're sitting in the theater in the dark the horror movie on the screen sometimes seems so real that it's hard to tell the difference between the real world and the movie world.

The Tale: The struggling movie theater, the Rialto, is paid a visit by a mysterious filmmaker calling himself Doctor Vink. He has a vampire film he wants to show that he guarantees will draw an audience, but what he doesn't tell them is that the vampire in the movie is alive. He crosses between the silver screen and our world to wreak havoc, and the only way to kill him might be to kill him in the film.

Closing Campfire: Frank ends his tale and wonders who's going to the triple horror feature now. David and Kiki agree that it's getting late and decide to go home instead, leaving their tickets with Frank. Gary wonders what Frank is going to do with them since he said he's never going back, but he assures Gary that they're only movies, and after all what's the worst that can happen.

Seeing as there's an extra ticket, Gary invites himself and they head off to the horror movie fest.

Review: This is my favorite episode of Season 2, probably because I am a huge film aficionado and frequently take in double and triple features at my local theaters here in Los Angeles, but also because it features the return of Doctor Vink, the villain who changes jobs like a snake changes skins. Last we saw Vink, he was a hermit in episode one, and now he is an eccentric filmmaker, later he'll own a fancy restaurant known for its dangerous soup. The creepy stuff doesn't really get going until the last five minutes, but the characters and the location makeup for its lack of horror throughout. If you like old movies and old movie theaters, then this one will not only be a hoot, but be quite nostalgic, as well. I wish we had seen more of Nosferatu, but we get enough for him to make an impression, and I'd say that's good enough.

Series Mythology

- The film playing at the Rialto at the beginning is titled *The Bosticks of Beacon Hill*, which is not a real film, but might be a reference to the supporting character Bostick from the Season 1 episode, "The Tale of the Twisted Claw."

- Christopher Heyerdahl, who played Nosferatu, will return to the series in the fourth episode of Season 2, "The Tale of the Thirteenth Floor."

- Harry Standjofski, who played Mister Kristoph the theater manager, will returned to the series in the Season 6 episode, "The Tale of the Wisdom Glass."

- This is Frank's second turn at the campfire and Vink's second appearance. In fact, except for two episodes, whenever Frank tells a tale, Vink is the main antagonist!

EPISODE 16:

"The Tale of Locker 22"

U.S. Airdate: July 3, 1993

Written by: Chloe Brown

Directed by: David Winning

Guest Cast: Karen Elkin, Cory King, John Koensgen, and Jennifer Irwin.

Favorite Line: "We can't both be crazy."-Chris

Opening Campfire: The gang spends a few moments considering all the gory, gruesome characters that will be featured in Kristen's tale tonight, because apparently she has a rep for gore-soaked stories, although she's only told fairly vanilla stories, like "Tale of the Hungry Hounds," "Tale of the Prom Queen," and "Tale of the Final Wish," so I'm sure we must have missed the gore fests. She makes her usual grand entrance, dressed like a hippie. They wonder what the 1960s getup is all about, and she warns them, "If you don't heed the lessons of the past, you will be doomed to repeat them."

The Tale: Julie, formerly from Paris, is trying to settle into her new school in Canada, but when she's given locker 22, the former occupant, a girl from the 1960s named Candy, starts to haunt her. With the aid of a time-traveling bead necklace, Julie and her friend Chris discover that Candy died in an accidental explosion at the school and if they aren't careful that explosion might claim their lives as well.

Closing Campfire: Kristen ends her incredibly gore-free story and the gang responds with 1960s slang to show their appreciation. Frank botches it by saying "neat-o," and the gang laughs at his failure to grasp the flower child lingo. They get up and return their19 trinkets to Kristen as the show fades out and the campfire remains blazing.

Review: The strangest thing about this episode is that the bullies decide to pick on the cute French girl. In what universe would that ever happen? The bitchy cheerleading squad, yes, but not the two mouth-breathing morons. To me, that is the weirdest element of this episode. The time travel logic is a little fuzzy, so it's best not even discussed. This is more of a mystery episode than a scary one, and it basically works except for the aforementioned logic gaps. It's not a very fun episode in terms of humor or light moments, but it has a happy ending that feels organically earned.

Series Mythology

• Episode director David Winning's name cameos in the episode, appearing under Candy Warren's name in a list of students from 1968.

EPISODE 17:

"The Tale of the Thirteenth Floor"

U.S. Airdate: July 10, 1993

Written by: Anne Appleton

Directed by: Michael Keusch

Guest Cast: Trish Lindstrom, Aaron Ashmore,
Johni Keyworth, and Pierre Leblanc.

Favorite Line: "What do my jeans got to do with it?"-Billy

Opening Campfire: Gary, Frank, and Kiki are tending to the fire as flashlights beam down on them. They turn to find Betty Ann, David, and Kristen cloaked in shadows and holding the flashlights. Gary says they can lower the lights because he knows who they are, but Betty Ann wonders if you ever really know someone. The question of someone's true identity is interesting, and with this Betty Ann hops into her sci-fi story.

The Tale: Billy and his foster sister Karin become the test subjects of a strange toy company that has moved into the thirteenth floor of their apartment building. It turns out the toymakers may be out of this world, and they have their sights set on Karin for some unknown reason.

Closing Campfire: Betty Ann cautions us to look closer, even if we think we know someone. Gary grabs his trusty red bucket of water and adjourns the night with, "I declare this meeting, of the Midnight Society closed, whoever you are."

Review: This is a fun, sci-fi tinged episode, which is rare. On retrospect, the faceless aliens go through a lot of trouble to make a toy factory, when all they wanted was to get Karin's attention. Keeping that in mind, all the tests and games they ask her to play are essentially time wasters, since all they wanted to do was spirit her back to her home world. The surprise ending was very nice, and added an extra layer of depth to the so-called bad guys. Sometimes we work against our own good, and don't realize it until it's too late. The alien design was neat, and Réal Proulx killed it yet again with the candy-colored alien toy factory he built. This one was obviously inspired by the *Twilight Zone.*

Series Mythology

- Aaron Ashmore, who played Billy, will returns in Season 7's "The Tale of the Lunar Locust." He's also the twin brother of Shawn Ashmore, Iceman from the *X-Men* films.

- Pierre Leblanc, who played Raymond, will returns in Season 5's "The Tale of the Unexpected Visitor."

- Johni Keyworth, who played Gus the elevator attendant, appeared in Season 1's "The Tale of the Nightly Neighbors" as the blood-drained mailman.

EPISODE 18:

"The Tale of the Dream Machine"

U.S. Airdate: July 17, 1993

Written by: Darren Kotania

Directed by: David Winning

Guest Cast: Michael Hong, Nicole Lyn, Joel Gordon, and Rikee Madoff.

Favorite Line: "Go ahead, Gar, be crazy. Throw away the rules."-Frank

Opening Campfire: It's Kiki's turn, but she arrives late, and with laryngitis of all things. She's typed up her story and she asks Gary to read it out loud. He grabs the pages and begins to read that, ". . . once a story is written, it no longer belongs to the author, but has a life of its own, and for some stories that could be a very dangerous life indeed."

The Tale: Sean, a wannabe writer, finds a magic typewriter in a secret room of his new house with the power to make whatever he writes come true. This God-like power turns against him as his best friend and the girl he's secretly in love with fall in danger of his imagination.

Closing Campfire: Kiki has mysteriously disappeared during the tale, which is kind of impossible seeing as friends surrounded her. In her place in the storyteller's chair is her typewriter with a piece of paper in it. Frank pulls it out and reads what is ostensibly the ending of a new story, where a headless creature chases down the members of the Midnight Society. Remembering that written tales have power, the gang grows anxious, then skedaddles into the woods and onward to their homes.

Review: You get three horror stories for the price of one with this one, which has a special place in my heart because, as a writer myself, I want to believe that my words take on their own life and my characters live and breathe somewhere over the rainbow. This is a jam-packed episode, with plenty of spooky moments and twists and turns. I'm surprised so much was able to fit within the small running time and still be incredibly satisfying. I would give this one the award for second best episode of Season 2, in my opinion.

Series Mythology

- Joel Gordon, who plays Sean's pal Billy, returned in Season 4's "The Tale of the Long Ago Locket."

- Tim Post, who plays Blind Paul in Billy's story within the story, will return in Season 4's "The Tale of the Fire Ghost" as the titular character.

- Gary does not officially declare the Midnight Society meeting closed when he pours the water over the campfire.

- A photo of a bearded fellow, who may be James Ellington, the last owner of the Dream Machine, was of the series' prolific director of photography, Karol Ike.

EPISODE 19:

"The Tale of the Dark Dragon"

U.S. Airdate: July 24, 1993

Written by: Alison Lea Bingeman

Directed by: D. J. MacHale

Guest Cast: Chuck Campbell, Cara Pifko,
Eleanor Noble, and Richard Dumont.

Favorite Line: "Is there a Mister Sourdough here?" -Keith

Opening Campfire: Gary wanders into the campfire to find it empty. Something pops under his feet and he bends down to find the remnants of a balloon and another one magically appears in his hand, which we can assume he picked up off camera. The gang jumps out with a shout of surprise. It's Gary's birthday, and David has prepped a special tale in honor of this most auspicious occasion. He tells Gary he borrowed one of his magical characters, and Gary wants to know which one, but David won't spill until the tale is told. However there can only really be one magical character worth borrowing, right?

The Tale: Keith wishes he could be more confident and powerful, so after seeing an ad in a comic book, he heads to the infamous Sardo's Magic Mansion to buy the potion that will give him everything his heart desires. The potion, bought at a rock bottom price from Sardo, seems to work at first, but quickly turns against him as he begins to regress into a monstrous form that may end his cool streak quicker than it started.

Closing Campfire: This is one of quickest campfire end sequence ever. David ends the story and turns to Gary to wish him a happy birthday. Gary drops a goofy smile and we fade to black. I really wanted to see them cut a cake or something. Oh well.

Review: Sardo is back in the house, spreading magic and madness like wildfire, and his scenes are always highly entertaining. The title is a bit misleading, because there is *no* dark dragon present, it's more a metaphor for the dark side of your personality, so it's kind of a cheat on the part of the episode's writer, Alison Lea Bingeman, who will go on to write two more episodes. Chuck Campbell as Keith is a likable lead. The template, taken from *The Strange Case of Dr. Jekyll and Mr. Hyde,* (we get a glimpse of Robert Louis Stevenson's book in the opening), works well here against teen inadequacy and high school drama. This is a fun, twist-filled episode that will resonate with a lot of folks, just remember: here there NOT be dragons.

Series Mythology

• Second appearance of Sardo, who apparently returned unscathed from the crystal ball he was trapped inside of from the last episode, somehow lived, thank God!

• You get a glimpse of the x-ray specs sitting on the counter of Sardo's Magic Mansion, referencing his last episode from Season 1, "The Tale of the Super Specs."

• Eleanor Noble, who plays Keith's dream girl Shelly, will returns in Season 7's "The Tale of the Time Trap."

EPISODE 20:

"The Tale of the Frozen Ghost"

U.S. Airdate: August 14, 1993

Written by: Naomi Janzen

Directed by: Ron Oliver

Guest Cast: Melissa Joan Hart, Andrew Henry, Sandra Scott, and Sara Lee Stadleman.

Favorite Line: "GHOSTS?"-Charles

Opening Campfire: It's the hottest night of the year and Gary wonders if sitting around a roaring campfire is a good idea. Kristen arrives wearing a jean jacket and everyone wonders how she's not melting. She sits and promises that they will all be wearing jackets when she's done, because she has a story guaranteed to give everyone a massive case of the shivers.

The Tale: Charles and his babysitter Daphne head to the home of his estranged Aunts while his parents are at a wedding, leaving them at the mercy of two old ladies and a ghost boy who is cold and makes sure you know it.

Closing Campfire: Realizing the story wasn't clear enough, the Midnight Society fills in the blanks for us. It is by far the most exposition-heavy closing campfire so far. The gang explains why the boy was frozen and where the gold came from at the end, which are elements that the tale should have filled us in on. Kristen's promise of shivers did not come to fruition, seeing as it was a happy ending, and a lame one at that. Gary closes this meeting of the "heat wave society," as David recommended due to the boiling night, and douses the campfire on Kristen's last time in the storyteller's chair.

Review: Why didn't they just make Charles and Daphne siblings? It's really odd that Charles is going to spend time with his estranged Aunts and the parents send a babysitter with him, when that is essentially what the Aunts are for. If he has a babysitter, why not just leave him home? But that, sadly, isn't the silliest element of this episode. It turns out the frozen ghost that was plaguing Charles just wanted his red jacket all along. What the heck does a ghost need with a jacket, and why would that keep him grounded on earth? We get a tag at the end that reveals the Aunts discovering a pile of gold thanks to the object that the coat was wrapped around, but it seemed beside the point. The frozen ghost kept saying it was cold and wanted its jacket, that was it, and because of that utterly goofy plot point, this episode is weak and one of my least favorite of the series.

Series Mythology

• Melissa Joan Hart, who played Daphne, was shooting her well-known series, *Clarissa Explains It All,* at the same time as her guest appearance in this episode.

• This is sadly Kristen's last tale as a member of the Midnight Society (and it *still* wasn't a gore-fest).

EPISODE 21:

"The Tale of the Whispering Walls"

U.S. Airdate: July 31, 1993

Written by: Alison Lea Bingeman

Directed by: D. J. MacHale

Guest Cast: Vivian Liu, Tamar Lee, Ryan Gifford, and Robert Higden.

Favorite Line: "He was a creep, remember?
Now he's a ghost creep!"-Andrew

Opening Campfire: It's a full moon on a leap year, February 29th, and as the gang arrives at the campfire, they find a hooded figure in a papierer maché skull mask waiting for them. Betty Ann is revealed behind the grim visage and she promises a story about the spirits who hunt and prowl on this particular night.

The Tale: Thanks to a shady detour on the highway, two siblings and their babysitter run afoul of the mysterious Master Raymond, a ghost that is only allowed to roam the earth on the leap year during a full moon to collect souls. When their babysitter Louise is taken, Andrew and Claire must join forces to get her back before she becomes a permanent resident of Master Raymond's spook house.

Closing Campfire: Betty Ann closes the tale by warning us that Master Raymond's house still stands and people still disappear when the moon is full on a leap year. She doesn't say "the end," but Gary reminds the group that it's time to go. The problem is that Betty Ann's story has warned them about the dangers of this very night, and no one wants to be the first to leave the relative safety of the campfire light.

Review: I had high hopes for this episode, because the old dark house template is a strong one, and this episode plays off of those conventions to a point. Weary travelers lost in the middle of nowhere, a mysterious mansion and mysterious owner to go along with it, and a ghostly mystery tied to the past. The problem is the mystery is never satisfyingly resolved, nor is an explanation even attempted, and to top it all off the ghost is defeated by an electric hand fan and sunlight, which means his kryptonite is wind and light. The two leads are fine and the plotting is steady for the most part, but there are too many loose bits and the ending resolution is too goofy to be very effective as a standout tale from the series.

Series Mythology

- Zeebo's Laughing in the Dark ride is mentioned, making this the first of many references to the cigar-smoking ghost clown's legacy.

- The jukebox in The Whisper Inn plays an old-timey version of the show's theme music.

- Una Kay, who played the so-called Elegant Lady, will return in Season 6's "The Tale of Oblivion."

- Betty Ann's last tale for Season 2.

EPISODE 22:

"The Tale of the Full Moon"

U.S. Airdate: August 21, 1993

Written by: Ron Oliver

Directed by: Ron Oliver

Guest Cast: Dominic Zamprogna, Jesse Lavendel,
Peter Colvey, and Ellen David.

Favorite Line: "How do you like that? Pure silver!"-Jed

Opening Campfire: Gary announces that tonight is special because it is the one-year anniversary of the start of the show, which was the night that David brought Frank to the Midnight Society to be vetted. Kristen and Kiki reference Doctor Vink, so we know he's become a part of the Midnight Society repertoire. It's tradition to celebrate the anniversary with a tale, and Frank's got just the one to go with a night like this, one with a full moon glowering down on them.

The Tale: Jed is investigating a recent slew of pet disappearances and discovers that his new neighbor has issues with the full moon that bring the beast out in him.

Closing Campfire: The gang surprises Frank with hot dogs as an anniversary present, because what better way to say they care than to enjoy some "roast frank." They spear their wienies and huddle closer to the fire to enjoy their anniversary dinner.

Review: This is a really fun episode, with a perfect resolution. Everything from the set up to the reveal and the twist ending makes this a standout episode for Season 2. The werewolf makeup is great, even though we only really get to admire it better in the third act. This one is basically another riff on *Fright Night*, but it's a sturdy basis from which to work on, and we get a traditional monster for once in this series, instead of some of the more uniquely wacky ones. The switch from dark to light at the end works also, because the characters are believable and the situations add up organically. Despite the bizarreness of the ending, we buy it because it ties itself into a neat and tidy knot.

Series Mythology

- Dominic Zamprogna, who played Jed, will returns in the thrilling Season 4 two-parter, "The Tale of Cutter's Treasure."

- One of two episodes in which prolific series director Ron Oliver handles both writing and directing duties. The other one is the famous Season 4 episode: "The Tale of the Ghastly Grinner."

- Peter Colvey, who plays the boyfriend, will return in Season 4's "The Tale of the Long Ago Locket."

- Carl Alacchi, who plays the werewolf, is Mister Braun in Season 1's "The Tale of the Nightly Neighbors," which is funny because both episodes are similar.

- Frank's last tale for Season 2.

EPISODE 23:

"The Tale of the Shiny Red Bicycle"

U.S. Airdate: August 28, 1993

Written by: Cassandra Schafhausen

Directed by: David Winning

Guest Cast: Matthew Edison, Jamieson Boulanger,
Benjamin Shirinian, and Mark Camacho

Favorite Line: "Looks like someone's gonna fall asleep
in his Corn Wackies."-Leonard, (aka dad)

Opening Campfire: David and Kristen arrive at the campfire to find the others roasting marshmallows. David's beloved bicycle has recently been stolen and they commiserate over the loss, but the good news is that it inspired David's tale for the evening.

The Tale: The death of his best friend Ricky was a childhood trauma that has haunted Mike for years. Now a teenager, Mike finds himself haunted by Ricky himself and his shiny red bicycle. But is it revenge, or has Ricky returned to help Mike and pay him back for trying to save him all those years ago?

Closing Campfire: David closes the tale by letting us know that Ricky's previously undiscovered body was found the next day, bringing the tale to a somewhat happy conclusion. Betty Ann hands Gary the bucket and he closes the meeting, after which they all walk off into the woods introspectively.

Review: This is a great episode, and one with a satisfying beginning, middle, and end. The three-act structure is rarely as clean as it is here, but we get it all laid out, and it even includes a third act twist that changes the way we view the situation and the characters. This is one of the better episodes of Season

2, and carries likable performances, and suspenseful plotting. This isn't one of the scary episodes, but it's definitely one worth the time and effort to enjoy. It's not a slow burn ghost story, but it shares much of the same territory as a tale told in that manner. If episodes like this teach us anything, it's that people don't just suddenly go crazy. If they say they see something, well then they SEE something, folks! This episode is also a testament to friendship, and should be viewed by all.

Series Mythology

- Mark Camacho, who plays Leonard Buckley, was a delivery guy in Season 1's "The Tale of the Nightly Neighbors."

- Pauline Little, Aunt Dottie from Season 1's "Tale of the Lonely Ghost," returns to the series in this episode as Ruth Buckley, and will return again in Season 5's "The Tale of Prisoners Past."

- Jason Alisharan, who playeds Frank, considers this one of his favorite episode.

EPISODE 24:

"The Tale of the Magician's Assistant"

U.S. Airdate: September 11, 1993

Written by: Cassandra Schafhausen

Directed by: Ron Oliver

Guest Cast: Noah Plener, James Bradford, Sally Singal, and Wendii Fulford.

Favorite Line: "Shandu, can do!"-Todd Marker

Opening Campfire: Gary reveals that Mr. Drago, Frank and Betty Ann's homeroom teacher, is a prestidigitator, which is professional jargon for magician. "I guess you shouldn't judge people, you never know when they might surprise you," Kristen says, and that just so happens to be exactly what Gary's tale is all about.

The Tale: Todd Marker becomes the assistant to Shandu the magician, only to discover that the old man wields real magic from a twisted wand. An ancient demon craves the wand and will do anything to get it, even if Todd becomes a pawn in his plans.

Closing Campfire: Gary ends the tale by letting us know that Todd never saw Shandu again. He douses the campfire without officially closing down the meeting, and they all wander off into the darkness, except for Frank. He stays behind to grab the stick that Gary was holding throughout the telling of the tale, considering the possibility that this could actually be a wand. Kiki returns to get him, and feeling dumb he drops the stick and follows her into the woods, leaving the would-be wand behind.

Review: A riff on the *Fantasia* tale *The Sorcerer's Apprentice*, which is also the title of an episode in Season 1, this spookier variation gives us a demon instead of dancing hippos. The world of magic is an interesting one, and will become a cornerstone of the series, most notably through Gary's tales. I liked that our hero doesn't steal the wand for selfish reasons, but to help his single mother. Shandu is a fun character, and had the potential of becoming the good Doctor Vink, but sadly he never makes another appearance in the series.

Series Mythology

- The writer of this episode, Cassandra Schafhausen, only wrote two episodes for the series; this one, and the previous episode, "The Tale of the Shiny Red Bicycle."

- James Bradford, who plays Shandu, will return in Season 7's three-part "The Tale of the Silver Sight" as General Laing Candle.

- Mark Bromilow, who plays the Nazrak demon, will return in Season 4's "The Tale of Cutter's Treasure" as Mr. Noise.

- Shandu is no doubt referencing Bela Lugosi's 1932 film, *Chandu The Magician.*

EPISODE 25:

"The Tale of the Hatching"

U.S. Airdate: September 25, 1993

Written by: Chloe Brown

Directed by: D. J. MacHale

Guest Cast: Illya Woloshyn, Heather Brown,
Liz MacRae, and Pierre Lenoir.

Favorite Line: "I may be a chicken, but I'm smart."-Augie

Opening Campfire: The gang shows up to find David already tending the roaring campfire and looking upset. Kristen tells us his parents had to move across town and he had to change schools. Kiki rags on him but David shut her down by explaining how difficult it is being the new kid. In fact, he figured he'd make the best of it by coming up with a story inspired by his situation.

The Tale: Brother and sister, Augie and Jazz, are sent to a boarding school where the rules are not only strict, but the entire student body seems to be enslaved by the will of an ancient race bent on the re-population of Earth by monstrous reptiles.

Closing Campfire: David drops the mike on his tale which demonstrates why new schools could be hazardous to your health, but we don't get a satisfying wrap up to his woes. Gary stands and declares the meeting closed, and then urges them to go straight home. Frank wonders why, and Gary reminds them menacingly that tonight is a school night. Maybe David feels better, maybe he doesn't, but it seems as if there is a new appreciation for the new kid on the schoolyard.

Review: This *Invasion of the Body Snatchers*-inspired tale can only be described as monster-tastic! It also owes a lot to the great TV mini-series, *V*, which featured reptilian aliens working toward conquering mankind, but this episode definitely stands on its own. With superior makeup and monster effects work, and a compelling plot that leads to a goopy, though brief conclusion, this episode is another standout for Season 2. Tons of green slime must have been used to make this show happens, and nothing makes a horror fan happier than a slime-covered monster and two unwitting heroes with which to best it.

Series Mythology

- Liz MacRae, who plays Mrs. Wilson, will return to the series in Season 4's "The Tale of the Fire Ghost," and Season 6's "The Tale of Bigfoot Ridge."

- Philip Spensley, who plays Mr. Taylor, will return to the series in Season 7's "The Tale of the Silver Sight Pt.1."

- ells tThis is David's final tale as a member of the Midnight Society.

EPISODE 26:

"The Tale of Old Man Corcoran"

U.S. Airdate: October 2, 1993

Written by: Scott Peters

Directed by: Ron Oliver

Guest Cast: Adam Bonneau, Michael Alexander Jackson, Jonathan Cameron, and Tamar Kozlov.

Favorite Line: "Remember friends as you pass by, as you are now so once was I, remember in life that you must die."-Kenny

Opening Campfire: Kiki wanted the gang to play hide and seek to get them in the mood for her story. Gary wonders how a kid's game would get them ready for a scary tale, and Kiki assures them that hide and seek isn't like any other game. Her story is about hide and seek, but with a ghostly twist!

The Tale: Jack and Kenny are new in town. The local kids invite them to play hide and seek in the nearby cemetery that carries the legend of a ghostly caretaker named Old Man Corcoran, who died while digging a grave, but there may be more to the ghostly legend than they are aware of.

Closing Campfire: Kiki brings her tale to a close and wonders if anyone wants to play that dumb kid's game again? They share glances and start calling "not it," leaving Frank holding the bag. He lowers his head in shame and starts counting as the Midnight Society in its current incarnation runs off into the woods for the last time to hide. Strangely, Gary is missing from the campfire, as we fade out of Season 2.

Review: This final episode of Season 2 with the original cast of *AYAOTD?* is almost entirely set in a cemetery at night, and it's a dead-on perfect setting, pun intended. This is a fun and spooky episode with the right amount of atmosphere and an eerie twist ending that puts it firmly in *Twilight Zone* territory. The more you think about the ramifications of what the kids were trying to do to Jack and Kenny, the more chilling this episode becomes, joining the ranks of Season 1's "The Tale of the Dark Music" in sheer cold-blooded creep-factor. It's also funny that Kiki always seems to tell the ethnic episodes, since characters of other ethnicities only seem to take center stage in her tales. This was a great way to sign out of Season 2.

Series Mythology

- Look closely at the tombstones, and you will find a reference to this episode's director, Ron Oliver, on the tombstone reading "Ron Oil."

- Tamar Kozlov, who plays Cissy Vernon, first appears in the memorable Season 1 episode, "The Tale of Laughing in the Dark."

- David Francis, who plays Old Man Corcoran, was last seen as Giles in Season 1's "The Tale of the Hungry Hounds," and will return to the series in Season 5's "The Tale of Station 109.1."

- Kristen and David's final night at the campfire.

THE TALE OF SEASON THREE

Original U.S. airdate: January 8, 1994–April 16, 1994

Midnight Society Year Three Roster:

Gary (Ross Hull)

Betty Ann (Raine Pare-Coull)

Frank (Jason Alisharan)

Kiki (Jodie Resther)

Tucker (Daniel DeSanto)

Sam (JoAnna Garcia)

EPISODE 27:

"The Tale of the Midnight Ride"

U.S. Airdate: January 8, 1994

Written by: Darren Kotania

Directed by: D. J. MacHale

Guest Cast: Tighe Swanson, Rachel Wilson,
François Gauthier, and Arthur Holden.

Favorite Line: "Tucker, this better be good, or
I'm going to let Frank pound you."-Gary

Opening Campfire: We begin Season 3 with some sad news. Gary informs us with the following, "Well, friends come and friends go, and I'm sorry to say that two of our good friends have gone. David and Kristen's families have moved. We won't be hearing their stories anymore, but they'll always be a part of the Midnight Society. We'll miss them, but that means we have room for two new members." Betty Ann informs us that her friend Sam wants to join, but her initiation story isn't ready. Gary understands and wants her to take her time. He has someone he wants to sponsor for membership tonight and it turns out to be Tucker, his annoying kid brother, who isn't very liked by the rest of the group. Gary says his parents won't let him come anymore if he can't bring Tucker, so the gang has no choice but to give the little guy a chance to tell his initiation story.

The Tale: Ian has just moved to Sleepy Hollow, New York, and when he tries to ingratiate himself with the cool kids, he butts heads with the Brad, the jock ex-boyfriend of Katie, the girl that Ian wants to put the moves on. Brad reveals that the legend of Sleepy Hollow is a true story, but Ian doesn't believe him until the legend quiet literally rips itself free of the shadows and chooses him as a modern-day Ichabod Crane.

Closing Campfire: Tucker concludes his first tale and Gary takes the gang's temperature. Kiki pats his shoulder and says, "You'll do." Betty Ann gives him a high-five and tosses him an, "Excellent!" Frank walks up and grimaces, saying, "Just keep him out of my face." Tucker shouts with joy and runs off to catch up with his new pals, leaving Gary to douse the flames and mumble, "I hope I'm not going to regret this."

Review: We experience the greatest shakeup in the Midnight Society, (until the fall of the old regime in Season 6, that is), with the start of Season 3. We lose David and Kristen and gain Gary's little brother Tucker in this episode, and Betty Ann's friend Sam in the third one. I'm glad the show, and by default the characters, acknowledge the passing of David and Kristen, a courtesy that was not extended to Eric at the start of Season 2, but here it shows that not only does the Midnight Society inhabit a "real" universe of their own, but gives us, the fans and Midnight-Society-members-by-proxy, a bit of closure. Tucker's story isn't just an updating of Washington Irving's *The Legend of Sleepy Hollow* with teens; it also resonates with his current position. The story is about a new kid, who has to participate in an initiation ritual, which is exactly what Tucker is participating in. This is a great, perfect-for-Halloween-night episode. The stuff with the Headless Horseman is exciting and the moment when he oozes out of the shadows into reality to chase Ian down is one of the most memorable in the series. Director D. J. MacHale and writer Darren Kotania do a great job of infusing life into the old scary tale, and offer up a satisfying return for the Midnight Society.

Series Mythology

- Tucker goes on to inherit the mantel of Midnight Society leader from his brother Gary in Season 6, when the show is revived for two more years with a mostly-new Midnight Society. Next to Gary, Tucker is the second most-recurring member of the Midnight Society.

- Actor Francois Gauthier, who plays the Headless Horseman in this episode, will go onreturns to do stunts in the 1999 TV movie *The Legend of Sleepy Hollow.*

- Actor Arthur Holden, who plays the pale Ichabod Crane, will returns to the series twice more in Season 5's creeper, "The Tale of the Dead Man's Float," and Season 6's "The Tale of the Wisdom Glass."

EPISODE 28:

"The Tale of Apartment 214"

U.S. Airdate: January 15, 1994

Written by: Scott Peters

Directed by: Scott Peters

Guest Cast: Lea-Helen Weir, Denise McLeod,
Beth Amos, and Marie-Chantal Savard.

Favorite Line: "You get a discount living with a ghost."-Tibold Holstrom

Opening Campfire: Tucker is digging through the bag of midnight dust, curious to figure out what it *really* is, but Gary arrives and snatches it away as he says, "Don't touch the pouch." That should go on a t-shirt, right? Gary wonders if Sam will make an appearance, and Betty Ann promises next week for her debut, because it's Kiki's turn tonight. Frank arrives and complains of being "dead" because he was helping his brother move all day. The gang commiserates over how terrible moving is. Kiki, however, loves it, and what a coincidence because her story is about moving—oh, and promises—but mostly moving.

The Tale: Stacy Cooper moves into a new apartment building, and makes friends with a lonely old woman named Madeline, who is much too old and set in her ways to do anything but haunt her apartment, in more ways than one.

Closing Campfire: Gary searches for the bag of midnight dust, and Tucker reveals that his sticky fingers were behind the disappearance. Gary takes it back, annoyed now more than the others by his brother. He declares the meeting closed, but reminds us that next week Betty Ann's pal Sam is up for initiation, which we shouldn't miss. The gang disperses into the woods as Gary looks around for his red water bucket, which has mysteriously also gone missing. Tucker is the most likely suspect.

Review: This is probably the sweetest and most heart-warming episode in the series. It manages to paint a believable picture of friendship between Stacy and Madeline, then gives us the goods with some angry ghost moments, and finally subverts all that by making us get teary-eyed in a twist that is not only earned, but very much appreciated. This isn't exactly an all-out scary tale, though there are moments. It's really about people and how we will always need someone to look out for us, or at the very least care that we are around. It's great, dramatic stuff that works beautifully. There is a great mirror gag, where it appears as if the camera is staring right into a mirror, and yet is unseen in it. Those tiny technical details give the show style in its effortlessness, which I assume was certainly not easy to pull off. This is one to watch with the whole family, especially dear old Grandma!

Series Mythology

- Episode writer Scott Peters, and future creator of the TV series, *The 4400,* and the 2009 version of *V*, wrote six episodes for *AYAOTD?*, six episodes for *Goosebumps*, and six episodes for the revamped *The Outer Limits* in the late 1990s.

- InIn the opening campfire, Tucker plays a prank and steals the midnight dust. Gary demands that he returns it, and we get a glimpse of the white fire-eating dust, which in reality was non-dairy creamer with a bit of pyrotechnic magic added to the campfire to make it spark.

EPISODE 29:

"The Tale of Watcher's Woods"

U.S. Airdate: January 22, 1994

Written by: Gregory Kennedy

Directed by: David Winning

Guest Cast: Jewel Staite, Kendall Saunders, Tom Rack, and Sheena Larkin.

Favorite Line: "The babe's got bite!"-Tucker

Opening Campfire: Lightning crashes above the campfire on this auspicious night. Sam, a potential new member, sits by the campfire wearing a bag for a helmet. The gang arrives, and Betty Ann unveils Sam, who happens to be a girl. Frank instantly takes a liking to her, but she takes an instant disliking to him. Gary is also instantly smitten and we can tell not only by the puppy dog eyes, but by his first words to her, "You're perfect! . . . ." Sam knows the initiation rules and has a story for them that will assure her a place at the campfire.

The Tale: Kelly and Sarah discover that the legend of the ghost of Watcher's Woods is real, and when Kelly is trapped by three Macbeth-style witches, Sarah must retrieve an item from the past to help break a spell and put the restless spirits at ease before they are both trapped in the woods with the witches forever!

Closing Campfire: Sam ends her tale and wonders what they all thought. Gary calls a huddle, and the Midnight Society puts their heads together to deliberate. Seconds later, Gary turns to her and says, "I don't know how to tell you this," which Sam reads as an intro to a rejection, but it turns out to be the opposite. "It's going to be hard to call someone like you Sam," Gary finishes. With that weighted sentence, Sam is inducted into the Midnight Society, and becomes the cute girl that will drive Gary and Frank mad!

Review: This is a fun, woodsy episode that deals with the old trope of the haunted forest. The addition of the witches and their benign origins adds a nice layer and twist to the proceedings. I also appreciate the fact that the two leads were basically enemies, but bond together through their ordeal and a real character change occurs. I wanted to see more of the Watcher, who appears as a creepy zombie in one of the best jump scares in the series, but he only gets a few moments of screen time and fails to leave a true monstrous mark. Jewel Staite as Kelly is a great bitchy girl, and her turn to the nice side is believable and satisfying.

Series Mythology

- Sheena Larkin, who plays Boss Hag, returns to the series after her turn as Nanny in Season 1's "The Tale of the Lonely Ghost." She will returns two more times and then portrays Grandma Aggie in Season 7's three-parter, "The Tale of the Silver Sight."

- Early role for *Firefly* star Jewel Staite, who will returns to the series in Season 4's "The Tale of the Unfinished Painting."

- Babs Gadbois, who plays the lovely Fat Hag, will return to the series in Season 5's "The Tale of the Mystical Mirror" and Season 6's "The Tale of the Walking Shadow."

EPISODE 30:

"The Tale of the Phone Police"

U.S. Airdate: January 29, 1994

Written by: David Preston

Directed by: Jean-Marie Comeau

Guest Cast: Marcus Turner, Ryan Kent, Marlowe Dawn, and Nancy Wood.

Favorite Line: "The End!"-Tucker

Opening Campfire: Frank arrives to find the gang waiting around for Tucker, who's supposed to go tonight. Gary's giant cell phone rings and it turns out to be Tucker. Gary sets up a speaker for the phone (remember this was the 1990s) and *through* it Tucker plans to tell his tale of the scariest object in anyone's home: the phone! Why, you ask? Because when you pick up the phone you make a connection, and it may not be a connection you want to make.

The Tale: Jake and Chris love to make crank calls, until Jake's sister warns them that they could get into trouble with the phone police, who makes sure no one is monkeying around with the phone lines. Curiosity leads them to discover that the phone police is indeed an actual thing, but it may be too late for Jake to fix is phone etiquette.

Closing Campfire: Tucker, on the other end of a cell phone, appears behind Frank and yells "The end!" into his ear. Frank jumps up and the tension is relieved with a laugh from the others. Tucker hangs up the phone and Gary declares the meeting closed.

Review: This is an Orwellian nightmare of an episode, couched within the world of prank calls. I like the idea of a Phone Police, but it feels more like a cautionary tale you tell annoying pranksters than a satisfying scary tale. It's got some suspenseful moments, but plays more like an action-thriller than a straight horror story, and so for me it stands outside of the type of thing I expect from this show. That can be a bad thing sometimes, but this time at least the pacing and the script were fun enough to help me not sweat the small stuff. There is a bizarre moment where Jake's sister, Annie, played by Marlowe Dawn, pours herself a drink, walks around a kitchen island, and pours it into the sink without even taking a drink. It was basically a bit of actor business that went south, which doesn't happen often, but when it does it's hilarious to watch.

Series Mythology

- References elements of George Orwell's novel *1984*.

- Griffith Brewer, who plays the Phone Clerk, returns to the series after his brief appearance in Season 1's, "The Tale of the Capture Souls," and will returns two more times to the series in Season 4 and Season 6.

- Richard Jutras, who plays the mouse-headed Pizza Guy, will returns in Season 6's "The Tale of Vampire Town."

EPISODE 31:

"The Tale of the Dollmaker"

U.S. Airdate: February 5, 1994

Written by: David Preston

Directed by: David Winning

Guest Cast: Maia Filar, Amanda Walsh, Eve Crawford, and Sam Stone.

Favorite Line: "It was the house that got her!"-Uncle Pete

Opening Campfire: Tucker races to the campfire. It's Betty Ann's turn tonight, and Gary has told him she tells really weird stories, so the pressure is on, as Sam indicates. Betty Ann pulls out a porcelain doll, and Tucker instantly loses interest. He pretends to go to sleep, and Gary chides him, but Betty Ann doesn't care and continues with her tale of why some dolls look more lifelike than others, which restores Tucker's attention.

The Tale: Melissa has gone to spend the summer with her aunt and uncle and visit with her friend Susan, who lives next door to them, but she quickly learns that Susan's family has moved away because Susan mysteriously vanished, and it might have something to do with the strangely ornate dollhouse in her attic.

Closing Campfire: Betty Ann is surprised to find Tucker awake when she ends her tale. He grumbles that it was pretty good for a doll story. As they get up to leave, Kiki finds a doll that Betty Ann has left behind, and it looks almost exactly like Tucker; right down to the backward-facing orange cap. Tucker wonders where she might have gotten something like that. Betty Ann takes it away and assures him ominously, "That's a whole other story."

Review: This is an interesting story because the title references a "doll-maker," however we never meet an actual person that is the "dollmaker." The title must be referring to the dollhouse as the "dollmaker," which is an interesting twist of words, however I feel they should have just called it "Tale of the Dollhouse," because the expectations of discovering a Doctor Vink-style dollmaker were summarily dashed. This is kind of a sad story revolving around a missing kid, which always pulls at my heartstrings, but throw in the supernatural and a happy ending and it makes it a very rewarding episode, as well. In a way I wish there was more to the mythos of the dollhouse but, like Michael Myers in *Halloween,* it's scarier that we don't know anything.

Series Mythology

• Amanda Walsh, who plays Susan, will returns to the series in Season Five's "The Tale of the Door Unlocked."

• This is the second in an informal trilogy of episodes of which writer David Preston wrote that aired consecutively, starting with "The Tale of the Phone Police," followed by this one, and ending with the next episode, "The Tale of the Bookish Babysitter." He also wrote Episode 10 for this season.

EPISODE 32:

"The Tale of the Bookish Babysitter"

U.S. Airdate: February 12, 1994

Written by: David Preston

Directed by: Iain Paterson

Guest Cast: Natalie Radford, James Sherry, and Lynne Adams.

Favorite Line: "Would you stop trying to be such a guy all the time!"-Frank

Opening Campfire: Sam arrives with a bundle of wood in her arms to help feed the fire, and Frank chivalrously springs to her aid. She tells him she's got it, but he un-chivalrously tells her that they're too heavy for her and she should stop acting like a guy all the time, which prompts her to agree and drop the logs on his toes. Tucker and Gary arrive to see Frank nursing his fresh injury, they also find Kiki and Betty Ann pouring over a leather-bound book. It's Betty Ann's turn again and Gary wonders if the book pertains to her story. Guess what? It does! Her story is about stories, which confounds the group.

The Tale: Ricky is twelve years old and feels he doesn't need a babysitter, but his mother disagrees. Luckily (or unluckily) his mother hires Belinda, a unique babysitter who helps Ricky's imagination run away with him with the aid of the right book.

Closing Campfire: Tucker reaches for the book in Betty Ann's hands, interested in taking a look through it, but she warns him that he's way too young for it. He pries it away anyway and opens it to read a passage that explains how that stupid, little jerk Tucker stole the book from the beautiful and intelligent Betty Ann. "Gotcha!" she yells, and the gang filters back into the woods with giggles, leaving Tucker with the sting of being pranked.

Review: This is by far my favorite episode of Season 3. Maybe it's because I'm a writer and I love imagination, and it scratches that itch that Season 2's "The Tale of the Midnight Madness" scratched, but this is a great episode. Imagination is a powerful thing and here it is used to scare and excite, and works as great advertisement for the power of books. This is hands-down the most fun episode of the season and one to re-watch. Belinda is an awesome idea for a recurring character, she could have worked in a library next time, or a bookmobile, but alas she never returns to the series, and that's a real loss.

Series Mythology

- This episode's story is credited to Cliff Bryant and Alice Elliott, and not only is this the only credit for both of them for the show, but it is Cliff's only credit whatsoever.

- Speaking of credits, the actors who plays the Ghost King, the Knight In Armor, The Little Girl, and the Witch, who I think was a man, go uncredited in this episode for some unknown reason.

EPISODE 33:

"The Tale of the Carved Stone"

U.S. Airdate: February 19, 1994

Written by: Susan Kim

Directed by: Ron Oliver

Guest Cast: Frank Gorshin, Richard Dumont,
John White, and Aidan Pendleton.

Favorite Line: "Eternal pain seems rather harsh."-Sardo

Opening Campfire: The Midnight Society, minus Gary, arrives at their spot to find a mysteriously cloaked figure with a big, black hat standing by the fire. Freaked at first, they quickly come to the conclusion that it must be Gary. That is until Gary shows up behind them! Gary confesses to setting up the dummy and unwraps the cloak and hat from around a small pine tree. He tells them the outfit belonged to strange order of monks that lived hundreds of years ago, and he's got a story to tell about their legendary magical powers over nature, and possibly time itself!

The Tale: Alison is new in town, and desperate to make friends. Unluckily for her, but luckily for us, she walks into the Magic Mansion and our old pal Sardo (no 'Mister', accent on the '*do*') sells her a so-called Egyptian Friendship Stone. Of course, as things go with Sardo's trinkets, the end result isn't what the purchaser paid for and Alison discovers the stone's time-travel abilities, which aid her when Brother Septimus, a mysterious, cloaked man, comes searching for the stone that belongs to him.

Closing Campfire: Gary informs us that Brother Septimus was never seen again, and Alison never forgot Tom, the first friend she made in her new home. He closes the meeting and douses the fire as the gang comes up to congratulate him on a story well told. Betty Ann grabs the hat off his head, flops it on, and walks away with it.

Review: This is a fantastic episode. What starts out as the usual new-kid-tries-to-be-popular story, ends up becoming a time-traveling chase around an old house, and manages not only to make sense, but gives us a very sweet and happy ending to boot! The cast here is in fine form, especially Frank Gorshin, who really shines, as opposed to a few other guest star appearances that floundered. It's a pity that Brother Septimus never returns, but at least he gets a fun episode and a creepy role to chew on.

Series Mythology

- Aidan Pendelton, who plays Alison, will return in Season 5's "The Tale of Badge."

- Sardo's third appearance on the show, and he manages to throw out a brief mention of the popularity potion from Season 2's "The Tale of the Dark Dragon."

- Frank Gorshin, who plays the creepy Brother Septimus, is most well-known as The Riddler on the Adam West-led *Batman* TV series (1966-1967).

EPISODE 34:

"The Tale of the Guardian's Curse"

U.S. Airdate: February 26, 1994

Written by: Chloe Brown

Directed by: D. J. MacHale

Guest Cast: Danny Cooksey, Martin Doyle,
Vanessa King, and James Carroll Jordan.

Favorite Line: "I wonder if she likes to ski?"-Josh

Opening Campfire: Gary chases Tucker into the campfire area, where Frank grabs him and holds him still. Sam steps in to play mom, and Gary explains that Tucker stole his ankh. His what now, you ask? The ankh is an ancient Egyptian symbol that means life, and Tucker explains that he needs it because his story tonight is all about ancient symbols, particularly those referring to life.

The Tale: Mina the guardian, an ancient mummy, awakens and ruins the ski weekend for Josh and Cleo, whose father is the head Egyptologist of the museum that she is shambling around in. Is she friend or foe? It's up to Josh and Cleo to track her down and find out.

Closing Campfire: Tucker wraps up his story and reminds us that immortality may be the worst curse of all, and then walks off into the forest. Gary concedes that his story was pretty good, and then realizes that his little brother still has his beloved ankh. He rushes off after Tucker, leaving Sam and the others behind to douse the campfire.

Review: This is an okay episode, but while it's another good example of the series using a classic monster as source material, sadly, the mummy effects are a little hokey, and the love-at-first-sight ending is even hokier. The mummy doesn't even make an appearance until the tail end, and it's most likely because it looked pretty goofy. The lead kids are good, and the premise is fine while not unique or groundbreaking, but the lack of a monster, or any real narrative thrust, hurts it, in my opinion. There is an interesting twist in the story towards the end, but it isn't the typical thing we've come to expect, and while the unexpected is usually always welcomed, here it doesn't really work with how *AYAOTD?* functions, in my opinion.

Series Mythology

• Daniel DeSanto, who playeds Tucker for five seasons, also stars in *Return of the Mummy,* the *Goosebumps* episode that also features a mummy!

• Vanessa King, who plays Cleo, will returns in Season 4's "The Tale of the Fire Ghost."

• Danny Cooksey, who plays Josh, was most well-known for his forty-eight-episode run on the popular series, *Diff'rent Strokes* (1978).

EPISODE 35:

"The Tale of the Curious Camera"

U.S. Airdate: March 19, 1994

Written by: Susan Kim

Directed by: Ron Oliver

Guest Cast: Eddie Kaye Thomas, Richard McMillan, Christian Tessier, and Katherine Giaquinto

Favorite Line: "Don't push me, you little skid mark!"-Frank

Opening Campfire: The gang giggles over younger school pictures of themselves, and after they make fun of each other, Sam wonders why they had to bring them anyway, and Betty Ann explains that photos tell the future. She claims you can learn a lot from pictures, the question is do you want to know what's coming down the line, or is it better not knowing what the future holds?

The Tale: Matt Dorney feels powerless until he is given a strange old camera that grants him the power to force bad luck onto anyone he takes a picture of. He quickly realizes the dangers inherent, and discovers that the strange gremlin that haunts the camera will not relinquish his new master so easily.

Closing Campfire: Betty Ann ends her tale and wants to take a group photo, at which point she takes out the same exact cursed camera that was featured in the episode. The gang scrambles to get the hell out of there, leaving Betty Ann and Gary alone. Gary reveals that it's just a prop from his dad's magic store, (which we visited in Season 1's "The Tale of the Super Specs"), and he wonders why they were so afraid. Then the camera takes a selfie of Gary and

Betty Ann by itself, and the duo exchanges a worried glance. Gary takes the photo and, without looking at it, he tosses it into the campfire.

Review: This is an -intricately plotted episode, and it's the kind that really allows the show to shine because the writing shines. What starts out as a bullied kid wanting to be bully-proof, becomes what at first appears to be about a future-predicting camera, but turns out to be a gremlin-haunted item that causes bad luck. It's those fun twists and turns that keep the series fresh and the episodes memorable. We never see the gremlin in the flesh, only a strange little drawing of it, but it somehow works. Keeping the mystery in the shadows really helps with the mood of the piece. Thankfully, the finale is also satisfying.

Series Mythology

- Christian Tessier returns to the series after his tussle with the infamous Zeebo in Season 1's "The Tale of Laughing in the Dark."

- Bill Rowat, who plays Mr. Dorney, will returns in Season 7's "The Tale of the Silver Sight" Part One.

- Eddie Kaye Thomas, who plays Matt Dorney, is most well-known as a member of the group of pals in the popular *American Pie* film franchise.

EPISODE 36:

"The Tale of the Dream Girl"

U.S. Airdate: March 26, 1994

Written by: David Preston

Directed by: David Winning

Guest Cast: Fab Filippo, Andrea Nemeth,
Shanya Vaughan, and Barbara Jones.

Favorite Line: "It's me, isn't it?"-Johnny

Opening Campfire: Kiki and Tucker arm wrestle, because Kiki called him a runt, and the battle ends with Tucker losing, but he blames it on the fact that he was distracted by Betty Ann and Sam's arrival at the campfire. It's Sam's turn tonight, and she promises a tale about something really scary: true love! It's something that most people live for. Some would even die for it.

The Tale: Johnny finds a girl's high school ring in his locker and becomes haunted by a beautiful girl, who died in a tragic accident. She wants Johnny for some reason, and with the help of his sister Erica, he's going to find out why.

Closing Campfire: Sam ends her feel-good ghost story and Tucker expresses his appreciation, which Kiki uses to continue her runt-based insults, and they chase each other off into the woods. Gary douses the fire quickly and hustles over to walk off into the woods next to Sam.

Review: This is a remarkably powerful episode, and deserves a second viewing immediately right after. I've got to admit that this episode's final moments brought tears to my eyes. This is absolutely a highlight of Season 3. Tragic love stories have an incredible power, and this one, which is really a love story between a brother and a sister who couldn't say goodbye, works on many levels. Again, the writing here is top notch, going from ghost story to tragic romance to bittersweet ending. This isn't an episode that will make you afraid of the dark, but it's one that will linger with you, and, in my book, that's even better. This isn't exactly directly aimed at the episode, but Fab Filippo, who plays Johnny, has the strangest hair I've ever seen; it's beyond description.

Series Mythology

• There seems to be some controversy about this episode, which some consider the inspiration for the M. Night Shyamalan hit film, *The Sixth Sense* (1999), but as far as my research goes, it hasn't been conclusively proven that that is indeed the case, however the stories are remarkably similar.

• The main character's name, Johnny Angelli, has got to be a reference to the popular 1962 song "Johnny Angel," about a girl pining for a boy who doesn't know she exists. Keeping this in mind, the episode also references the 1959 song with a similar name, "Teen Angel," that also involved a high school ring and a girl dying in a train-related accident, which is exactly what happens in the episode's story.

• Michel Perron, who plays the bowling alley manager, will return in Season 6's "The Tale of Vampire Town."

EPISODE 37:

"The Tale of the Quicksilver"

U.S. Airdate: April 2, 1994

Written by: Wendy Brotherlin

Directed by: Michael Keusch

Guest Cast: Tatyana Ali, Kyle Alisharan, Stuart Stone, and Jocelyne Zucco.

Favorite Line: "What a ride!"-Doug

Opening Campfire: Tucker arrives, playing a flute about as badly as he dresses. It's supposed to be a magic flute from his dad's shop that makes it rain, but it doesn't work. In fact, Tucker is bummed that none of his dad's magic stuff ever works. Kiki warns him not to say that, because you never know the true power of something magical. Those powers can be used for good, but if you have no clue what you're doing then that same magic can turn against you, and she'll show us what she means.

The Tale: Two brothers, Aaron and Doug, move into a new house that is haunted by a Quicksilver poltergeist named Laura, who tried to trap an ancient ghost in a rock, but failed and was killed by it.

Closing Campfire: Tucker learns that if you're going to use magic, you should use it right. At which point he plays his rain flute and the skies open up. The gang scatters to find a dry spot in the forest, and Tucker looks up at the brand-spanking new rainstorm and swears he didn't do it. But maybe, just maybe, he did.

Review: This has got to have the dumbest explanation for a ghost ever. Laura is not just a ghost, she's a poltergeist known as a Quicksilver because she leaves the letter "Q" wherever she haunts. I can believe some crazy stuff, but that's just too goofball for me. This episode could have worked, but the cheesy elements like trapping the ghost in a chunk of rock and the leaving of the green "Q," which only happens twice, amount to a really dopey plot with not much narrative clout. The cast in general is fine, but they aren't served by the outlandish, and complex story. I thought that Laura and Connie being twins would pay off, but it didn't and felt unnecessary. I also wish we knew more about the hooded ghost, but we don't. It missed the mark by cramming too much in.

Series Mythology

• Kyle Alisharan, who plays Aaron, is Jason Alisharan's brother.

• Ivan Smith, who plays Mr. Johnston, will returns to the series in Season 5's "The Tale of a Door Unlocked," and Season 6's "The Tale of the Wisdom Glass."

• Director Michael Keusch only directed two episodes, Season 2's sci-fi tinged "The Tale of the Thirteenth Floor" and this one.

• Tatyana Ali, who plays both Laura and Connie, is most well-known as Ashley Banks in the now-classic sitcom *The Fresh Prince of Bel-Air* (1991-1996).

EPISODE 38:

"The Tale of the Crimson Clown"

U.S. Airdate: April 9, 1994

Written by: Darren Kotania

Directed by: Ron Oliver

Guest Cast: Michael Barry, Christopher Redman,
Susan Almgren, and Wally Martin.

Favorite Line: "Nobody will help you, Sam.
Nobody wants to." ~Crimson Clown

Opening Campfire: Frank boldly asks Sam out on a date, but she is put off by his forwardness. Tucker arrives on Gary's shoulders, because Gary is his slave now. Apparently Tucker found a poem that Gary wrote, and much to Gary's chagrin he is now in servitude to his bratty brother in order to keep his mouth shut, but it's okay, because Gary has a special story in mind for tonight, and it just so happens to be a cautionary tale that bids them to remember that what comes around, goes around.

The Tale: Sam is a little selfish jerk of a brother and poor Mike has had enough of him when Sam steals his money to buy himself a video game, instead of a present for their mom's birthday. Mike spots a creepy crimson-suited, purple-haired clown in the store, and warns Sam that the Crimson Clown gets bad kids. Sam doesn't believe him at first, but he changes his mind when the Crimson Clown shows up at his house and starts stalking him.

Closing Campfire: Tucker is moved, or maybe scared, into remorse, and returns the poem to Gary. Frank approaches Sam, and noticing this, Gary tosses the poem into the fire. Frank pushes hard for her answer concerning their date, but she feels he needs to cool off, and she dumps the water bucket on his head; Gary smiles and offers to walk Sam home. She agrees, and as they all walk off we focus on the poem burning in the fire and we see that 'Samantha' was written across it, so now we know who the poem was for.

Review: Okay, so the Crimson Clown kicks Zeebo's butt. I know Zeebo gets all the love, but think about it. Zeebo doesn't really do anything. The Crimson Clown is all kinds of crazy scary; everything from stretching arms, to an inflating head, to a creepy voice, and whatnot. It would have been phenomenal to have a Zeebo versus Crimson Clown episode, but unfortunately we never got that. Despite the fact that the horrid Sam doesn't really apologize to his brother after being converted to the good side, and there is no explanation as to how Mike got their mom the present without any money, this is a great episode with some truly chilling moments… especially if you hate clowns.

Series Mythology

- A direct reference to the infamous Zeebo the clown, from Season 1's "The Tale of Laughing in the Dark," appears in the title and art work of the video game: Zeebo's Big House.

- The actual Crimson Clown was put on eBay and sold for $11,597.

- Christopher Redman, who plays Mike, will return to the series in Season 4's opener "The Tale of the Renegade Virus."

- Susan Almgren, who plays Mrs. Carter, will return in Season 4's two-parter, "The Tale of Cutter's Treasure."

EPISODE 39:

"The Tale of the Dangerous Soup"

U.S. Airdate: April 16, 1994

Written by: Chloe Brown

Directed by: D. J. MacHale

Guest Cast: Neve Campbell, Aron Tager, Greg Haberny, and Tracy Davis.

Favorite Line: "It knows what scares you."-Doctor Vink

Opening Campfire: Frank walks around holding a box, asking the Midnight Society what their fears are. Gary isn't good with heights, Kiki is scared of dogs because she was bitten by one as a kid, Sam is scared of birds because she fears they'll fly into her face, Betty Ann is scared of her attic, and Tucker says he isn't really afraid of anything. Frank admits he's afraid of the dark, much to Kiki and Gary's joy, and in fact fear is what his tale is about.

The Tale: Nonnie and Reed work at the most popular restaurant in town, where the chef serves a dish called 'the dangerous soup,' which goes for $100 a bowl and people are gobbling it up. The problem is that the chef is our old pal Doctor Vink, and the secret ingredient in the so-called dangerous soup may be fear itself.

Closing Campfire: Tucker felt the story was weak, because if there were nothing you were afraid of, then the fear room wouldn't work. This prompts Frank to pick up the box, with a mysterious hole in it that he was holding at the beginning, and instruct Tucker to reach into the unknown. Tucker approaches the box cautiously, then changes his mind and runs away. Gary wonders what was in the box and Frank opens it to reveal that it contained exactly what Tucker was afraid of: nothing. Gary grabs the bucket and douses the Season 3 campfire.

Review: This is a great episode, not just because the much-beloved semi-villain Doctor Vink returns and he's moved up in the world to become a famous chef, but also because it features an early performance from Neve Campbell. The logic behind the gargoyle statue that somehow knows your fear and can turn it into yummy tasting liquid is silly, but somehow Vink makes it beside the point. Neve and Greg Haberny are great, sympathetic leads, and the restaurant location is a unique setting without feeling too constrictive story or budget-wise. This was a great way for Season 3 to go out. We'll have one more season with Frank, and then we lose him, but Vink returns in spades next season!

Series Mythology

- Doctor Vink's restaurant, The Wild Boar, is a callback to the wild boar brain, a true wonder of nature, featured in the series opener and his first appearance, "The Tale of the Phantom Cab."

- Martin Watier, who plays Paul, will return in Season 7's "The Tale of Many Faces."

- Neve Campbell, who plays Nonnie, is, of course, most well-known for her role as final girl extraordinaire Sidney Prescott in the *Scream* (1996) film franchise.

THE TALE OF SEASON FOUR

Original U.S. airdate: October 1, 1994–January 21, 1995

Midnight Society Year Four Roster:

Gary (Ross Hull)

Betty Ann (Raine Pare-Coull)

Frank (Jason Alisharan)

Kiki (Jodie Resther)

Tucker (Daniel DeSanto)

Sam (JoAnna Garcia)

EPISODE 40:

"The Tale of Cutter's Treasure: Part 1"

U.S. Airdate: October 1, 1994

Written by: Chloe Brown

Directed by: D. J. MacHale

Guest Cast: Charles S. Dutton, Dominic Zamprogna, , Aron Tager, and Richard Dumont.

Favorite Line: "Now, have you seen our vomit?"-Sardo

Opening Campfire: "Tonight is a special night," Gary informs us as we swoop down onto the campfire from high above. "Normally, when we meet around this fire to tell our tales, each one of us has our special brand of terror." Gary then goes on to define each one's tale-styles with Tucker's being about adventure, Betty Ann's about the macabre and grotesque, Kiki's are about real people trapped in an unreal world, and Sam's are about heroes searching for truth. "No two stories are alike, that's because no two of us are alike," he says, and Frank walks up behind Gary to reveal that tonight both him and Gary will combine forces to tell the tale. "Because it's so major, it needs the best of both of us!" Frank explains gruffly, and they both take a spot in the storyteller's chair for the series' first and only two-part tale.

The Tale: Rush visits Sardo's Magic Mansion to buy his bratty brother a Shandu magic set to keep him busy while their parents are away for the weekend, and unwittingly opens an old chest that awakens the ghost of an angry pirate, craving revenge.

Closing Campfire: The story is brought to an abrupt stop when a rainstorm lets loose and drenches the gang. Everyone is into it, and wants Frank and

Gary to keep going, but the duo adjourns for the night with a promise of finishing next time.

Review: This is a red-letter episode; a true e-ticket event for the series. We get some fun Sardo face time, and only a hint of Doctor Vink, but we know he's there and he'll make his swansong appearance in the second half of this tale. There is not much explaining of the events in this episode, so the characters (and by default the viewer) are being thrown around willy-nilly trying to make sense of the pirate hauntings. This wouldn't work on its own, but then again it wasn't designed that way. Charles S. Dutton is perfectly hammy, yet manages some serious gravitas in his brief reveal at the end. The rest of the cast is pretty good, but the real fun is yet to come.

Series Mythology

- Not only does this episode feature the ultimate team up of Doctor Vink and Sardo, but they manage to throw in a reference to the magician Shandu, from Season 2's "The Tale of the Magician's Assistant," which is a tale Gary told.

- Coincidentally, Mark Bromilow, who plays Mr. Noise, was also the Nazrak Demon in "The Tale of the Magician's Assistant."

- Sardo mentions the popularity potion again from Season 2's "The Tale of the Dark Dragon."

- Emily Hampshire, who plays Sandy, returns will return iin Season 5's "The Tale of the Vacant Lot."

- Ajay Fry, who plays Tony, will returns to the series in Season 7's "The Tale of the Time Trap."

- Susan Almgren, who plays Mrs. Carter, returns to the series after appearing in Season 3's "The Tale of the Crimson Clown."

EPISODE 41:

"The Tale of Cutter's Treasure: Part 2"

U.S. Airdate: October 1, 1994

Written by: Chloe Brown

Directed by: D. J. MacHale

Guest Cast: Charles S. Dutton, Dominic Zamprogna, Aron Tager, and Richard Dumont.

Favorite Line: "I don't know who you guys are, but I don't think I'll ever forget you."-Rush Keegan

Opening Campfire: Frank and Gary arrive to find the gang eagerly awaiting the rest of their story. After a brief recap, they jump right in.

The Tale: The pirate ghosts have kidnapped Rush's brother. He learns about Jonas Cutter, a knife-happy pirate, when he seeks help from the mysterious barber, Doctor Vink. Legend states that anyone who opens the chest must do battle with Cutter's ghost, so to save his kidnapped brother he accepts his destiny and goes after Cutter in his underground lair.

Closing Campfire: Frank and Gary bring their story to an end, and the gang, with big smiles, agrees unanimously that it was awesome. Gary declares the meeting closed and douses the fire on the Doctor Vink stories.

Review: There's a great Indiana Jones feel to this second half, which not only manages to give us a satisfying explanation for the pirate tomfoolery, but delivers a fun, *Goonies*-style supernatural adventure. Dutton continues to rock as a true Bond villain-like pirate, and though it might not ever appear on his acting reel, he really is a lot of fun here. The eventual end of Cutter isn't exactly what you might expect, but it makes sense within the context of a kid's show. The team up of Vink and Sardo is just too awesome to overlook, and is definitely a highlight, but thankfully the episode would have worked without it. This episode finds Vink as a barber, and as close to a good guy as he ever comes in the series, which is a nice way for the character to go out because this is Doctor Vink's final appearance. I've chosen Rush's last line as my favorite line of this episode, because it's basically us, the audience, talking about Vink and Sardo. Whoever Vink was, we'll never forget him. Luckily, we get one more adventure with Sardo next season!

Series Mythology

- Doctor Vink holds yet another business now called the Wild Boar Coiffure, a twenty-four-hour barbershop, which again references Vink's bizarre love of Wild Boar.

- Dominic Zamprogna, who plays Rush, returns after his tussle with the neighborhood werewolf in Season 2's "The Tale of the Full Moon," which was coincidentally a tale told by Frank.

- Doctor Vink doesn't correct anyone in this episode, because Rush gets the name precisely right, but he does manage to warn him that he is most definitely *not* a nut bag.

- This is one of two stories to be novelized from the series proper.

EPISODE 42:

"The Tale of the Renegade Virus"

U.S. Airdate: October 8, 1994

Written by: Andrew Mitchell & Gerard Lewis

Directed by: Ron Oliver

Guest Cast: Christopher Redman, Micah Gardener,
Paul Cagelet, and Eric Fink.

Favorite Line: "Kiss your brain goodbye!"-Virus

Opening Campfire: Gary was late because he was dealing with a computer virus that ate his book report. He plans to find out who planted it as soon as he eradicates it. Betty Ann warns that viruses can be dangerous, but Gary knows. He tells us a virus is a disease, and once it gets inside something it takes hold, so imagine if something like a computer virus got inside the world's greatest computer: the human brain?

The Tale: Simon gets a chance to try out a new virtual reality game his teacher Mister Poe invented, unaware that his brother has installed a virus into the game to pay him back for all the mischief he's had to endure. Now, Simon must not only play, but survive.

Closing Campfire: Tucker says what he liked about the story is that no matter how bad it got Simon always forgave his brother, Evan. Gary says he liked that the virus is still alive and if Tucker wasn't careful it could jump into his computer, which sends Tucker running off into the woods, almost ratting himself out as the source of Gary's own virus. Gary cheers triumphantly and puts the fire out.

Review: We get another interesting melding of sci-fi and horror with this outing, and it pays off wonderfully. I really wish Erik Fink had returned to reprise his role as Mister Poe, he had the eccentric chops to be a new Sardo or Vink, but this is sadly his first and last appearance as the series' own Doc Brown. The same can be said about Paul Cagelet, as the silver, Metaluna Mutant-looking virus. He is so much fun to watch that a repeat performance with the virus, maybe in another, bigger location would have been fantastic, especially with how this episode finishes, but it was not meant to be. As this show stands, however, it uses the fears of what virtual reality is capable of to give poor Simon a very vivid nightmare, much to our delight. It's a blast. Beware of technology, friends!

Series Mythology

- Christopher Redman returns to the series after sicking a monster clown on his bratty brother in Season 3's "The Tale of the Crimson Clown."

- On Simon's nightstand in the opening of the episode is a copy of *The Omen* novelization. No real connection to the series, but interesting to note the first time a real a movie is referenced.

- The giant lock on Simon's bike is an Oliver brand, which doesn't exist, but was a reference to episode director Ron Oliver.

EPISODE 43:

"The Tale of the Quiet Librarian"

U.S. Airdate: October 15, 1994

Written by: Susan Kim

Directed by: David Winning

Guest Cast: Shannon Duff, Aaron A. McConnaughey, Anna MacCormack, and Jory Steinberg.

Favorite Line: "Chilly. Very chilly."-Jace Ellman

Opening Campfire: Tucker arrives at the campfire, locked under Frank's elbow and complaining. Kiki tells them to keep quiet, in fact he tells all of them she wants absolute silence, but Gary says that that would be impossible, because where there's life there's sound. But what if there could be total silence? If you take away sound, you take away life.

The Tale: While working on a school project together, Laurie and Jace run into a ghostly Librarian who traps children in an alternate dimension reading room where she wants the children to remain quiet . . . dead quiet!

Closing Campfire: Speaking of libraries, Kiki has some books she has to return and asks if anyone wants to come with her to drop them off in the night slot. Her story, having creeped them out, causes the Midnight Society to abandon her to deal with the library on her own, leaving Kiki smiling because her story was a success.

Review: There's something cozy, yet eerie about libraries. Maybe it's all about those ideas and voices trapped on paper, waiting for mouths to speak and ears to listen. I love libraries, and I've always wanted to spend a night in one. This episode allows me to carry that out vicariously, and just as I figured there *is* something different about the library when the sun sets. While the way Mercy Macgregor, the Quiet Librarian, and her sound-sucking box are defeated doesn't really make a lot of sense and the plot doesn't really kick in until the halfway point, the cast is great and the setting is obviously wonderful, so it highly entertains, and manages to give us a nice character arc for Jace and Laurie, too.

Series Mythology

- Justin Borntraeger returns to the series after his run in with reptiles in Season 2's "The Tale of the Hatching."

EPISODE 44:

"The Tale of the Water Demons"

U.S. Airdate: October 22, 1994

Written by: Scott Peters

Directed by: Ron Oliver

Guest Cast: Tony Sampson, Charlie Hofheimer,
Griffith Brewer, and Luis de Cespedes.

Favorite Line: "Every second I spend with you my brain shrinks."-Dean

Opening Campfire: Frank arrives to find the campfire empty, but finds Sam's bag with her diary sticking out. Being Frank, he sneaks a peek and reads that she treats Frank badly because she has feelings for him and doesn't know how to tell him. The gang arrives and Frank hastily returns her diary to her bag, only to confront her with the truth he's learned. She claims that the diary doesn't belong to her, and Gary examines it to discover that the handwriting is Tucker's. The wily trickster did it to prove a point for his story. You shouldn't mess with other people's stuff, no matter how much you're tempted.

The Tale: Shawn and Dean meet Captain Abraham Westchester, who once collected treasures from sunken ships, and is now cursed by water demons that want revenge for his watery grave robbing.

Closing Campfire: Frank liked the story, but it doesn't get Tucker off the hook for the diary. Gary douses the fire and everyone except for him and Kiki walk off. Kiki finds a bag and wonders to whom it belongs. Gary recognizes it as Tucker's and opens it to find all of his stuff, including a pair of Super Specs and fake vomit, inside of it. Along with all that is a note from Tucker thanking Gary for letting him borrow all this stuff, but wonders what

Gary is doing rummaging through *his* knapsack. Didn't he learn anything from his story?

Review: This episode is a straight rip off of John Carpenter's great horror film, *The Fog* (1980), and that's not necessarily a bad thing. Again we get two antagonistic leads, who band together to survive a common struggle, and manage to wrap up the conflict within the tale in a neat and tidy way. It's got some fun water zombie makeup and some great creeper moments, but the artifacts on display all seem to be pirate related in some way, whereas the titular Water Demons are all Titanic-style folks from the early 1900s, so there's a disconnect there with what was expected in my opinion. While the idea of ghosts returning to look for their stolen goodies isn't a novel idea, it's nice to see the show play with mood and new kinds of creatures.

Series Mythology

- Charlie Hofheimer, who plays Dean, will returns in Season 5's "The Tale of the Unexpected Visitor."

- Griffith Brewer, who plays Abraham Westchester, is almost a series regular, having appeared in the "Tale of the Captured Souls" and "The Tale of the Phone Police" before this one. He will go on to appear one more time in Season 6's "The Tale of the Forever Game."

- In the boathouse that Shawn hides in during his initial run in with the water demons, there is a life preserver with the name "Lithuania" stenciled on the side. There is no ship with this name, so it's probably a reference to the *RMS Lusitania*, which was famously sunk by a German U-boat during World War I and prompted America to join the fight.

EPISODE 45:

"The Tale of the Long Ago Locket"

U.S. Airdate: October 29, 1994

Written by: Gerald Wexler

Directed by: David Winning

Guest Cast: Will Friedle, Paul Hopkins, Kim Johnson, and Joel Gordon.

Favorite Line: "I guess that means you're history." -Tucker

Opening Campfire: The gang arrives to find Sam engrossed in a history book. Frank asks her if she couldn't find something more boring, and she wonders why he asked her to study history with him after school if it was so boring. Frank says he's fun to hang out with, as opposed to some other guys, and he tosses a withering glance at poor Gary, the other seeker of Sam's affections. History, as it turns out, is what Sam's story is all about, because history always repeats itself and if you don't learn from the past you'll be doomed to repeat it.

The Tale: Jimmy Armstrong slips through a time warp in the woods that places him in the middle of the Revolutionary War, where he meets an ill-fated soldier who is trying to get back to the woman he loves, teaching Jimmy to live for the now.

Closing Campfire: Frank invites Sam to the Phantasmagoria concert, but she turns him down because she's already going with Betty Ann and Gary, who bought the tickets. Tucker walks over to console Frank, but manages to make it a dig. This prompts Frank to chase Tucker off into the woods, leaving Kiki to douse the flames.

Review: This is an interesting time-travel episode, but there is zero explanation given for why Jimmy is able to travel. It appears Jimmy can slip in and out of the time warp so it doesn't feel like a real threat exists, making this one a more interesting than scary episode. Will Friedle makes for a good, likable lead as Jimmy, and Paul Hopkins is suitably frantic as the fugitive Lt. William. Their scenes are great, and the unrequited love that bonds them makes for great story-telling stuff, so you can look past the lack of explanation. What I can't look past are the goofy drawings inside the locket, which we get a peek at towards the end. Now that's scary!

Series Mythology

- Paul Hopkins, who plays Lt. William, will returns to the series in Season 7's "The Tale of the Last Dance."

- Joel Gordon, who plays Josh, returns to the series after nearly becoming zombie food in Season 2's excellent "The Tale of the Dream Machine," also directed by David Winning.

- Peter Colvey, who plays the Redcoat Captain, returns to the series after playing a werewolf's twin brother in Season 2's "The Tale of the Full Moon."

- Victor Knight, who plays Mr. Olshak, will returns to the series in Season 7's "The Tale of the Photo Finish."

- Rachelle Gait, who played Mrs. Ritter, returns to the series after her Dark Lady appearance in Season 1's "The Tale of the Super Specs."

EPISODE 46:

"The Tale of the Silent Servant"

U.S. Airdate: November 5, 1994

Written by: Wendy Brotherlin

Directed by: Jean-Marie Comeau

Guest Cast: Jesse R. Tendler, Kimberley Warnat,
Brian Dooley, and Tyler Labine.

Favorite Line: "The servant will hear it nevermore, for the
true master is dead, and the beast runs free!"-Crazy George

Opening Campfire: Gary and Sam cuddle by the fire, stoking it with sticks, while Tucker reads a comic. Frank and Kiki arrives, not surprised to find Betty Ann missing, after what she did. Betty Ann walks up behind them and fills in the others as to what exactly she did, which was prevent her friends from sneaking into a second movie after the one they went to let out by. She thought it was wrong and had to decide between standing up for what was right or staying silent. "I hope this is about your story," the impatient Tucker chimes in, because apparently he hates to hear people talking about non-story related things. But don't worry Tucker, because Betty Ann, with her sparkly-gold Elton John vest, does have a story about the power of silence.

The Tale: Jarred and Anne discover an abandoned scarecrow, who comes to life with a magic chant and becomes their servant, fixing things around Anne's farmhouse. All is hunky dory, until they realize that their silent servant acts upon every whim, even the dark ones they wish they could take back.

Closing Campfire: Betty Ann ends her story and Gary declares it to be "great," which it was. Frank and Kiki confer as the others leave, then approach Betty Ann and invite her to the movies; they even offer to pay for her ticket. Betty Ann accepts gratefully. Frank throws in the caveat that he gets to pick the movie, to which the girls roll their eyes. "What, I pick good movies!" Frank exclaims as he puts his arms around them, and they walk into the woods while he details all the elements his choice in cinema will include.

Review: Four seasons in and we get our first farm-based episode, using one of the great spook-figures, the sentient scarecrow. This is a great episode that manages to include twisted wish fulfillment, a series motif, and some eerie monster moments. The plotting is great here, and the finale makes perfect sense within the context of the "curse" of the dragon bone. I was thoroughly impressed by the episode, and while we don't see a heck of a lot of the scarecrow in action, it is a menacing presence and works great just standing there, but I am glad we get to see him sort of in action toward the end. The episode ends with a cliffhanger, but neither the silent servant, nor Crazy George, return to the series to see the story continue.

Series Mythology

• The series comes full circle, in a way, when Brian Dooley returns as Uncle Pete, after having appeared as Flynn in the premiere episode "The Tale of the Phantom Cab."

• This is an early role for Tyler Labine, who plays Mark, and would go on to a great TV and film career that includes the memorable films, *Tucker and Dale vs. Evil* (2010) and *Rise of the Planet of the Apes* (2011), among others.

EPISODE 47:

"The Tale of the Room for Rent"

U.S. Airdate: November 12, 1994

Written by: Lucy Falcone

Directed by: Will Dixon

Guest Cast: Alison Hildreth, Melissa Altro,
Walter Massey, and Andreas Apergis.

Favorite Line: ". . . it's never too late for true love to be rekindled."-Sam

Opening Campfire: Sam is finishing a birthday card for her Grandmother that she has been putting off for weeks, because she's been busy volunteering at the library and at a local hospital. Frank is a big fan of procrastination as he exhibits when he says, "Why do today what you can put off till tomorrow." Sam disagrees with that. You should never leave something undone, because you never know if you're going to get a chance to finish it. "Always say what you have to say, and do what you have to do," because you never know when death might get in the way of second chances.

The Tale: Jessie freaks out when she realizes the new boarder in her Grandpa's home is a ghost, though no one but her best friend Alex believes her. He seems to be targeting her Grandpa, but is he friend or foe?

Closing Campfire: Sam ends her tale and Betty Ann finds it quite sad, because Samuel and Sara lost so many years together. Sam replies, "They say that nothing is ever lost, it just comes back in a different way." Gary closes the meeting and Sam hops up with her Grandma's letter, which she has to get in the mail. They follow her off into the woods.

Review: The biggest complaint I have about this episode is why Samuel didn't recognize Jacob. Old war buddies remember everything of their experiences and those that they shared them with. Why would Samuel not recognize the man who not only died in his place, but also was in competition for the same woman's affections? This is a pretty big plot hole, and maybe you can chalk it up to old-man-brain. The rest of the episode is pretty good. Alison Hildreth is particularly good as Jessie, and it's a shame she didn't do much acting past this episode. I like the ghost being greedy and wanting to take Grandpa Samuel's body, but then the show manages to twist it and give us a happy ending. It manages to be spooky and heartwarming all at the same time. Series regular Sheena Larkin is really great here, and so is Walter Massey as Samuel, but him not recognizing his friend is a really big problem, in my opinion.

Series Mythology

- Sheena Larkin is back! She plays yet another character, this time as Sara Simpson the psychic. She will returns four more times, or twice if you consider Season 7's "The Tale of the Silver Sight" one long episode. We see her again sooner than that in Season 6's "The Tale of the Walking Shadow."

- Walter Massey, who plays Grandpa Samuel, will returns to the series in the final season's epic "The Tale of the Silver Sight."

- Andreas Apergis, who plays Jacob the Spirit Man, will returns to the series in Season 5's "The Tale of the Night Shift."

- The horror movie on TV is Doctor Vink's vampire opus *Nosferatu, The Demon Vampire*, which featured prominently in the mayhem of Season 2's "The Tale of the Midnight Madness."

- This is director Will Dixon's first of three episodes. He will directed two more in Season 5, and write the excellent Season 5 opener, "The Tale of Dead Man's Float."

EPISODE 48:

"The Tale of the Ghastly Grinner"

U.S. Airdate: November 19, 1994

Written by: Ron Oliver

Directed by: Ron Oliver

Guest Cast: Amos Crawley, Heidi Burbela,
Neil Kroetsch, and Missy Christianssen.

Favorite Line: "John, I'm making pizza waffles.
You want one?" -Marsha Wood (Mom)

Opening Campfire: Frank arrives to find Gary and Tucker having difficulty starting the campfire, because the wood is wet. Kiki comes to help and says they need paper. Frank spots a folded comic book in Tucker's back pocket and grabs it for the fire, but Tucker snatches it back, sighting its importance. Betty Ann arrives and snatches it away from Tucker again, explaining that she could use it for her story tonight. She posits the questions, "You ever wonder where they get the ideas for these things? What if it's not made up? What if comic books were something more?"

The Tale: Wannabe comic book artist, Ethan Wood, discovers a comic book titled *The Ghastly Grinner*, which is more than just paper and ink, it's a portal to another dimension, one in which the Grinner is very real and very dangerous.

Closing Campfire: Betty Ann finishes her tale by telling us it will be continued next issue, which it never is, but the Ghastly Grinner does make a few referential appearances later on. Gary calls the tale ghastly, but he means it as a compliment, and declares the meeting closed.

Review: I wish Belinda, the bookish babysitter, worked at the comic book store, that would have been a great way to bring her back into play. Still, there is a lot to like here in what I would call the most iconic episode of Season 4. The tale of a boy artist who uses his art to save the day is some sweet, sweet wish fulfillment stuff. Writer/director Ron Oliver does a great job of delivering a memorable monster and a satisfying, roller coaster ride of an episode. I loved the backhanded insult at lazy couch potatoes when the spud-like parents munch junk food and watch TV while calling comic books an addiction. The dialog works well here and allows the characters to seem lived-in, which is hard to do in a one-off, but everyone here seems like actually people and not just fodder for a story. The Grinner should have become a Vink-like character, but we will see him again here and there in less threatening forms later on.

Series Mythology

- Despite the Nickelodeon rules of not showing kids how to start fires, this episode is the first time we see the campfire actually being lit when Kiki stokes it to life.

- We get references to a ton of *AYAOTD?* episodes in the comic book shop, including the titular creeper from "The Tale of the Crimson Clown," the Watcher's zombie face from "The Tale of Watcher's Woods," the knight from "The Tale of the Bookish Babysitter," and an ogre I'll be honest and say I can't place.

- Ethan holds up the back of the comic to reveal an advertisement for two books, one of them is for the *AYAOTD?* book series, making it the first time the show went meta.

- Heidi Burbela, who plays Hooper, will returns in Season 6's "The Tale of the Walking Shadow."

- Penny Mancuso, who plays Marsha, will returns in Season 7's "The Tale of the Time Trap."

- Terrence Labrosse, who plays Mr. Wrightson, will returns in Season 5's "The Tale of the Jagged Sign."

- According to director Ron Oliver, there once existed an indie band named Hooper Picalarro. They were so enthralled by this episode they decided to dedicate their band name to the heroine.

EPISODE 49:

"The Tale of the Fire Ghost"

U.S. Airdate: December 10, 1994

Written by: Scott Peters

Directed by: Jean-Marie Comeau

Guest Cast: Myles Ferguson, Vanessa King,
Michael Copeman, and Larry Day.

Favorite Line: "Adios, hotshot!"-Jimmy

Opening Campfire: Kiki and Sam argue over a sweater that Kiki lent her, but was stolen from Sam's locker. Tucker arrives with the bucket of water and trips, spilling it, giving Gary good reason to yell at his clumsy little brother. Betty Ann stands and whistles, silencing everyone. She wants them all to calm down and get on with the story. It's Tucker's turn, and he tells us, "It might be kind of hard to cool down, cuz my story has to do with fire."

The Tale: Jimmy and Roxy are left alone in a fire station when their fire-fighter dad sets off to fight a blaze, and they fall prey to a fire ghost who has come looking for revenge. Luckily Jake, another firefighter, is there to lend a hand, but he may not be what he appears to be.

Closing Campfire: Sam gives Kiki money to replace the sweater that got stolen, but Kiki understands it wasn't her fault so she only takes half the money. Gary is still miffed about the spilled water, but Tucker says they can just throw dirt on the flames. The fire goes right out, and Gary admits that it wasn't a bad idea. They walk off, but we see smoke plume from the dead fire, perhaps where the ghost of it still lingers.

Review: This is an interesting, self-contained episode, and I love the idea of fire wanting revenge, I just wish something more was done with the plot. The way the fire ghost is defeated is fairly quick and not as clever as it could have been, but it offers a few good scares and a neat fire-ghost-demon thing. I love the fire station location and they do a good job of using the space, but I wish more happened story-wise. Also, I know cops in Canada carry guns, so why does the police officer in this episode only have a nightstick and a flashlight, and the world's baggiest shirt? He turns out to be the fire ghost, of course, but still if he put in the effort of making a flashlight and nightstick, why not make a gun and a shirt that fits? It's nitpicking maybe, but this is a review, after all. I also wished they hadn't have skimped on the fire ghost and given us something truly memorable, instead of a dude with soot on his face, but maybe this was lower-budget episode.

Series Mythology

- Vanessa King, who plays Roxy, returns to the series after escaping the clutches of a mummy in Season 3's "The Tale of the Guardian's Curse."

- Larry Day, who plays Dan Preston, will returns to the series in Season 6's "The Tale of the Hunted."

- Tim Post, who plays the fire ghost, returns to the series after playing a black-robed zombie in Season 2's "The Tale of the Dream Machine."

- Liz MacRae, who plays Linda Preston, first appears in Season 2's "The Tale of the Hatching," and will returns for a third and final appearance in Season 6's "The Tale of Bigfoot Ridge."

EPISODE 50:

"The Tale of the Unfinished Painting"

U.S. Airdate: January 7, 1995

Written by: Lucy Falcone

Directed by: David Winning

Guest Cast: Jewel Staite, Joel Keller, Vivian Reis, and Jessica Reed.

Favorite Line: "Sometimes an artist's vision will simply end before it's completed. I keep these as a reminder that art is a struggle." -Mrs. Briar

Opening Campfire: Tucker's worried because it's his turn tonight, but he hasn't been able to crack a new tale. His big brother Gary comes to his rescue, much to his delight, covering up for his brother because he knew Tucker was having trouble and it just so happens that he has been hit with inspiration for a new tale. In fact, inspiration is what his tale is all about.

The Tale: Wannabe artist Cody discovers an art gallery run by the mysterious Mrs. Briar, who collects unfinished paintings and offers student painters a chance to finish them, in exchange for their souls.

Closing Campfire: Kiki wonders if Tucker will be ready for next week and he says he absolutely will. Gary closes the meeting and the others scatter into the woods leaving the brothers behind. "I owe you one," says Tucker to his big bro. Gary shrugs it off and wonders if he'll be ok for next week. Tucker hopes so. He just needs some inspiration and wonders what inspired Gary's story. It was Tucker's difficulty being creative that helped Gary see the potential story there, to which he adds, "at least you're good for something."

Review: This episode explores the power of art to not only capture the imagination, but also the body and soul. As a creative individual I know how easy it is to be caught up by the creation process, and how it can sometimes seem otherworldly in terms of inspiration. I can't paint worth a heck, but in writing I find I can lose myself very easily. This episode deals with painters, and while the mediums are different, the transcendent qualities are the same, making this for me a very unique episode in the series because it explores that power of art over reality. The episode doesn't get really weird until the end when the Hunter, a severed blackened head in the paintbrush closet, starts talking, promising immortality. There seemed to be more to Mrs. Briar and her powers, and while we don't get a clear explanation, I'm fine not knowing whom the Hunter was and what he wanted with the trapped girls. Jewel Staite returns, playing a nice girl this time, and she is a likable lead that allows us to buy the unbelievable and root for her. It's all solved a bit too neatly, but I understand it's tricky to fit in only so much within the tight run time. All in all, it's a fun watch. The Hunter could have returned to the series once more, popping up in someone else's cabinet, but this is the last time we see this bizarre soul-collection creature.

Series Mythology

• Jewel Staite, who plays Cody, returns to the series after tangling with the Watcher's witches in Season 3's "The Tale of Watcher's Woods."

• Amanda Gay, who plays Jenna, will returns to the series in Season 7's "The Tale of Many Faces."

EPISODE 51:

"The Tale of the Closet Keepers"

U.S. Airdate: January 14, 1995

Written by: David Preston (story by Michael Kevis)

Directed by: Iain Paterson

Guest Cast: Bethanny Nurse, Tommy J. Michaels,
Peter Messaline, and Rebecca Drysdale.

Favorite Line: "I don't believe it, you look like . . . like a girl!"-Tucker

Opening Campfire: Kiki is up tonight, despite what was set up previously with Tucker. Tucker states that Kiki just told one, and wonders if maybe she threatened to pound Gary if he didn't let her do it again. Frank, who arrived with Sam amid giggles, agrees that she probably could pound poor Gary. Betty Ann arrives and introduces Kiki dressed in . . . well, a dress! It's the first time the gang sees her in one and it blows their collective minds. She did it to make a statement, because everyone's got more than one side to them. She goes on to say, "What you don't know about somebody could turn out to be the one thing your life depends on."

The Tale: Stacy, a lonely deaf girl, stumbles into an alien plot to kidnap children using high-frequency audio waves to help populate an intergalactic zoo. Luckily, Stacy's handicap becomes her greatest asset against the other-worldly zoologists.

Closing Campfire: Kiki uses sign language to bring her tale to an end and Gary declares the meeting closed. Betty Ann rushes over to Kiki and invites her to go shopping the next day, but Kiki pulls out her trademark orange cap, slips it on backwards and says, "Get real." She hustles off into the woods with a laugh and the others follow.

Review: We've grown to learn in this show that if a character has a defect, or in this case a handicap, then it will become a strength that will help him or her survive the terrors in their path. This is another sci-fi tinged episode, where we meet a new race of alien, but get expressionistic backgrounds similar to the ones in the last alien episode, "The Tale of the Thirteenth Floor." Stacy is deaf, and, due to that, she is the series' first and only silent heroine. This element is unique and it adds a very interesting layer to an episode that is basically *The Great Escape* (1963) with sci-fi trappings. I wish I knew more about the aliens and the Keeper guy with the rotted teeth, but the real story here is Stacy's triumph over adversity and it's enough to keep us glued to our seats.

Series Mythology

- Brigid Tierney, who plays Emma, hasn't been in the series before, however her brother Jacob Tierney has. He appeareds as Eric, the long lost member of the Season 1 Midnight Society.

- Bethanny Nurse returns to the series after dealing with a sad ghost in Season 1's "The Tale of the Lonely Ghost," and it turns out she isn't actually deaf, because she is perfectly fine in that second episode of the series, making her performance here even more impressive.

EPISODE 52:

"The Tale of Train Magic"

U.S. Airdate: January 21, 1995

Written by: Gerald Wexler

Directed by: D. J. MacHale

Guest Cast: Gregory Smith, Jesse Moss, Colin Fox, and Ray Aranha.

Favorite Line: "Ray Lawson, this is not
my train, and we're getting off!"-Tim

Opening Campfire: Sam paces the campfire anxiously because Frank is running late to what will become his last tale. It's hard to tell if she's worried for him or annoyed by his lateness, but she grabs her bag and runs off to either look for him or head home, and walks into a flashlight beam accompanied by the sound of a train chugging towards her. Frank appears, holding said flashlight and a boom box blaring the train sound effects. Gary predicts Frank's tale is going to be about trains, and he's correct, but that's not all.

The Tale: Tim loves trains and hopes to become a conductor when he grows up, but when he runs into a ghostly conductor with evil designs on Tim's future, he begins to rethink his career goals.

Closing Campfire: "So, Tim learned about two kinds of magic. Train magic, and the kind of magic that happens between brothers, and friends," Frank says, ending his story and his run as a member of the midnight society. After those parting words, Gary stands and declares the meeting closed, dousing the flames on the Season 4 campfire and officially ending Frank's tenure. They walk off into the woods, congratulating Frank on a job well done.

Review: I like how the episode starts out as a possibly sweet story about a boy and a ghost train and turns into a freaky tale about a boy and a ghost train, led by a wicked ghost conductor. The magic element doesn't really make much sense here, as it all seems more paranormal than witchcraft, which is what I imagined I would get with "magic" in the title. Make no mistake, this is a haunted ghost train story, and while I feel the name is misleading, the episode works great. It comes up with a great, believable back-story for the ghosts and Gregory Smith as Tim does a wonderful job of giving us a great lead to root for. Also, the way it's solved makes perfect sense, which not only makes for a satisfying ending, but also ties the whole episode together. This wasis a good episode for the season to go out on, even if Frank's creation, Doctor Vink, didn't appear in it for a final hurrah.

Series Mythology

- The videogame, Zeebo's Big House, makes yet another appearance, referencing both Season 1's "The Tale of Laughing in the Dark" and Season 3's "The Tale of the Crimson Clown."

- Jesse Moss, who plays Hank Williamson, will returns to the series in Season 5's "The Tale of C7."

- Susan Glover, who plays the Parasol Lady, returns to the series after her otherworldly appearance in Season 2's "The Tale of the Thirteenth Floor."

- Terence Bowman, who plays the Gambler, will return to the series in Season 7's "The Tale of the Stone Maiden."

- Frank's final tale as a member of the Midnight Society.

THE TALE OF SEASON FIVE

Original U.S. airdate: October 7, 1995-April 20, 1996

Midnight Society Year Five Roster:

Gary (Ross Hull)

Betty Ann (Raine Pare-Coull)

Kiki (Jodie Resther)

Tucker (Daniel DeSanto)

Sam (JoAnna Garcia)

Stig (Codie Wilbee)

EPISODE 53:

"The Tale of the Dead Man's Float"

U.S. Airdate: October 7, 1995

Written by: Will Dixon

Directed by: D. J. MacHale

Guest Cast: Margot Finley, Kaj-Erik Eriksen,
Michael Ayoub, and Aimée Castle.

Favorite Line: "Don't push it, grungy boy."-Sam

Opening Campfire: "Tonight's one of those meetings I always have mixed feelings about," Gary begins, visibly lighting the campfire with a match. "It's sad because Frank's family moved, and we lost one of our members, but it's exciting because we have to find a new member," and boy, does Tucker have a candidate for them: his pal Stig! The gang instantly hates Stig, whose first act of business is to smooch Kiki on the cheek, but Tuck begs them to give him a chance. "Is this about telling a good story, or winning a popularity contest?" wonders Stig. "I figure I got to impress you guys, so I'm taking my best shot."

The Tale: Zeke and Clorice discover a hidden pool inside their school that was built over an old cemetery. One of the bodies was left behind, and the ghoulish ghost gets his revenge by drowning anyone brave enough to swim over its grave.

Closing Campfire: Stig brings his tale to a close and Tucker looks to the gang with a big smile. "Tell me that wasn't the best," he says, and rightly so. The gang puts their heads together to vote, and in the meantime Stig takes the chance to explore inside the bag of midnight dust and give the powder a lick. They catch him at this really bizarre act, and I believe that event is what cost him the immediate election. They have decided to let him come to a couple more meetings and tell another story, and if they don't think he's "a total puke," as Kiki puts it, then he's in. Stig agrees to the terms. Gary douses the fire and he flirts with Sam as they disappear into the shadows.

Review: The real estate and job market must be very unsteady in Canada, because Frank's absence is explained away when Gary tell us that his family moved, which was the same thing that happened to Kristen and David at the beginning of Season 3. Maybe they should have just mysteriously killed him off or something, but that might have been too grim of a choice for a kid's show. Stig, however divisive, becomes a great addition because he brings a different kind of energy to the group, and his stories are actually the best in the season. This premiere story is by far the scariest of the season and an all-time favorite of mine. The red-tinged zombie is one of the most amazing creatures created for the series; it is jaw-droppingly awesome. This is another episode that uses chemistry to save the day, like Season 1's "The Tale of the Sorcerer's Apprentice," and while it doesn't make a lot of sense that chemicals would "kill" or banish a ghost, it ties things up neatly for the characters in terms of their development. However, I cry foul that the gang doesn't accept Stig, because his story is without a doubt the scariest one the series has had since season's three's "The Tale of the Crimson Clown."

Series Mythology

* Jay Baruchel, who would go on to big Hollywood hits like *How to Train Your Dragon* (2010) and *This is The End* (2013), appears here for the first of what will be a total of four times, making him the most recurring young actor in a stand-alone tale in the series' history. He next appears in Season 6's "The Tale of the Zombie Dice."

- This is a crucial episode for the series mythology, because it features the first and only time an initiate storyteller doesn't quite make the cut.

- The school, at least location-wise, appears to be the same one featured in Season 3's "The Tale of the Midnight Ride." This episode also stars Arthur Holden, who playeds Ichabod Crane in that episode.

- The only episode written by director Will Dixon, who will go on to direct Season 5's next episode, "The Tale of the Jagged Sign."

- Marcel Jeannin, who plays the red Corpse, will returns in Season 6's "The Tale of the Walking Shadow."

EPISODE 54:

"The Tale of the Jagged Sign"

U.S. Airdate: November 4, 1995

Written by: Susan Kim

Directed by: Will Dixon

Guest Cast: Jennifer Meyer, Hillary Hawkins,
Marcia Bennett, and Terrence Labrosse.

Favorite Line: "Go on, eat the Brussels sprouts I told them, but
don't say I didn't warn you when the gas starts acting up!"-Mr. Duncan

Opening Campfire: Sam arrives to find Tucker sitting next to Stig, who still wears the initiation bag over his head. He's decided not to remove it, until the group can accept him for who he is, but it isn't going to sway them, and he isn't getting in this week because it's Kiki's turn in the storyteller's chair. Stig remains stubborn and keeps the sack on his head. Kiki tells us she got her idea for tonight's tale from a book on symbols, most of which we would recognize, unless we had a bag over our heads. But what if there was a symbol you couldn't recognize, and what if it was a warning?

The Tale: Claudia is spending the summer at her aunt's old folks home, and with the help of a neighbor girl she discovers a ghost boy in the woods, who pines for the love of a girl that looked remarkably similar to Claudia.

Closing Campfire: Betty Ann asks Stig what he thought, and Stig whispers to Tucker that he can't breathe. Tucker rips the bag off his pal's head and Stig demands to go again next week because the bag on his head is not as comfortable as he apparently imagined it would be. Gary agrees to give Stig his second shot next week, but Sam covers his eyes with her bandana because he's not a member yet and the way to the storytelling spot is still a secret to non-members. She tells him to keep the bandana, then wipes her hands on poor Kiki as she leads the way into the woods.

Review: Yet another summer vacation story where a kid is abandoned by botanist parents, and the mistaken identity of a ghost leads to a happy reunion. Nothing original here in this very serviceable episode that recycles series tropes. If this were Kiki's initiation story, she would most certainly not make the cut. The ending is especially goofy when the statue of the doves become real doves somehow and fly away. Maybe the power of love did it, I don't know.

Series Mythology

- Terrence Labrosse, who plays Mr. Duncan, returns to the series after tangling with the titular Season 4 creeper in "The Tale of the Ghastly Grinner."

EPISODE 55:

"The Tale of Station 109.1"

U.S. Airdate: November 11, 1995

Written by: Scott Peters

Directed by: Ron Oliver

Guest Cast: Gilbert Gottfried, Zachary Carlin,
Ryan Gosling, and David Francis.

Favorite Line: "Boy, if I had a dime for every time somebody
tried to weasel out of death, it would actually do me no good at all,
because I'm dead. What do I need money for? What am I going
to do, I'm dead. What am I going to do, buy gum?"-Roy

Opening Campfire: "It's do or die time," Gary says, ripping off Stig's blind-fold. Gary tries to return the bandana to Sam, but she refuses it. Tonight is Stig's second chance to impress the Midnight Society, and they promise to be fair. "So, what do we need these things for anyway?" Sam asks, holding up a mini boom box that she brought. Stig instructs the gang to tune to their favorite station and when he says so they all turn their radios on at the same time, causing a discordant noise that only Tucker seems to appreciate with some vicious head banging. Stig tells them to turn them off and Kiki wonders what that proved. Stig explains that "There are tons of invisible radio signals flying all around us," and with so many signals floating around there is no way to tell what could be hidden within them.

The Tale: Jamie decides to play a prank on his death-obsessed brother Chris by locking him in a hearse. While trying to find a way out, Chris turns on the radio and hears a radio station that beckons to the newly departed. He tracks the station's physical location down and discovers a way station into purgatory.

Closing Campfire: "If you don't let me in after that story, you haven't been listening to me," Stig says, prompting the gang to huddle up again. Stig turns on the radio and blares some random rock instrumental, causing the gang to look over and shake their heads, shaming him into turning his radio off. After a few more seconds, they turn to him and reveal that it was a unanimous decision: he's in! Stig celebrates by wrapping his arms around poor Sam. She pushes him away and runs off. "Control him, or I'll throw you both out," Gary warns, as Tucker and Stig high five triumphantly.

Review: Chris is a potential future serial killer, and the most disturbing element of this episode is that the parents are avoiding his incredibly unhealthy hobby and not getting this maniac kid some professional help. If it weren't for the events of this episode, which scare him straight, this would have been a Ted Bundy in the making. In any case, we get a very unique take on the afterlife, in a *Beetlejuice* (1988) kind of way. Gottfried is amazing as Roy, the station owner and announcer, and without him this episode might have felt flat. The suspense elements work, and I like the idea of having the death-obsessed Chris realize the truth behind his obsessions, but man he starts off so bleak it's hard to accept him as a sympathetic lead. Gosling's Jaime is barely in the tale, but he does a good job with what little he is given in his first role ever.

Series Mythology

- Stig's second crack at joining the Midnight Society is a series first. This is also his final tale, but he was not really an official member of the Midnight Society.

- Ryan Gosling, later a Hollywood superstar, makes his big debut here with this episode.

- David Francis, who plays Daniel Carpenter, returns to the series for the third time. He last appeared as the titular caretaker in Season 2's "The Tale of Old Man Corcoran."

- Jason Cavalier, who plays Sid the Mechanic, will returns to the series in Season 6's "The Tale of the Misfortune Cookie."

- Bill Corday, who plays the scared guy being thrown into purgatory, will returns to the series in Season 6's "The Tale of Oblivion."

- You have to freeze-frame it to make it out, but there is what appears to be a crew person's foot in the foggy void beyond the doors to the afterlife when they close after rejecting Chris. Look towards the bottom right-hand corner to see the goof.

EPISODE 56:

"The Tale of the Mystical Mirror"

U.S. Airdate: November 18, 1995

Written by: David Wiechorek

Directed by: Craig Pryce

Guest Cast: Lexi Randall, Laura Bertram,
Jayne Heitmeyer, and Genevieve Ferderber.

Favorite Line: "So, what are you, a beauty or a beast?"-Tucker

Opening Campfire: Gary arrives to find Tucker and Stig cooking hotdogs over the campfire. This isn't a cookout, so he makes them put it away, much to Tucker's dismay. The girls arrive, discussing makeup. Betty Ann's parents want her to wear some for a family portrait, but she's not into changing the way she looks to fit someone else's idea of what beauty is. In fact, that's what her story is about. "Some people spend a whole lot of time worrying about their looks, but looks can be deceiving," she says, "and sometimes, mirrors lie."

The Tale: Cindy discovers that her new boss, Ms. Valenti, a fashion plate with model-like good looks, is actually an old witch, who turns beautiful girls into dogs for use in a youth potion, and Cindy's best friend Laurel has been dog-eared for her supernatural kennel.

Closing Campfire: "Are we done now?" Asks Stig, excitedly, and Gary responds affirmatively with a sad look on his face. "Then let's eat!" Stig grabs the buns and Tucker grabs a giant pole studded with ready-to-cook hot dogs. The gang huddles around the fire for what has now become a cookout.

Review: The witch turns girls into dogs? As unbelievable as most of these episodes get, this element is probably the biggest head-scratcher in the entire series. Also, we later find out as Betty Ann wraps up the tale that Ms. Valenti's home and store disappeared after her death, but how in the world is that possible? I buy that she is an ancient witch, but that she has power over buildings, I cannot. We never learn why the girls have to become dogs either, which adds to this episodes con side. On the pro side, the lead girls are great, and Ms. Valenti's disappearing act at the end is well done, but beyond that I feel the series is repeating itself again, much like Kiki's "Tale of the Jagged Sign" a few episodes back. Nothing new or remarkable here, save for a few bizarre plot points.

Series Mythology

- Zeebo the clown is referenced yet again in another of Betty Ann's stories, when Cindy states she'd look like Zeebo with any amount of makeup on.

- The popularity potion from Season 2's "The Tale of the Dark Dragon" can be seen in the medicine cabinet; this tale was told by David as Gary's birthday present, so its appearance here can either be accidental, or referential as far as it relates to the desires of the lead characters in both tales.

- Laura Bertram, who plays Laurel, returns to the series after helping reunite a mother and daughter in Season 1's "The Tale of the Lonely Ghost."

- Babs Gadbois, who plays Old Ms. Valenti, returns to the series after playing the unfortunately titled Fat Hag in Season 3's "The Tale of Watcher's Woods." She will sbe back in Season 6's "The Tale of the Walking Shadow."

- Andrea Lui, who plays Vicki, was apparently twelve years old but pulls off a much older aura, no doubt thanks to all the makeup.

- Director Craig Pryce's first and last episode for the series, but earlier he directed Neve Campbell, *AYAOTD?* alumni from "The Tale of the Dangerous Soup", in her first film, *The Dark (1993)*

- Writer David Wiechorek's first and last script for the series.

EPISODE 57:

"The Tale of the Chameleons"

U.S. Airdate: December 2, 1995

Written by: Mark David Perry

Directed by: Iain Paterson

Guest Cast: Tia Mowry, Tamera Mowry,
Samantha Chemerika, and Spencer Evans.

Favorite Line: "Bite you once, bite you twice.
A little water, pay the price."-Evil Chameleon

Opening Campfire: The gang arrives to find a bag sitting in the storyteller's chair. Tucker rushes to see what it is, being the type to touch a hot frying pan without thinking, but Betty Ann warns him away. Her new pet Spike is in the bag, and she's afraid Tuck will scare him, because "He's just a baby, strangers disturb him." They all take turns guessing what kind of pet Spike is, but Betty Ann assures them he's a little more exotic than the usual pet store fodder. In fact, he gave her an idea for a story.

The Tale: While visiting a local pet store, Janice is bitten by what appears to be a regular chameleon, but turns out to be a shape-shifting creature that wants to switch places with her and live among mankind as Janice.

Closing Campfire: Betty Ann ends her tale and Tucker wonders if Spike is a Chameleon. She bids them forward and pulls out a baby snake from what appears to be a birdcage. The sight of the reptile sends the gang scrambling into the woods from fear. Betty Ann wraps it around her neck and says, "Just wait till they see you when you grow up." She stands and douses the campfire, seeing as Gary has fled in panic.

Review: This is really fun episode, because it mixes two different genres: the werewolf mythos, and the alien invasion tale. We are told that there are thousands of shape-shifting lizards out there, and so are only glimpsing the tip of the iceberg. That alone is a frightening thought, because if chameleons can look like us, then there's no stopping them! I will say the rhyming chant that is said throughout is a little goofy, and takes the alien invasion aspect out of play, placing it more in the fairy tale/werewolf category, but I like the way writer Mark David Perry played with the conventions here. I also like how the hero point of view switches from Janice to her friend Sharon, it adds another layer to the proceedings. It's further icing on the creep cake that the episode has a heck of an ending, the kind that I really wish the series had done more often.

Series Mythology

- Betty Ann's final tale as a member of the Midnight Society, and she officially signs out by dousing the campfire for her first and only time.

- No actual chameleons were harmed in the making of this episode—because they were iguanas! The iguanas weren't hurt either, as far as I can tell.

- Samantha Chemerika, who plays Sharon, is credited here as Samantha Aboud. She returns to the series after tangling with Bobcat Goldthwait's Sandman in Season 2's "The Tale of the Final Wish."

- Amanda Strawn, who plays Mrs. Robinson, returns to the series after appearing in Season 2's "The Tale of the Shiny Red Bicycle," and will close out the series by returning in Season 7's final episode, "The Tale of the Night Nurse."

- Don Jordan, who plays Mr. Robinson, returns to the series after playing another dad in Season 1's "The Tale of the Captured Souls."

- Tia and Tamera Mowry are most well-knownwell known for their popular TV series *Sister, Sister,* which ran for six years, during which this episode was filmed.

EPISODE 58:

"The Tale of Prisoners Past"

U.S. Airdate: December 9, 1995

Written by: Alan Kingsberg

Directed by: Ron Oliver

Guest Cast: Christopher Castile, Dan Petronijevic,
Martin Neufeld, and Aline Vandrine.

Favorite Line: "Is tonight nonfiction night?"-Gary

Opening Campfire: Kiki walks through the woods with her arm around Tucker, which makes you wonder what their friendship entails beyond the campfire light, when a paint-spattered Gary rushes Tucker and nearly tackles him. Turns out Tucker ditched Gary and left him to paint the den alone. Tucker pleads innocence, but Gary isn't buying it. Luckily, Kiki steps in and diffuses the situation. Back at the campfire, Sam and Betty Ann watch Stig ring out water from his socks and Betty Ann commiserates how much she hates stepping in water. "Who says I stepped in water?" The girls cringe at the thought of Stig's damp feet being the cause of the moisture. Kiki and the boys arrive, prompting Sam to jump up and say excitedly to Gary "Yes, absolutely! I can't wait!" This catches Gary unawares, but Tucker changes the subject because he wants to start. Stig offers Gary a chance to wipe up the paint and hands him the wet sock, which Gary quickly recognizes and tosses back. "My story's kind of fitting, it's about two brothers that don't get along for a lot of reasons," begins Tucker, causing Gary to raise an eyebrow.

The Tale: Stepbrothers Jason and Scott are forced to bond when they unwittingly let the ghost of prisoner One-Eyed Jack free, but he needs them to do one more thing for him, whether they like it or not.

Closing Campfire: Tucker brings his story to a close, but Gary is unmoved. Sam jumps up and says "Saturday night! Can't wait," to our befuddled leader. Tucker takes him aside and reveals that the reason he wasn't able to help him paint was because he was waiting in line for five hours to get Gary tickets to Lollapalooza, and that he told Sam that Gary wanted to take her, because Gary wouldn't be able to ask her himself. Gary melts instantly and thanks his brother. Tucker expects a hug, but Gary rushes off to walk into the woods with Sam and discuss their plans. Stig does the honors and douses the fire.

Review: We get another mistaken identity ghost tale here, but some neat lighting gags and effects—coupled with a unique new setting—make this one a fun watch. The chemistry between Christopher Castile as Jason and Dan Petronijevic as Scott is believably acrimonious, and their patching up at the end is satisfying without feeling too saccharine for its own good. Ron Oliver's direction is great here and keeps things jumping visually. Praise also goes to writer Alan Kingsberg, who debuts here with the first of five episodes he will write for the series, for his striking and sad conclusion, which rang true as opposed to forced.

Series Mythology

- Martin Neufeld, who plays One-Eyed Jack, will return in Season 7's "The Tale of the Stone Maiden."

- Jennifer Seguin, who plays the Tour Guide, returns to the series after getting lucky in Season 1's "The Tale of Jake and the Leprechaun."

- Pauline Little, who plays the Librarian, appears here for her third and final time after playing Aunt Dottie in Season 1's "The Tale of the Lonely Ghost" and Ruth Buckley in Season 2's "The Tale of the Shiny Red Bicycle."

- Almost the exact same scare gag happens in the Microfiche room that was featured in Season 1's "The Tale of the Prom Queen."

EPISODE 59:

"The Tale of C7"

U.S. Airdate: December 30, 1995

Written by: David Preston

Directed by: David Winning

Guest Cast: Jesse Moss, Tegan Moss, Jane Wheeler, and Stephanie Bauder.

Favorite Line: "Can't you hear the music?"-Lisa

Opening Campfire: Tucker arrives with Stig, beating himself up that he can't remember something he wanted to share with the gang. "That's sort of what my story's about," says Sam. "About memories, but not any memories. It's about the kind we share." She reaches into her bag and pulls out items that helped inspire some of her stories, like the locket that helped her come up with Season 4's "The Tale of the Long Ago Locket," her brother's school ring that inspired Season 3's "The Tale of the Dream Girl" and the whistle for her initiation story "The Tale of Watcher's Woods" that same season. She explains that shared memories are important, because they bring us together as friends, but what if we didn't have these memories? "It would be like we had no past and no friends," she eerily expounds.

The Tale: Jason and Lisa move into an old house by a lake with their single mother and discover a dusty jukebox that summons a ghostly girl who drowned in the lake whenever the track C7 is played.

Closing Campfire: Sam ends her tale and lightning flashes with a roar of thunder. Tucker finally remembers what he was going to tell everyone, that a big storm was coming tonight. Gary stands to close the meeting and douse the campfire, but the heavens open up and send the gang scrambling for shelter.

Review: This episode had promise, but ultimately the way the mystery is solved is utterly implausible and serves no purpose toward making the leads proactive in the story's development. If simply playing C7 on the jukebox was all it took to reunite the lost, ghostly lovers, then how did that not happen already, and why didn't it happen the first night when Jason played the track. The ending isn't just incomprehensible, but it feels rushed, which adds to marks against it. The two kids are good, and the first half of the episode works as a moody ghost story should, but the wrap-up falls flat. Also, the fact that Lisa is somehow dragged out to the lake and magically returns isn't exactly explained. She can't swim, and she's old enough to know better, so was it intimated that the ghost girl was seducing Lisa out to sea to drown her like she died? Now *that* would have been a great twist! Also, not sure what Sam is talking about in the beginning, because this episode has nothing to do with memories or keepsakes or friends.

Series Mythology

- Writer David Preston's last of six scripts for the series, which started with Season 3's "The Tale of the Phone Police."

- Jesse Moss, who plays Jason, returns to the series after appearing in Frank's closing tale in Season 4's "The Tale of Train Magic."

- Tegan Moss, who plays Lisa, is Jesse Moss's real-life sister, and while she never returns to this series, she went on to play young Dana Scully in *The X-Files*.

- Jane Wheeler, who plays Ellen, returns to the series after appearing in the fairytale-centric Season 2 episode "The Tale of the Final Wish" Season 2.

- Lisa is reading the Ghastly Grinner comic with the *Are You Afraid of the Dark* novels advertisement that featured prominently in Season 4's "The Tale of the Ghastly Grinner," which was a tale told by Betty Ann.

EPISODE 60:

"The Tale of the Manaha"

U.S. Airdate: January 13, 1996

Written by: Gerald Wexler

Directed by: Will Dixon

Guest Cast: Michael Yarmush, A. J. Buckley,
Matthew Stone, and David Deveau.

Favorite Line: "How to survive in the bush by Oscar BUTTS?"-Lonnie

Opening Campfire: Gary and the girls arrive to find a frantic Stig warning them about a giant monster that almost got him. They think he's pulling their leg until a monster actually jumps out of the woods at them. The girls jump, but Gary recognizes Tucker's shenanigans and unmasks him. Tucker was setting the mood for his story, which concerns a monster in the woods that is more fact than fiction.

The Tale: Young campers embark on a vision quest into the woods with a jerky camp counselor and unwittingly disturb an ancient Native-American spirit and his Manaha, a group of Bigfoot-like creatures who aren't looking to cuddle.

Closing Campfire: " . . . size has nothing to do with how brave you are," Tucker explains, concluding his tale. Suddenly, a strange animal noise echoes through the forest. "And maybe being small also means you got to run faster!" Tucker shouts, beating feet into the woods. Gary douses the flames and races away with the girls after his brother and Stig.

Review: This is the most disappointing and ludicrous episode in the season, and it hurts me to say that, but this is my opinion, so I feel I should be honest. I'm a huge Bigfoot fan, so the chance of seeing some Bigfoots in action excited me, but what we get is vague shadows and magic mumbo jumbo. There are too many problems with this episode, so I'll point out only a few. How does Jonah conclude that the Manaha will only hurt you if you believe in them? Lonnie and Eddy don't believe in them and they are taken. The only one who does believe in their existence is Jonah, and he is safe for the most part. Also, if he knows the Manaha aren't "real", why does he prep his pals as backup Manaha to scare away the Native American guy, who quite possibly might be fake, too? Come to think of it, the Native American guy makes no sense either. He says he uses the Manaha to scare away kids, so why is *he* scared when Jonah summons his Manaha army? He knows this kid can't have ancient magic, and he knows the Manaha are powerless if you don't believe in them, so why is he so scared by them? This episode is completely illogical and very disappointing. It has such a promising start, but is unfortunately overwhelmed by its ridiculous plot holes.

Series Mythology

- David Deveau, who plays Eddy and loves his pasta with a light tomato-garlic sauce, will returns to the series as Andy, a full-fledged Midnight Society member for season's six and seven.

- The Manaha is real, or at least in mythological terms. He is better-knownbetter known as the Wendigo, a demonic beast man from Native-American legend.

- The Ghastly Grinner comic makes yet another appearance in this episode, and it's apparently the first edition of volume six, which means in some alternate world Sylvester Uncas continued making the dimension-hopping villain's adventures. Funny thing is the front and back covers are exactly the same as the first issue.

- Michael Yarmush, who plays Jonah, will returns to the series in Season 7's "The Tale of the Reanimator."

- James Hayes-Liboiron, who plays Steve, will returns to the series in Season 6's "The Tale of Jake the Snake."

- Tucker's last tale for Season 5, and as a lowly junior member of the Midnight Society. When next he spins a yarn, he'll be the top dog.

EPISODE 61:

"The Tale of the Unexpected Visitor"

U.S. Airdate: January 20, 1996

Written by: Alan Kingsberg

Directed by: Jacques Laberge

Guest Cast: Charlie Hofheimer, Chris Wilding, Tommy Mezey, and Natalie Hamel-Roy.

Favorite Line: "You have a story about a snoring aunt?"-Tucker

Opening Campfire: The gang arrives at the campfire to find Kiki already there, and passed out. Stig grabs the bucket of water and plans mischief, but Gary stops him as Kiki rouses. She hasn't gotten any sleep in three days thanks to her Aunt Stephanie, who is visiting from out of town and apparently snores like a lawn mower. The good thing is, she got a story out of her noisy houseguest.

The Tale: Bandmates Jeff and Perch contact an alien race accidentally when Perch uses Jeff's dad's satellite to send their first song into space, attracting glowing aliens who want to play with them.

Closing Campfire: Kiki ends her tale and Gary douses the fire. She asks everyone to let her sleep at their house, but they turn her down for various reasons. She looks around and finds Stig smiling at her. She hasn't asked him . . . yet.

Review: This episode is best described as a homespun take on the film, *Contact* (1997). Thanks to the magic of 1990s computers, two kids make contact with a glowing alien that tries to trap them in his glowing spider web. We later learn that the alien came to play, which means his idea of playing is to terrorize the humans and keep them encased in a glass tube after smothering them in a web. Aliens have a strange way of playing. My biggest issue with this episode is that Perch, while trapped and weakened by the alien, somehow knows that music, specifically the D sharp note, will free him and Jeff's brother, Bobby. How the heck did he figure that out? The end resolution is funny, but a bit too simple. The webs don't make a heck of a lot of sense, seeing as the glowing aliens are humanoid and not arachnid in any way. In fact, not much makes sense in this episode, but it kind of works because you're dealing with aliens, and aliens can play games by their own rules.

Series Mythology

- Charlie Hofheimer, who plays Jeff, returns to the series after playing the goodie-goodie in Season 4's "The Tale of the Water Demons."

- Pierre Leblanc, who plays Jeff's Dad, returns to the series after getting otherworldly in Season 2's "The Tale of the Thirteenth Floor."

- Director Jacques Laberge's first of two episodes he directs. The second one is Season 6's "The Tale of the Wisdom Glass."

EPISODE 62:

"The Tale of the Vacant Lot"

U.S. Airdate: January 27, 1996

Written by: Gerald Wexler

Directed by: Lorette Leblanc

Guest Cast: Jean Marie Barnwell, Aloka McLean,
Erin Simms, and Andrew W. Walker.

Favorite Line: "I always get what I want."-Marie

Opening Campfire: Kiki asked the gang to bring the most valuable thing they own, so now it's show and tell time. Gary goes first by showing off his autograph of Harry Houdini, which has got to be ridiculously priceless. Sam lifts up a bracelet that belongeds to her great grandmother, Tucker reveals his Hank Aaron rookie card in its Lucite coffin, and Betty Ann holds up a battered, leather-bound copy of the poems of Edgar Allen Poe printed in the 1800s. Stig doesn't bring anything, and when questioned by Gary, he covers up the real reason by calling it all lame. Kiki holds up a snow globe with a white unicorn inside of it. "Weak, that isn't worth anything," Tucker shouts, being the sensitive, caring soul he is. "Maybe not to you, but there's different kinds of value," Kiki replies. "Everything has value, everything has a price. In my story, you have to make sure the price you pay doesn't turn out to be more than you bargained for."

The Tale: Catherine is unpopular and uncoordinated until she finds a Grecian-style store in a vacant lot where a veiled woman named Marie promises to give her all that her heart desires, but for a price that may be too steep to pay.

Closing Campfire: Kiki ends her tale and Gary quickly closes the meeting and douses the fire. Sam walks off with the others and Gary asks her to wait up for him so they can leave together. How adorable. Tucker and Stig linger, and Tucker wonders why Stig didn't bring anything for show and tell. "Everybody brought this really cool stuff. Mine was so stupid I didn't show it," Stig says, and upon Tucker's prompt to see what it is Stig shows him a picture of him as his goldfish, Moldy. "A fish? Your most valuable thing is a fish?" Tucker runs off with the picture to show the others, much to Stig's dismay.

Review: This episode feels like the series recycling itself, because while the elements are different, it's too similar to Season 2's "The Tale of the Dark Dragon," where a boy wanted to be better looking and more popular and hideous disfigurement ensues. I like Jean Marie Barnwell as our plucky heroine, but the plot feels too derivative and never as engaging as it should be until the final five minutes or so. Tack on top of all that an ending that comes out of left field and makes absolutely no sense, not even in a fantastical sense, which only serves to end the episode quickly instead of satisfyingly, and you kind of have a bummer episode.

Series Mythology

- Kiki's final tale as a member of the Midnight Society.

- Andrew Walker, who plays Eric, will returns to the series in Season 6's "The Tale of the Secret Admirer."

- Emily Hampshire, who plays Heather, returns to the series after her romantic interlude in Season 4's "The Tale of Cutter's Treasure Part 1."

- This is director Lorette Leblanc's directorial debut on the series, after working as continuity for ten previous episodes, including Season 1's stellar "The Tale of Laughing in the Dark," and will direct five more episodes all the way into Season 7.

- This is writer Gerald Wexler's final screenplay for the series. He penned four episodes, starting with Season 4's "The Tale of the Long Ago Locket."

EPISODE 63:

"The Tale of a Door Unlocked"

U.S. Airdate: February 3, 1996

Written by: Scott Peters

Directed by: Ron Oliver

Guest Cast: Richard Dumont, Michael Maccarone,
Shawn Potter, and Elana Nep.

Favorite Line: "That's in the fine print of any oral contract."-Sardo

Opening Campfire: Gary holds up a crystal ball and tells us that it offers a glimpse into the future. He proceeds to walk around and read everyone's futures. He sees that Kiki will become a famous singer due to her incredible voice, and Jodie Resther has in reality become a very well-knownwell known singer. Betty Ann's compassion and intelligence will lead her into medicine, Stig will become a pro wrestler, which he is excited about, and Sam's love for adventure will make her a famous explorer. Tucker is last, and it turns out his fate is to clean elephant cages at the zoo. "What does that thing say for you, smart guy?" Gary sees a story in his future, "a story about looking into the future."

The Tale: Justin, hoping to find a way to tell if a girl will go out to the dance with him or not, buys a small door that the eccentric Sardo swears will show him the future. Through the door, Justin glimpses a beautiful, young girl dying in a fire. None of it makes any sense to him, until a new girl shows up in class and it's the very same one he glimpsed beyond the little door.

Closing Campfire: Tucker snatches the crystal ball from Gary and uses it to predict Gary's annoyance. Kiki takes it and predicts, "I see a little guy, and he's being pounded by a big guy with glasses. Oh, nasty." Tucker turns to his brother and Gary slowly steps forward, which sends Tucker fleeing. Gary thanks Kiki, and douses the fire.

Review: Structurally, this episode plays like a murder mystery. We know someone is going to die, but we don't know why, when, or how. With that dynamic in play, there is some real energy to the episode, even if in retrospect it feels a bit lackluster. There aren't any scares in this episode, but that doesn't seem to be the goal. I am happy to report that this episode has a very satisfying and believable ending, which ties all of it together very neatly, but it's really Richard Dumont's energetic return as Sardo that saves this episode from mediocrity.

Series Mythology

- Prolific series director Ron Oliver's seventeenth and final episode for the series, which began way back with the first aired episode, "The Tale of the Phantom Cab."

- Scott Peters' final screenplay for the series, which started all the way back with Season 2's "The Tale of Old Man Corcoran."

- Shawn Potter, who plays Ben, will returns to the series two more times. He will next be seen in Season 6's "The Tale of Jake the Snake."

- Anthony Etesonne-Bedard, who plays Michael, will return to the series in the epic three-parter, "The Tale of the Silver Sight" in Season 7.

- Amanda Walsh, who plays the so-called Girl with the welcome cake, was last seen as the doll girl in Season 3's "The Tale of the Dollmaker."

- Ivan Smith, who plays Mr. Birney, was last seen in Season 3's "The Tale of the Quicksilver," and will return to the series one more time in Season 6's "The Tale of the Wisdom Glass."

- Sardo's final appearance in the original incarnation of the series and as a product of Gary's stories, but we shall see him again two more times. Next up for him is Season 6's "The Tale of Oblivion."

- Sardo throws in a mention to the Super Specs that introduced us to him in Season 1's "The Tale of the Super Specs."

EPISODE 64:

"The Tale of the Night Shift"

U.S. Airdate: February 10, 1996

Written by: Chloe Brown

Directed by: D. J. MacHale

Guest Cast: Emmanuelle Chriqui, Oren Sofer,
Jorge Vargas, and Elizabeth Rosen.

Favorite Line: "I got to see the morgue. For real."-Bud

Opening Campfire: Gary and Sam bump into each other awkwardly upon arriving at the campfire, prodding Sam to say she's going to get some more firewood. Gary sits next to Betty Ann, and she wonders if Gary finally revealed his true feelings to Sam. "Oh yeah," says Gary. "I said 'Sam, we've known each other for a long time, and I think you know how I feel about you, so maybe we should just talk about it and decide if we should go out for real.'" Did it work out for good old Gary? Nope. "She said she liked me too, but didn't want to get into a relationship right now because she had a lot going on," Gary sighs. "Bottom line is she doesn't want to have anything to do with me." Stig, Tucker, and Kiki arrive, interrupting Gary's vent. The newest member wonders who's up tonight, and it just so happens to be Sam. Looks like she's been saving this particularly story for a long time, and tonight's the best night for her to tell her tale about illusion and deception.

The Tale: Volunteer nurse Amanda teams up with Colin, a patient at the hospital, to defeat an ancient evil when a vampire is set loose and her coworkers join the forces of darkness in search of human blood.

Closing Campfire: Sam ends her tale and Gary hops up, not planning to hang out. Sam asks him to stick around, and Stig and Tucker ohh and ahh. Betty Ann ushers them away, but not before she tosses Gary a big smile. Kiki mentions that it's getting a little hot, but Betty Ann returns and drags her away, leaving the lovebirds alone. Sam explains that her story was about someone being so busy that they missed out on possibilities. "Well," she says, "I was thinking about what you said, and maybe you and I have some possibilities." Gary melts and turns into a big goofball with the news. He wants to douse the fire and take her somewhere, but Sam says, "no, not yet. I want to watch for a little while longer." She takes his hand and leads him to the storyteller's chair, where they sit down together to watch the fire. According to the airdates, this is the second to last episode, however in some instances this shows up as the finale of Season 5, and thus the close of the original Midnight Society. Without a doubt, this ending with Sam and Gary finally hooking up and sitting together to watch the campfire is the more satisfying and perfect ending for the series, so airdates be damned!

Review: Now, this is a fun, scare-packed episode! It's got monsters, suspense, and blood, plus a fantastic twist ending that actually works. I think this one is my second favorite of Season 5, after the awesome opener "The Tale of the Dead Man's Float." Emmanuelle Chriqui, who has gone on to a great career, is a wonderful heroine, and Elisabeth Rosen is creepily awesome as the vampire's disguise. The vampire's green-apple demon face is a bit hokey, but it's a small gripe. The biggest fault the episode has, and most of the episodes this season, is that the ending is rushed and the way it is solved makes no sense. I can buy that burning the coffin kills the vampire, and that killing the vampire cures the victims as is according to lore, but save for Felix the maintenance kid, why would they not remember what happened to them? I'll forgive this sloppy plot point because the episode is otherwise enjoyable. This episode also wins for best closing campfire. Now that Frank is out of the picture, Gary has the chance to finally make his move. I'm glad it works out for our fearless leader. This ending always puts a smile on my face.

Series Mythology

- Sam's final story as a member of the Midnight Society (and I'm glad they used her final time to wrap up the will-they/won't-they between her and Gary).

- Elisha Cuthbert, who would return as a full-fledged Midnight Society member for Seasons 6 and 7, makes a brief appearance in this episode.

- Sam, who wasn't a member of the Midnight Society when Zeebo first appeared, references the clown here for the final time; maybe she adopted it through osmosis.

- Writer Chloe Brown's (aka D. J. MacHale's) final script for the series. He began using this pen name all the way back to the first episode, "The Tale of the Phantom Cab."

- D. J. MacHale's final episode as director for the series, which started all the way back with the pilot, which is the current episode 4 "The Tale of the Twisted Claw."

- Andreas Apergis, who plays the Vampire, returns to the series after being the jerky Spirit Man in Season 4's "The Tale of the Room for Rent."

- Kathleen Fee, who plays Nurse Hantin, will return to the series two more times. She will next be seen in Season 6's "The Tale of the Gruesome Gourmets."

- Irene Contogiorgis, who plays the so-called Beautiful Girl, will return to the series in Season 7's "The Tale of Many Faces."

EPISODE 65:

"The Tale of Badge"

U.S. Airdate: April 20, 1996

Written by: Wendy Brotherlin

Directed by: Iain Paterson

Guest Cast: Aidan Pendleton, Judy Sinclair,
Roland Smith, and Dylan Provencher.

Favorite Line: "The end."-Gary

Opening Campfire: The final campfire for the original incarnation of the Midnight Society is in full blaze as Stig appears with a bundle of wood to keep it roaring. Gary is late, and Stig wonders what happens if he doesn't show. It wouldn't be a problem, because Tucker slips on a pair of glasses and pretends to be Gary, doing his stuffiest impression of his brother. Stig asks fake Gary if he likes Sam, and Tucker expounds, "Oh, Samantha. What a babe! I have a picture of her in my room. It's right next to my bed. In fact, I declare this meeting closed so I can go home and look at it right now." He stands to leave and runs into a sour-faced Gary. Gary isn't mad, because Tuck just proved a point for his final story tonight. Everyone has a special talent. In Tuck's case, it's that he's a complete idiot, but some people have hidden talents, that are waiting for someone or something to shine a light on them.

The Tale: Gwen, envious of her overachieving brother, learns that she comes from a long line of witches tasked with keeping a Grinch-like goblin named Badge trapped inside a chunk of green stone, and when her brother accidentally lets him out, she must put her new powers to the test.

Closing Campfire: Gary ends his story, prompting Stig to stand and announce that he has a special talent. Everyone expects something disgusting to happen, but he howls into the night, arousing the howls of real wolves in the distance. The eerie sound motivates the girls to rush away, never to be seen by campfire light again. Gary doesn't officially close the final meeting, but he douses the fire and runs off after the others, leaving Stig, who we shall also never hear from again, alone. He realizes he's been ditched and he chases after them, leaving the Season 5 campfire to steam out of existence.

Review: This is a very special episode for many reasons. The main reason is because it adjourns the final meeting of the original members of the Midnight Society, though there is some confusion based on airdates. Certainly the fact that Gary and Sam aren't together puts the actual placement of this episode, story-wise, somewhere earlier in the series, but I am placing it at the end here according to the airdates to avoid too much confusion. However, it is hard to believe we've been with Gary, Betty Ann, and Kiki for five years. While Tucker will return to revive his brother's Midnight Society in Season 6 a few years later, the rest of the original cast, save for Gary, will disappear into the real world.

The episode itself is very interesting if we take a meta look at it. It's about a person with a talent that uses it to keep the monsters at bay. The same can be said of the Midnight Society, who kept away the monsters by speaking about them and taking the teeth out of the horror. Once again Aidan Pendleton is a great lead heroine, and does a wonderful job here. The makeup for Badge is top-notch stuff, and while Roland Smith is a bit hammy I suppose the role of the mouse-like goblin does call for a bit of cheese. The one weird element is that the kids call their grandma by her name, so I wasn't sure if they were related until the end, and maybe that was intentional, but it's a very teensy gripe.

This is a solid episode, with an ending that ties up all the loose ends and actually pays off elements implanted as seemingly throwaway character fluff. It's a great episode for the original series to go out on, because it's all about gaining power over the darkness and after all, that's a campfire's main goal. I still get misty eyed at the closing campfire, even though the show is far from over, I know the Midnight Society will never be the same again.

Series Mythology

- The final episode of the series' original run, and the end of the Midnight Society's original membership.

- This is Gary's last story as a member of the Midnight Society, but he will return in Season 7's "The Tale of the Silver Sight" to aid the new Midnight Society in their biggest adventure ever.

- Aidan Pendleton, who plays Gwen Reilly, returns to the series after traveling through time in Season 3's "The Tale of the Carved Stone."

- James Rae, who plays Mr. Reilly, will returns to the series in Season 6's "The Tale of the Hunted."

- Writer Wendy Brotherlin's last of three scripts for the series, which began all the way back with Season 3's "The Tale of the Quicksilver."

- Codie Lucas Wilbee, who plays Stig for Season 5, joins Season 1's Eric, played by Jacob Tierney, as the only other single-season Society member.

Creator D. J. MacHale, surrounded by *AYAOTD?* props!
Photo by Jonathan Wenk

Cast and crew in front of Shandu's wagon: featuring Ross Hull,
Raine Pare-Coull, and D. J. MacHale in center, with writer/director
Ron Oliver in front row with leather jacket and sunglasses, posing between
the head for the werewolf from "The Tale of the Full Moon" and
fellow director David Winning. Photo courtesy of Ron Oliver

The Midnight Society. Photo courtesy of Ross Hull

Ross Hull and Daniel DeSanto, behind the scenes tomfoolery.
Photo courtesy of Ross Hull

Ross Hull having lunch with Jodie Resther. Photo courtesy of Ross Hull

Ross Hull with Raine Pare-Coull. Photo courtesy of Ross Hull

D. J. MacHale directing Laura Bertram on "The Tale of the Lonely Ghost."
Photo by Jonathan Wenk

D. J. MacHale taking bite out of Nosferatu on the set of "The Tale of the
Midnight Madness." Photo by Jonathan Wenk

D. J. MacHale with Bobcat Goldthwait and Samantha Chemerika, cast of "The
Tale of the Final Wish." Photo courtesy of D. J. MacHale

The man, the myth, *the* Sardo (accent on the "do"), Richard M. Dumont.
Photo courtesy of Richard M. Dumont

Ron Oliver deciding shot size on "The Tale of Prisoners Past."
Photo courtesy of Ron Oliver

Behind the scenes with director Ron Oliver and the Virus itself, Paul Cagelet, from "The Tale of the Renegade Virus." Photo courtesy of Ron Oliver

Writer/direct Ron Oliver with Amos Crawley and Heidi Burbela, the young cast of "The Tale of the Ghastly Grinner." Photo courtesy of Ron Oliver

Ron Oliver posing with Neil Kroetsch as the titular villain from "The Tale of the Ghastly Grinner." Photo courtesy of Ron Oliver

Director Ron Oliver with young Ryan Gosling from "The Tale of Station 109.1."
Photo courtesy of Ron Oliver

Ron Oliver with comedian Gilbert Gottfried from "The Tale of Station 109.1."
Photo courtesy of Ron Oliver

Ron Oliver directing Gottfried, with Karol Ike in white hat (director of photography for multiple episodes), in "The Tale of Station 109.1." Photo courtesy of Ron Oliver

Six of the *AYAOTD?* novels, featuring glow-in-the-dark cover art. Photo courtesy of Jose Prendes

Cast and crew in the "coldest bloody winter" director Ron Oliver's ever experienced. Photo courtesy of Ron Oliver

The Midnight Society between takes. Photo courtesy of Ross Hull

THE TALE OF SEASON SIX

Original U.S. airdate: February 27, 1999-May 15, 1999

Midnight Society Year Six Roster:

Tucker (Daniel DeSanto)

Megan (Elisha Cuthbert)

Quinn (Kareem Blackwell)

Vange (Vanessa Lengies)

Andy (David Deveau)

EPISODE 66:

"The Tale of the Forever Game"

U.S. Airdate: February 6, 1999

Written by: Mark David Perry

Directed by: Iain Paterson

Guest Cast: J. Adam Brown, Tod Fennell, Sarah Gadon, and Kyle Downes.

Favorite Line: "It's this tree, I know it.
This is what's keeping us in here."-Monica

Opening Campfire: It's been a few years now. The storyteller spot sits abandoned, covered in forest debris, until a figure pushes through the surrounding tree line, revealing itself to be our old pal Tucker, now a few years older. Someone shouts his name and he spins around to meet the first of our new members, Quinn, who hopes this is the place they were looking for. "This is it," Tucker says with a smile. Megan, another new member, runs up behind them, freaking out. "I walked into something stringy," she complains, and Tucker helps remove a web from her hair. Andy, another new guy, shows up with some fresh wood for the fire, and proceeds to trip and eat dirt. Tucker, showing us he's gone from the obnoxious little brother to the caring leader, makes sure his buddy Andy is ok. Then Vange, our final new member, arrives. She's mad that they didn't wait up for her. Quinn tosses an insult, and Vange tosses a branch back at him. Tucker breaks it up and restores peace, asking everyone to grab a log and sit. "We closed off the trail, and no one's been back since we left," Tucker begins to explain. "The rules are simple, this is all about telling a tale. I know you guys, just like my brother Gary knew the friends he brought here. We all love stories that are weird and scary, and this is the secret place where we tell these stories, because when we enter the circle, we leave reality behind, and enter a dark world where anything can happen." He digs his hand into the stump by the storyteller's chair and discovers that the midnight dust is still there. "Vange, Megan, Andy, Quinn, are we ready?" Tucker asks and this new team nods excitedly. "Then the first one's mine," he says and submits the first story for the approval of the new Midnight Society.

The Tale: Peter finds himself magically trapped inside an old tree, playing a board game that uses his little sister Monica and his best friend Mark as pawns, and if he loses he might be trapped inside that tree forever.

Closing Campfire: "That's how it works. Next time someone else tells a story," Tucker says, bringing his story to a close. "So, are we going to keep this going?" Andy and Vange are in immediately. Megan is hesitant, but she agrees. "You let anybody know I'm a part of this, and you're going to answer to my buddy, Señor Fist," Quinn threatens, but Tucker laughs it off because he knows he's won him over. The new gang walks off into the woods, discussing how cool their new club is, leaving Tucker to admire the rekindled fire. With a knowing smile he says, "We're back."

Review: This is a very special episode, because after an almost three year hiatus, the show was revived and injected with new blood both in front and behind the camera. D. J. MacHale no longer worked physically on the show, but Paul Doyle stepped in as show runner for the final two seasons. This was a wonderful episode in terms of introducing the new batch, and as a fan, I really appreciated that the reestablishing of the Midnight Society was a big event, instead of just throwing us into the middle of an established group. Now, on to the tale.

There are so many leaps in logic in this episode, but I suppose to keep the story contained within its allotted runtime a few leaps need to be made. I love the idea of a game that influences the world around the players, and I love the monster effects for the Burden Beast, but the overall logic of this episode is bit too loosey goosey for it to amount to real tension or suspense. It is a heck of a fun episode though, and there is never a dull moment, so at the very least it's a good watch.

Series Mythology

- This is the biggest shakeup in Midnight Society history, where four of the members are new faces, and only Tucker, an alumni from way back in Season 3, acts as the anchor and de facto leader to the new batch.

- There were plans to make an actual Forever Game board game, but they sadly fell by the wayside and it never came to fruition.

- Tod Fennell, who plays Mark, will returns to the series in Season 7's epic "The Tale of the Silver Sight."

- Kyle Downes, who plays Nathaniel, will returns to the series later this season with the fun episode "The Tale of Vampire Town."

- Carl Crevier, who plays the Burden Beast, will not appear in the series again, but he will go on to become a stand-in for actors such as Henry Cavill and Aaron Eckhart.

- Though uncredited for some reason, Griffith Brewer returns to the series to play the older Nathaniel in this episode. This is not only his second appearance on the show, but the second time he plays the older version of the young villain, seeing as he played the Old Man in Season 1's "The Tale of the Captured Souls."

EPISODE 67:

"The Tale of the Misfortune Cookie"

U.S. Airdate: February 13, 1999

Written by: Mark David Perry

Directed by: Adam Weissman

Guest Cast: Brandon Boey, Flora Chu, Ming Lee, and Belinda Hum.

Favorite Line: "One should find perfect existence
through imperfect existence."-David

Opening Campfire: Andy passes out fortune cookies to the gang and they tear into them to reveal what fate the cookie has in store for them. Tucker and Megan, sitting on a couch that they dragged out there, crack into theirs. "You're a beautiful star that shines in the night," Megan reads. "Yeah, that's about right." Tucker reads his, "Many will follow your wise guidance. Cool!" "Good for one free egg roll! I am all over this," Vange exclaims, reading her rewarding fortune. Quinn opens his and it's mysteriously blank. Vange doesn't fail to point out that it's a bad sign, because it means he has no future. "Yeah right," Quinn says and turns to Andy. "What's the point here, Gomer?" Well, Andy's first tale happens to revolve around fortune cookies, hence the visual aids.

The Tale: David wants fortune and fame instead of working himself to the bone at his family's Chinese restaurant, but when he gets a chance to glimpse what he deems a perfect life, he realizes he misses the things that really matter to him.

Closing Campfire: The gang, even Quinn, is blown away by Andy's tale. Megan wonders what his fortune cookie says. Andy opens it and reads, "Many do not hear your song, but it is beautiful." Quinn makes a face and Vange reminds him that it's better than his blank fortune. "Yeah, yeah, show's over," Quinn stands and ushers the gang away, offering to extinguish the campfire himself. Vange leads the way, off to get her freebie eggroll, leaving Quinn alone to douse the flames, but he reaches for another fortune cookie in the hat that Andy has left behind. He cracks it open and reads, "I told you, Quinn, only one fortune apiece." This angers the quick-tempered Quinn, and he threatens to turn Andy into dead meat as he rushes off to catch up to them.

Review: This tale is basically an Asian take on *It's A Wonderful Life* (1946), but with decidedly darker undertones. It's the devil's deal, in a sense. Get everything you think you want, but be careful what you wish for, because you may lose everything you have. It's a brilliant play on those concepts, and while it's not a scary episode, it is extremely thought provoking, and a great family conversation starter. I really liked how this episode was pieced together, and I would put it alongside Season 3's "The Tale of the Dream Girl" as one of the most feel-good episodes, delivering a satisfying and moving conclusions.

Series Mythology

- Adam MacDonald, who plays Eddy West, will returns in Season 7's "The Tale of Highway 13."

- Russell Yuen, who plays Mr. Chin the Cook, will returns in Season 7's "The Tale of the Laser Maze."

- Jason Cavalier, who plays the Warrior, returns to the series after fixing a hearse in Season 5's "The Tale of Station 109.1."

- The first and only episode to focus on the legends of a particular culture.

EPISODE 68:

"The Tale of the Virtual Pets"

U.S. Airdate: February 20, 1999

Written by: Alice Eve Cohen

Directed by: Iain Paterson

Guest Cast: Nicole Dicker, Alisha Morrison,
Jonathan Koensgen, and Christine Jack.

Favorite Line: "My mom's going to kill me."-Tom

Opening Campfire: Quinn is feeling chilly so he instructs Tucker to make him a big campfire tonight. Andy arrives with firewood, again, and manages to annoy Quinn . . . again. Megan arrives late and her very trendy pager goes off, thanks to her mom who apparently insists on talking to her. Megan pulls out her top-of-the-line flip phone and dials her mom up, inspiring the just arriving Vange to shout, "That is exactly what my story is about!" "What, spoiled rich chicks?" Quinn posits delicately. Vange is referring to technology, not Megan specifically. "If we need computers so bad and they're getting smarter all the time, does that mean people are getting dumber?" The answer is yes, of course, and Vange has a tale all about it.

The Tale: Aliens use a rogue computer program to switch places with human children who are addicted to technology, but luckily Kate is analog and may be the only hope to save her friends from being downloaded into oblivion.

Closing Campfire: Vange ends her story and warns us to be careful around our computers. Megan's pager goes off as Tucker douses the fire. She doesn't understand why her mother keeps bothering her, until she reads it and runs off scared. Tucker and Andy read her abandoned pager and race off after her.

Vange walks over and picks up the pager to show us that it reads, "FEED ME . . . FEED ME . . . ." Is this the beginning of a coming invasion? Nope. Quinn reveals that it took him an hour to figure out how to do that. "Always wanted one of these," Vange says, pocketing the pager. She walks off with Quinn and he reminds her that she owes him big time.

Review: This is horror for the Tamagotchi generation. If you know what those are, you'll understand immediately the reference, and if you have no idea what that is, God bless you. This episode starts off like *Invasion of the Body Snatchers* then devolves into a finale where our heroine has to essentially close an app, and yes it isn't very thrilling. I love the idea of the episode, but the moving parts were too goofball for me. Why does the Digger program use a bulldog for its mascot, and couldn't they come up with a better webpage layout? I get the dog as a virtual pet, but it's just a static image! Even Tamagotchi moved around, and they were subpar graphically. Why does the Digger program brand the recently body-snatched with a dog tattoo? I know they needed a way to tell the good guys from the bad guys, but a tattoo of a dog is a bit too silly. I did like how the writer brought mirrors into play in the finale, after mentioning it briefly in the department store, but beyond that touch the typing-commands-into-the-computer finale was less than exciting cinematically, and ended the goofy episode even goofier.

Series Mythology

- The supposed author for the book featured in the opening moments of the episode, "Advanced Computer Language," is I. Paterson, a reference to the episode director Iain Paterson, who here directs his sixth and final episode for the series, which started all the way back with Season 3's excellent "The Tale of the Bookish Babysitter".

- This is writer Alice Eve Cohen's first and only script for the series. In fact, it's her first and only TV writing credit.

EPISODE 69:

"The Tale of the Zombie Dice"

U.S. Airdate: February 27, 1999

Written by: Maggie Leigh

Directed by: Adam Weissman

Guest Cast: Scott Pietrangelo, Jay Baruchel,
Edward Yankie, and Daniel Skorzewski.

Favorite Line: "Oh, I'm a granny. A really smart granny."-Alex

Opening Campfire: Poor Andy and Quinn carry Vange to the campfire in a swivel chair. Tucker is surprised to see a real chair at the campfire and wonders what's going on. Apparently Megan has taken it upon herself, with the help of the boys, to bring in some real, comfier furniture for the Midnight Society's rear ends, because Megan does not sit on logs. She knows it's not traditional, and she bats doe eyes at Tucker, hoping he won't mind. "Why should I mind?" Tucker shouts and swan dives onto the couch, which last sat mildewing at the dump. Vange is up tonight and she's got a good one. Megan falls into the chair the boys just brought as Vange takes her place in the storyteller's chair. Andy and Quinn make a mad dash for the other half of the couch, and Andy gets there first. Quinn, playing it cool after losing the impromptu game of musical chairs, decides to just pull up a rock to listen to Vange's tale of games run amok.

The Tale: Kids are disappearing at Mr. Click's arcade, and when Alex's friend goes missing, he goes searching behind the scenes and discovers the hidden secrets of Mr. Click's lair and falls prey to them.

Closing Campfire: Vange ends her tale and the gang seems to really like it, but Tucker really, *really* likes the new furniture. Quinn seems to like it the most, because he's managed to gain a seat at the couch and fall asleep on it. The gang tiptoes away quietly and lets poor, tired Quinn snuggle up by the campfire all by his lonesome.

Review: This episode should have been the second storyone aired, and was probably intended that way, but I am putting it fourth here, according to my triple-checked airdate sources, because it's the only real form of order I can use. This is yet another game-based story, like the season opener, so maybe that's why it was decided to air them separately. This season seems to be game-based, what with the Forever Game, Digger's virtual pets, and now the Zombie Dice as elements for the tales. This episode has a great location in the underground video arcade, but it has the same story problem that Season 5's "The Tale of the Mystical Mirror" had. In that one, a witch turns girls into dogs. In this one, the mysterious Mr. Click shrinks kids and puts them in cages because apparently he knows people who want that. Jay Baruchel, who would go on to Hollywood stardom, ably handles the hero role here and he is genuinely likable. If only the underlying plot were a bit easier to swallow, this would have been a great episode. If Mr. Click needed kids, why bet with them using the Zombie Dice, why not just take them? Also, why the heck are they called Zombie Dice? If this had been about a board game that summons zombies that would have been awesome, but alas it's about shrunken children for some reason. I will say I loved the final wager that Alex tricks Mr. Click with, that was very well played, sir. Very well played, indeed.

Series Mythology

- Vange's last story for this season.

- Jay Baruchel, who plays Alex, returns to the series for his second of four appearances. He will return in Season 6's theater-based "The Tale of the Walking Shadow" and finally in Season 7's Sardo swansong, "The Tale of the Time Trap."

- Jane Gilchrist, who plays the simply titled Woman Teacher, returns to the series after playing yet another teacher in Season 1's "The Tale of the Sorcerer's Apprentice."

EPISODE 70:

"The Tale of the Gruesome Gourmets"

U.S. Airdate: March 13, 1999

Written by: Michael Koegel

Directed by: Lorette Leblanc

Guest Cast: Patrick Thomas, Justin Bradley,
Giovanna Carrubba, and Annakin Slayd (aka Andrew Farrar).

Favorite Line: "Careful, young man. One slip and
you're hamburger meat."-Mr. Collins

Opening Campfire: Megan wastes no time as she sets out a fancy table for a candlelit dinner for one and briefs the gang on the importance of eating, and how some people love a certain kind of food so much that they would do whatever it took to get it. She scoops some midnight dust into her wine goblet and tosses it into the fire to submit her tale.

The Tale: Tommy and David suspect that the new neighbors, Mr. Collins and Mr. Pimm, are cannibals, and while they search for proof of their dastardly diets, the boys discover that they may be on their menu.

Closing Campfire: Megan ends her tale, leaving everyone queasy. Tucker wonders what she brought to eat, and Megan pulls out a massive, meat-stuffed deli sandwich. "Something very special. It's my favorite," she says, and they wonder what it is. "Well, it's tasty. It's meaty. It's tongue!" She manages to gross the gang out and send them running for the hills, leaving her alone to dig into her monster sandwich in peace.

Review: This is the most fun episode in Season 6, and I would go so far as to say it's my second favorite of the season. The Midnight Society segments are short and snappy, but they work. The episode shines because of its simple Scooby-Doo construction. Are the neighbors cannibals or not? The hunt for the truth is exciting and fits the bill for what *AYAOTD?* should be. The ending seems to give us closure, but there is a small hint that the boys might have been right about these guys after all and I loved that. I wish the show had pulled the rug out from under us a few more times, helping to maybe undercut the silly plot lines. This is a not necessarily a scary episode, but it has its suspenseful moments and best of all it's really a blast to watch. Got to love those mistaken identity episodes, like Season 2's "The Tale of the Full Moon." This episode even manages to fit in a little homage to *Home Alone,* which would play like too much in another episode, but it works perfectly in the finale of this one. It's also nice that Mr. Pimm and Mr. Collins found an apartment with a professional walk-in freezer; maybe that was the selling point?

Series Mythology

- Patrick Thomas, who plays Tommy, will returns to the series in Season 7's "The Tale of the Photo Finish."

- Gordon Masten, who plays Mr. Collins, returns to the series after getting kids in shape in Season 1's "The Tale of the Twisted Claw."

- Kathleen Fee, who plays Dotty, returns to the series after joining the undead in Season 5's "The Tale of the Night Shift," and will return for a third appearance in Season 7's "The Tale of the Stone Maiden."

EPISODE 71:

"The Tale of Jake the Snake"

U.S. Airdate: March 20, 1999

Written by: Alan Kingsberg

Directed by: Mark Soulard

Guest Cast: Ricky Mabe, James Hayes Liboiron,
Shawn Potter, and Paul Rainville.

Favorite Line: "Answer me this: if Jake the Snake was
the greatest, how come nobody ever heard of him?
Because he turned into a nasty snake creature, that's why."-Zach

Opening Campfire: Andy arrives to find the campfire roaring, but the spot abandoned. He quickly worries and when the trees start shaking, seemingly on their own, he freaks and turns to run, bumping into a hockey-masked maniac. The maniac turns out to be Tucker, and the others were in on the goof, shaking the trees to spook poor Andy, who's turns out to be a good sport about the whole thing. "Whoa, rewind. Tucker just gassed you nasty and you're not ticked?" Andy is not, shrugging it off. "Friends are like that, Quinn. If you ever get one, you'll know," Vange zings Quinn. Coincidentally, friends, and to a degree hockey, are what Tucker's story is about.

The Tale: Wiley wants to make the hockey team desperately, but he sucks at the game, until a shadowy figure gives him an old hockey stick that belonged to a legendary player named Jake the Snake, who wasn't called that for nothing.

Closing Campfire: Tucker's story crosses the goal line and as he douses the campfire, he turns to apologize to Andy for giving him the shakes, but Andy has disappeared, much to everyone's surprise. Suddenly, the trees surrounding them start shaking and they figure Andy's trying to get his revenge, so they aren't falling for it. "Who you talking to?" Andy wonders, arriving back at the campfire as the gang calls into the bush, toward the thing they thought was Andy. At this point they realize that it wasn't him, and they all scramble away in fright. We never find out who really was out there in the woods, watching them.

Review: So, Jake "the Snake" Desmond was so named because he could snake through any defense on the ice. I can buy that, but it's still weird to name your tale after a famous wrestler. I thought Jake the Snake himself was going to show up and wrestle some monsters, but that was not the case. That's false advertising, my friends, but that's the least of the issues I have with this one. This episode is another example of the series repeating itself, and going super goofy with their repeat, sadly. I like the idea of a kid getting to play hockey the way he always dreamed he could and selling his soul in the process. That would have been Faustian, but adding the element of a hockey stick that slowly turns you into a snake, of all things, just stretches credulity to its breaking point. The ending consisted of Wiley simply hitting Jake the Snake, causing him to fall into the pit of snakes, and that somehow defeats him. This resolution is conveniently brief and nonsensical, but ultimately fruitless because Jake survives. Also, the fact that breaking the hockey stick would break the curse was too simple a solution to be satisfying. I know cg effects were in their infancy at the time, but looking back at this now the cg snakes looked like lame video game graphics. They were a product of their time, so I can't fault the show for that. Also, side note, I find it surprising that in a show made by Canadians, this is the first time we see anything related to hockey.

Series Mythology

- Among the list of names of the players who made the hockey team you can find a nod to Ned Kandel, the man who helped create the series with D. J. MacHale and was an Executive Producer.

- James Hayes Liboiron, who plays Wiley Helphin (spelled Halpin in the episode), returns to the series after encountering imaginary Bigfoots in Season 5's "The Tale of the Manaha."

- Shawn Potter, who plays Duchamp, returns to the series after being the cool kid in Season 5's "The Tale of the Door Unlocked," and will return for a third appearance in Season 7's "The Tale of the Lunar Locusts."

EPISODE 72:

"The Tale of the Hunted"

U.S. Airdate: March 27, 1999

Written by: Gaylen James

Directed by: Lorette Leblanc

Guest Cast: Charlotte Sullivan, Noah Klar,
Larry Day, and Jennifer Bertram.

Favorite Line: "Nice shooting, dead-eye!"-Quinn

Opening Campfire: Everyone arrives to find a sad and lonely Andy sitting by the campfire. He proceeds to bum everyone out by telling a story about how he used his slingshot to knock a mourning dove out of a tree, killing it. "It's been bugging me so much that it made me think of a story," he says dourly. "Things are born and things die. That's the way it goes. But if you're going to step in and take nature into your own hands, then you better be ready to handle the outcome."

The Tale: Diana is excited to go out on her first hunting trip with her dad, who wants to bag the elusive wolf known as The Blaze, but the mystical Blaze has something else in store for Diana because she awakens one morning to find that she has somehow become a wolf, and is now the hunted instead of the hunter.

Closing Campfire: Andy brings his tale to a somber conclusion, and it looks as if he was able to work out his feelings through the telling. Tucker douses the fire and the gang approaches Andy to pat him on the back for a job well done as they head off into the woods, together.

Review: This is a very interesting episode, in that it seems to be referencing one of the tales in Ovid's *Metamorphoses* featuring the goddess of the hunt,

Diana. Pretty heady stuff, and for an episode that speaks against animal cruelty I couldn't think of a finer companion piece. The show manages to flip the tables as to audience expectations. What began as a ghostly wolf story becomes a semi-soft werewolf tale that works as an analogy to the old refrain about walking a mile in someone else's shoes. This isn't a scary one, except for a few moments in the beginning, but it's one to watch with the animal lovers in your life.

Series Mythology

- Malamute Huskies stand in for the wolves in this episode.

- Larry Day, who plays Grant, returns to the series after dealing with a fiery spirit in Season 4's "The Tale of the Fire Ghost."

- Jennifer Bertram, who plays Laura, only appears this one time in the series, but,, she is the sister of Laura Bertram, who appears twice in the series, first in Season 1's "The Tale of the Lonely Ghost," and then in Season 5's "The Tale of the Mystical Mirror."

- James Rae, who plays Hank, returns to the series after worrying about his daughter in Season 5's "The Tale of Badge."

- This is writer Gaylen James' first and last script for the series. This season seemed to have a running theme of one-offs from multiple writers.

- Andy's last tale for the season.

EPISODE 73:

"The Tale of the Wisdom Glass"

U.S. Airdate: April 3, 1999

Written by: Mark David Perry

Directed by: Jacques Laberge

Guest Cast: Tyler Hynes, Tyler Kyte, Harry Standjofski, and Ivan Smith.

Favorite Line: "Duuudde!"-Allan Price

Opening Campfire: Quinn arrives in a huff, looking for poor, beleaguered Andy. Turns out Andy accidentally ratted him out to the principal, concerning a forged note from Quinn's mother, and he wants to punch his pal's lights out. Andy hasn't arrived yet, according to the other, but we get a privileged glimpse behind the ratty, dumpster couch and discover the scared Andy hiding quietly behind it. Quinn has a feeling Andy won't show, and it's a shame, because it's his first time at bat tonight and his story happens to be about the perils of ratting on your friends.

The Tale: A stolen video game leads new friends Jimmy and Allan into a real-world game room where wisdom rules and crimes are punished severely.

Closing Campfire: Andy reveals himself and before getting pulped, he explains that he called Quinn's mom and told her what happened. She was able to get Quinn off the hook for the two weeks detention he got for the forged note, which was based on a real note his mother had sent, but he had lost. Quinn, deflated, doesn't quite know how to say thanks. Then, he quickly realizes that Andy told his mom that he forged a note from her and thusly might be in worse trouble! Andy runs off, realizing he still has a target on his back and Quinn gives chase. The girls follow to help Andy, and Tucker douses the flames before beating feet after them.

Review: The digital-age has infected this season of *AYAOTD?*, and this episode plays in similar game-related ground that most of this season's episodes seemed to gravitate towards. This one goes from modern-age computer gaming to metaphysical parable, making it a very interesting and unique episode. What appears on the surface to be about a haunted computer game is actually a scary tale about the evils of stealing and the terrible things that can happen to you if you do it.

My favorite scene in this is when the kids are invited to the live tournament and walk into a low-budget version of *Eyes Wide Shut* (1999), which came out the same year as this episode and may have informed the costume department. I love that there wasn't a nice, happy, and rushed ending here. For a story to truly have an impact and be scary there can't ever be sunshine and rainbows at the end, in my opinion. That's the point of a scary story, it's supposed to remind you that sometimes it doesn't always turn out ok; sometimes you pay the price.

Series Mythology

- Harry Standjofski, who plays Phil, returns to the series after playing the movie theater manager Mr. Kristoph in Season 2's "The Tale of the Midnight Madness."

- Ivan Smith, who plays Trevor/ Judge Day, returns to the series after appearing twice before in Season 3's "The Tale of the Quicksilver" and Season 5's "The Tale of a Door Unlocked."

- Danette Mackay, who plays The Keeper, will return in the series finale as the titular villain in "The Tale of the Night Nurse."

- Arthur Holden, who plays the foppish Court Jester, returns to the series after appearing twice before; once as Ichabod Crane in Season 3's "The

Tale of the Midnight Ride" and as Mr. Brooks in Season 5's "The Tale of the Dead Man's Float."

- Director Jacques Laberge's second and final time behind the camera. His first episode was Season 5's outer-spacey "The Tale of the Unexpected Visitor".

EPISODE 74:

"The Tale of the Walking Shadow"

U.S. Airdate: April 10, 1999

Written by: Matthew Cope

Directed by: Lorette Leblanc

Guest Cast: Jay Baruchel, Kathryn Long,
Sheena Larkin, and Marcel Jeannin.

Favorite Line: "This was way more fun when
I wasn't the responsible one."-Tucker

Opening Campfire: We skip the fun character preamble stuff and slam into the intro of Megan's tale as the gang munches popcorn and slurps sodas. She gives us a spiel about ghost stories, and how everyone loves a good one, but what makes them scary? "They're about unfinished business," she explains. "Is the ghost here to do something friendly, or is it here to haunt the living to create some unspeakable evil? You never know, until the ghost strikes." They all agree that that is what makes a ghost story scary, which cues Megan to toss the midnight dust into the fire and begin.

The Tale: Ross has been cast as Macduff in his school's version of *Macbeth*, but when he arrives at the theater he discovers that the ghost of a previous actor who played Macbeth and died tragically has a bone to pick with this new Macduff.

Closing Campfire: "And speaking of unfinished business, you guys owe me for the popcorn and soda," Tucker stands, as Megan winds up her tale, and begins to tally the prices. This prompts everyone to give various reasons for why they can't pay before they rush off into the woods and leave poor Tucker to deal with the trash.

Review: This episode's title comes not from the comparison of ghosts to shadows, but to Macbeth's famous final monologue where he states, "Life's but a walking shadow, a poor player that struts and frets his hour upon the stage, and then is heard no more." I like this episode, because it gives us a familiar setting, which we haven't seen since Season 1's "The Tale of Jake and the Leprechaun," but deals more with the magic of the theater than anything else. Jay Baruchel once again ably plays a likable lead, and Sheena Larkin is as wonderful as always in her bit. I love the way the episode deals with the superstitions of the theater and the power of performance over life and death. The ending feels earned, and not haphazardly constructed, which makes it very rewarding. However, would the kids be clapping at the ghosts prancing around on the stage? I think they'd be screaming and running in panic, but maybe the magic of the theater held them in sway.

Series Mythology

- The show goes meta when Ross distinctly whistles the *AYAOTD?* theme song.

- Jay Baruchel, who plays Ross, returns for his third of four appearances. His final appearance will be in Season 7's "The Tale of the Time Trap." This is his second appearance this season, having earlier battled the game master Mr. Click in "The Tale of the Zombie Dice."

- The amazing Sheena Larkin, who plays Hermione St. Clair, returns to the series for her fourth time as a brand-new character. She will return once more in the Season 7 three-parter, "The Tale of the Silver Sight."

- Kathryn Long, who plays Vanessa, only appears in this episode of *AYAOTD?*, but she is best-known to TV horror fans from her appearances in *Goosebumps* as Carly Beth in the "The Haunted Mask" saga.

- Marcel Jeannin, who plays Adrian, returns to the series after playing the red Corpse in the great Season 5 opener, "The Tale of the Dead Man's Float."

- Babs Gadbois, who plays Gwen, returns to the series here for her third and final time. She previously appeared in Season 3's "The Tale of Watcher's Woods" and Season 5's "The Tale of the Mystical Mirror."

- Heidi Burbela, who plays Kim, the play's young director, returns to the series after tussling with the titular villain as Hooper Picalarro in Season 4's "The Tale of the Ghastly Grinner."

- Writer Matthew Cope's first and last script for *AYAOTD?*

- The light that comes on at the end of the episode is referred to in theater lingo as the "ghost light", which is always left on, even when all other lights are turned off and the building had been emptied. Maybe this means that Macbeth remains to fight again another day.

EPISODE 75:

"The Tale of the Oblivion"

U.S. Airdate: April 17, 1999

Written by: James Morris

Directed by: Jim Donovan

Guest Cast: Daniel Clark, Emma Taylor-Isherwood, Richard Dumont, and Alan Legros.

Favorite Line: "I've got to get out of this business."-Sardo

Opening Campfire: Tucker brings a ton of outdated stuff like 8-track tapes and Hula Hoops (which are still easily found and played with today) for the gang to paw through. Andy got his hands on some stilts and wonders if Tucker's tale is about stilts before he face-plants into the ground. But it isn't; it's about stuff that isn't necessarily around anymore. "So, much stuff disappears so completely that people barely remember it," Tucker says. "So, I was thinking, 'where do things go when nobody wants them anymore?'" My answer would be the trash, but Tucker's got a different tale to tell.

The Tale: Young artist Max buys a simple eraser from the eccentric Sardo, which means the eraser is more than simple. It gives Max the power to eraser anything he doesn't like out of existence, and with great power comes great corruption.

Closing Campfire: Tucker ends his tale and reveals a charcoal drawing he has done of the other members sitting around the campfire. They are impressed, but Tucker doesn't think it's very good and prepares to throw it into the fire. The gang races forward to stop him, and he agrees to hold on to it if they help him carry all the outdated junk back. They hop to it, believing that Tucker might have the power of life and death over them. But it's just a story . . . isn't it?

Review: Oblivion looks like an overstuffed garage, so visually it isn't very interesting, and kind of a letdown, but the rest of the episode is really quite unique and compelling. The power to do away with the things that are in your way is something many folks would love to have, and yes it would quickly be abused. This is another in the long ling of "be careful what you wish for" episodes, but I like the spin on it, and Sardo's presence adds a lot, as well. I love how Sardo just blunders into the adventures he's introduced into, and having him appear in episodes for the revival seasons was a nice addition for the fans. The Kronos guy was an odd touch, because I wasn't sure how he connected to the monks in the beginning, but hey I guess the show can add Vikings to its list of baddies.

Series Mythology

- Sardo returns for the seventh time! Richard Dumont will play the memorable magic shop owner one more time in Season 7's "The Tale of the Time Trap."

- Emma Taylor-Isherwood, who plays Shelley, will return to the series in Season 7's "The Tale of the Reanimator."

- Alan Legros, who plays Kronos, returns to the series after uncredited appearances in Season 3's "The Tale of the Guardian's Curse," and as the freaky titular villain in that same season's "The Tale of the Crimson Clown".

- Bill Corday, who plays Thelodius, returns to the series after his brief appearance as the scared old man in Season 5's "The Tale of Station 109.1."

- Matt Holland, who plays Chadwick, will return to the series as an eccentric game master in Season 7's "The Tale of the Laser Maze."

- Una Kay, who plays Mrs. Fitzgerald, returns to the series after her brief appearance in Season 2's "The Tale of the Whispering Walls."

- Writer James Morris will go on to write one more episode for the series, Season 7's "The Tale of the Time Trap," which will also feature Sardo.

- Sardo references Season 5's "The Tale of a Door Unlocked."

EPISODE 76:

"The Tale of Vampire Town"

U.S. Airdate: April 24, 1999

Written by: Alison Lea Bingeman

Directed by: Mark Soulard

Guest Cast: Kyle Downes, Richard Jutras, Michel Perron, and Greg Dunley.

Favorite Line: "If I'm going to hunt vampires, then I need to think like a vampire, and I don't think that they eat peanut butter."-Adder

Opening Campfire: Everyone sits around, waiting for Quinn. It's quite possible he won't show, because rumor has it he started a fight and was sent to the principal's office. Megan criticizes him for being a jerk and he arrives right on cue to respond with, "And that's the kind of thinking that makes me nuts." He's tired of being the guy who always gets blamed when bad stuff happens. "I've got a story about this very thing," he says, sitting down in the storyteller's chair. "It's about a guy who's a little different. He doesn't go along with what's normal, you know? People don't like things that aren't normal, it makes them uncomfortable, but that's the way my guy likes it . . . ."

The Tale: Adder Carballo, a young vampire enthusiast and hunter, has dragged his family to the small town of Wisteria to hunt for a supposed vampire on the loose, and discovers that vampires are indeed real and he's put himself within striking distance of their fangs.

Closing Campfire: Quinn ends his tale, and the gang approaches to apologize for thinking he was always the troublemaker. Tucker hangs back after the others have left and asks him who really started the fight. Quinn reveals that it was him after all, but the guy nabbed Quinn's lunch, so he deserved it.

Review: This is my absolute, #1 favorite episode of Season 6. It puts a big smile on my face, from beginning to end. Kyle Downes, as Adder, does a fantastic job of playing fanboy/vampire poseur and it is a hoot to watch. This episode reminds you that you must be careful what you wish for, like some of the best *AYAOTD?*, and it delivers a fun, spooky ride that fires on all cylinders acting and plot-wise. The monster effects are great and the catacomb setting is fantastic, making this one another great Halloween evening episode to add to your eventual marathon.

Series Mythology

• Quinn's last tale for Season 6.

• Kyle Downes, who plays Adder, returns to the series after leading the titular game in "The Tale of the Forever Game" at the beginning of this season.

• Richard Jutras, who plays Stanley, returns to the series after playing the less-than-crucial role of the Pizza Delivery Guy in Season 3's "The Tale of the Phone Police."

• Michel Perron, who plays Mueller, returns to the series after running the bowling alley in Season 3's "The Tale of the Dream Girl."

• Writer Alison Lea Bingeman returns to the series for her third and final time here, after writing two episodes in Season 2, "The Tale of the Dark Dragon" and "The Tale of the Whispering Walls."

EPISODE 77:

"The Tale of the Secret Admirer"

U.S. Airdate: May 8, 1999

Written by: Eric Weiner

Directed by: Mark Soulard

Guest Cast: Asia Vieira, Mark Hauser,
Andrew W. Walker, and Domenic Di Rosa.

Favorite Line: "Tell me I wasn't scared by a
pair of long Johns."-Meggie Evans

Opening Campfire: Megan has asked everyone to type up a secret confession to someone in the Midnight Society. Quinn, who is always too cool for school, thinks it's a dorky game, but Megan assures him that the game will be fun. She reaches into a hat, where she placed the notes, and pulls out a note for Tucker, two for Andy (one sweet and one reminding him to zip up his zipper), one for Vange, where the confessor admits that she reminds them of them, which leaves her confused, and a last one for Megan, where the confessor reveals that they have always considered her pretty. Quinn wonders if this has any bearing on her story tonight, and of course it does! "Getting secret notes is cool, especially if they're good ones like this. But what if you got a note that wasn't so great? What if it warned you about something evil? What would you do?" She asks menacingly, and answers with her tale.

The Tale: Meggie Evans thought she was the kind of girl nobody noticed, until she starts receiving mysterious notes from a secret admirer that may not be alive.

Closing Campfire: Megan ends her tale and Tucker asks her what it's like to have a secret admirer. She smiles and looks down at the note, only to realize that she read it wrong. She unfolds it and discovers that it's a confession to Quinn that reads, "I always wanted to tell you that you're pretty . . . pretty much a dork." Quinn, furious, stands and demands to know who wrote the note, but Vange reminds him that it's supposed to be a secret.

Review: This is a well-crafted take on the secret admirer plot, giving us a ghost story and a stalker story at the same time, and I really love how the story shifts gears for a surprising third act. I appreciate that the writer gives us an extra layer to the tale by revealing that the letters were directed at Meggie's mom, who had a run in with an admirer named Teddy Mars. Also what happened to Teddy was actually quite horrific. It turns this tale into more of a Freddy Krueger thing, than a Phantom of the Opera thing, which is where I thought it was heading. The explosion effects are lame, but that's part of the charm of the series. This is a great, re-watchable episode, and it's almost quaint compared to the techno-laced plotlines abounding through this season. This one feels like an old school *AYAOTD?* episode, and that's a good thing.

Series Mythology

- Asia Vieira, who plays Meggie, only appears in the series once, but she workeds with Daniel DeSanto, aka Tucker, on the long-running kid's series, *The Adventures of Dudley the Dragon.*

- Andrew W. Walker, who plays Bucky, returns to the series after appearing in Season 5's "The Tale of the Vacant Lot."

- This is writer Eric Weiner's first and last script for the series. He later went on to co-create *Dora the Explorer,* of all things.

- Megan's last tale for Season 6.

EPISODE 78:

"The Tale of Bigfoot Ridge"

U.S. Airdate: May 15, 1999

Written by: Randy Holland

Directed by: Lorette Leblanc

Guest Cast: Hayden Christensen, Brooke Nevin,
Sarah Edmondson, and Liz MacRae.

Favorite Line: "Don't blame me if you dump!"-Tucker

Opening Campfire: While waiting for Tucker to arrive, Quinn beats Andy at the hand slap game, thanks to his sluggish reflexes, and Megan bemoans how their couch gets so dirty. Vange jumps on the couch and reminds her that they are, after all, in the woods. Tucker arrives with his tricked out BMX bike, wearing his helmet and body pads. He's training for a race and everyone except for Vange doesn't understand why Tucker finds the possibility of breaking a bone fun. Extreme sports are dangerous, right? Well, Tucker's got a story about some extreme sports lovers, who face something much more horrible than a broken bone or a dislocated pelvis.

The Tale: Kirk and Dani go searching for their missing friend Gina up on Bigfoot Ridge, only to find her as an old woman being held captive by a soul-sucking creature that also wants to age Kirk and Dani like fine wine before eating them.

Closing Campfire: Tucker finishes his story, prompting Quinn to stand up and reappraise Tucker's bike. He tells them that bikes are pretty cool, and the best part is that if you have a bike you don't have to walk home. With that said, he jumps on Tucker's bike and pedals away. Tucker instructs the others to put out the fire as he gives chase, only to hear Quinn come to a crashing halt somewhere deep in the woods.

Review: Again, the show teases Bigfoot, but fails to deliver on the actual creature. This could be called sleight-of-hand to trick the audience, but I call it false advertising. In any case, the episode is actually really good and quite scary, which is an element that has been missing from most of the entries this season. I like the way this episode evolves from a missing persons search to a ghost story to a demon on the loose in a haunted cabin story. We don't get any details about the Umbra demon, a formless black shadow that takes the shape of its last victim, but that works toward making it scarier instead of confusing. The future Darth Vader, Hayden Christensen, does a good job here, as does Brook Nevin, who never gives up on her pal, and serves to remind kids of the strength of friendship. This is a great episode, and while it still doesn't give me a Bigfoot, it certainly gives me chills.

Series Mythology

- This is writer Randy Holland's first and last script for the series. However, he would go on to write fifty-four episodes for the long-running soap opera, *The Young and the Restless* (1973).

- Sarah Edmondson, who plays Gina, will return to the series in Season 7's "The Tale of Many Faces."

- Liz MacRae, who plays Marie, returns to the series after appearing twice before in Season 2's "The Tale of the Hatching," and Season 4's "The Tale of the Fire Ghost."

- For some reason, the actor that plays Old Gina goes uncredited.

- Tucker's last tale for Season 6, thus bookending the revival season.

THE TALE OF SEASON SEVEN

Original U.S. airdate: April 2, 2000-June 11, 2000

Midnight Society Year Seven Roster:
Tucker (Daniel DeSanto)
Megan (Elisha Cuthbert)
Quinn (Kareem Blackwell)
Vange (Vanessa Lengies)
Andy (David Deveau)

EPISODE 79:

"The Tale of the Silver Sight: Part 1"

U.S. Airdate: April 2, 2000

Written by: D. J. MacHale

Directed by: Mark Soulard

Guest Cast: Daniel DeSanto, Ross Hull, James Bradford, and Ryan Cooley.

Favorite Line: "I hope you know what you've gotten yourselves into.
No one who's touched the Silver Sight has
emerged undamaged."-General Laing Candle

Opening Campfire: Due to the fact that the "Silver Sight" trilogy doesn't work like a traditional episode, the format I've been using will be jettisoned, in favor of a more in-depth recounting of the "tale," which is the entire meat of this and the next two episodes.

The Tale: Gary and Tucker's grandfather dies mysteriously, leaving Gary a piece of an old record with the words "listen to the music" written on it. Turns out that in 1937 their grandfather started the Midnight Society with his five best friends, who found a charm called the Silver Sight that held a powerful black magic.

Horrible things started to happen, and all because one of the five friends was wielding the evil magic of the charm. One of the members hid it and made a recording on a record that he broke and separated between the friends, telling them where the charm was before he mysteriously died the next day.

Gary and Tuck's grandpa has tasked them with finding the remaining four members of the OG Midnight Society to get their pieces of the record in order to find the Silver Sight and destroy it once and for all.

Gary teams up with Tucker and his new crew, and everyone splits up to investigate. The brothers head to the home of General Laing Candle, and Tuck manages to grab his piece of record after fighting off reanimated suits of armor that nearly shred him to pieces, but as he flees to safety a ghostly little Waif boy warns him that it will only get worse from here.

Review: This is a fun episode, because you get to see the Midnight Society in action for once, taking center stage in the proceedings. D. J. MacHale, series creator, returns to write this epic trilogy along with Ross Hull, returning to fill the shoes of the senior Midnight Society president, Gary. This episode gets the ball rolling and offers up some scares and a fun fight scene for Tucker, which I'm sure was a highlight of Daniel DeSanto's run as Tucker. The exposition is a bit too much for the first half of this episode, but there is a lot of groundwork to lay out, and it's all quite compelling, so I can forgive it.

We get a meeting in the middle of this episode where they gather in Gary's dorm room, revealing that Gary probably left the Midnight Society due to starting college, and we see what the others have been up to so it nicely teases the adventures of the rest of the team: Megan smells for some reason, and Quinn is stealing a drawing from Laing Candle's home.

This episode doesn't really work on its own, but it's not designed to do so. The mysterious urchin kid known as the Waif is the real mystery here. How he is connected to everything remains to be seen, but with two pieces of the record in our gang's possession we are close to finding it all out.

Series Mythology

• Andy mentions the Magic Mansion, the home of Sardo.

• Ross Hull returns as Gary, bridging the old and new generation.

- Ian Beny Anderson, who plays Young Laing for this and the next two episodes, will return to the series later in this final season in "The Tale of the Time Trap."

- James Bradford, who plays the older General Laing Candle for this and the next two episodes, returns to the series after playing the memorable Shandu in Season 2's "The Tale of the Magician's Assistant."

- Anthony Etesonne-Bedard, who plays Young Bruce, returns to the series after getting into trouble in Season 5's "The Tale of a Door Unlocked."

EPISODE 80:

"The Tale of the Silver Sight: Part 2"

U.S. Airdate: April 2, 2000

Written by: D. J. MacHale

Directed by: Mark Soulard

Guest Cast: Elisha Cuthbert, Kareem Blackwell, Sheena Larkin, and Anik Matern.

Favorite Line: "Finish your tea, dear."-Mrs. Gregory

Opening Campfire: Due to the fact that the "Silver Sight" trilogy doesn't work like a traditional episode, the format I've been using will be jettisoned, in favor of a more in depth recounting of the "tale," which is the entire meat of this and the preceding and next episodes.

The Tale: The second part of the Silver Sight trilogy focuses on Quinn and Megan's search for the missing pieces of the record. Quinn is led to a junk-yard where he outruns a ghostly Rottweiler and meets a junk dealer, who will give him a piece of the record in exchange for a portrait of OG member Donna, that is being held at General Laing Candle's home, connecting that piece of the story that was seen last time.

Megan finds herself in a sewer, talking to the descendants of one of the early Midnight Society members, who have fallen on hard times. Laing Candle shows up and reveals himself as the traitor amidst the original Midnight Society who was using the Silver Sight for nefarious purposes, and is desperate to find it again. He chases Megan, but she manages to escape, only to run into the Waif kid who warns her away from the hunt by scaring her into believing she was going to be run over by a train. She makes it back to the sewer clan's abode and finds the piece of the record she was looking for, making the tally four pieces in all, with one remaining.

Review: The *Empire Strikes Back* (1980) of the Silver Sight saga offers some great action beats and some really fun stuff for the cast to do, not to mention some very dynamic locations that open up the world around them. Gary and Tucker don't really factor into this episode, and Vange and Andy, who have teamed up, aren't given much to do except set up their hunt which will continue in the concluding episode next. I love the way the stories are intertwined, and I am impressed that the young cast ably handles themselves with the expanded duties.

Elisha Cuthbert, who plays Megan and would go on to stardom in shows such as *24* and various films, really shines here as the pretty, plucky heroine. However, the Waif character is still confusing, because he seems to be aiding them in the search for the Silver Sight, but at the same time he is trying to warn them and scare them away from digging into the mystery, so what does he actually want? I wish they had chosen a side for him to be firmly on.

Series Mythology

- The first episode of the series where a campfire is not lit, and no story is introduced. We join our adventure already progress.

- Bill Rowat, who plays Mr. Gregory, returns to the series after playing dad to Eddie Kaye Thomas in Season 3's "The Tale of the Curious Camera."

- Tod Fennell, who plays a Jim Gregory, returns to the series after dealing with a ghoulish game in Season 6's opener "The Tale of the Forever Game."

- Philip Spensley, who plays Vince, returns to the series after dealing with reptiles in Season 2's "The Tale of the Hatching."

EPISODE 81:

"The Tale of the Silver Sight: Part 3"

U.S. Airdate: April 2, 2000

Written by: D. J. MacHale

Directed by: Mark Soulard

Guest Cast: David Deveau, Vanessa Lengies,
Ian Beny Anderson, and .Walter Massey.

Favorite Line: "The story ends here."-Ross

Opening Campfire: Due to the fact that the "Silver Sight" trilogy doesn't work like a traditional episode, the format I've been using will be jettisoned, in favor of a more in depth recounting of the "tale," which is the entire meat of this and the preceding two episodes.

The Tale: Andy and Vange get some supernatural face time with the smoke monster from *Lost* in an old well, but manage to find the final piece of the record. The gang gathers to hear the recording, but it's the clues written on the record that help Andy figure out where the Silver Sight is hidden.

They head to an abandoned amusement park, owned by the man who hid the charm and made the recording, and find the Silver Sight with ease. This brings out the Waif kid, who is apparently the Silver Sight's operating system, and when Gary asks what the charm does the Waif replies, "It's the power to conquer. Armies have won wars with it; kingdoms have toppled, cities have fallen."

Laing Candle shows up and reveals that the Waif is a demon, who torments the souls that are banished by the Silver Sight, but he wants Gary to hand it over to him anyway. The Waif warns that the old man means him and his friends harm and that he must wish Laing away before it's too late, but Gary realizes the real enemy is the Waif behind the Silver Sight, and by calling him an enemy, he manages to free the trapped souls and banish the black-eyed demon boy to the void. The gang is victorious and the Midnight Society finally gets to play the heroes. After the hubbub, Gary gets to say a final goodbye to his Grandpa Gene, and to us, the fans.

Review: This episode manages to not only give us a thrilling end to the hunt for the record, but gives us a satisfying conclusion that works organically, and makes the whole thing worthwhile. I love the theme park setting because it makes the episode feel expansive. The trilogy as a whole feels big and grand, and it is -much appreciated. The Waif being, who for all intents and purposes is the Silver Sight itself, still doesn't make much sense because while he helps a few times, there are more times where he is telling the gang to get lost, and isn't playing fair about it, either. Why would he want to warn them off when he is craving souls and needs their help?

Despite that little flaw, this is a really fun bunch of episodes. They aired on the same night as one whole chunk of movie, and then were split up later into episode installments. None of them works well on their own, so when you watch these you have to commit to the three-episode arc to really get the full enjoyment. This was a hell of a way for the series to kick off its final season, and I was very happy that D. J. and Ross return to not only give us the biggest episode of the series, but let us say hello and goodbye to our old pal, Gary, once more. The final scene of Grandpa Gene telling the tale to the original members of the Midnight Society is a perfect, poetic ending. I wish this had been the final episode of the series; it would have gone out with a grand flourish as a bookend, but we have ten more episodes to go, so hang on!

Series Mythology

• The busy bee, Sheena Larkin, who plays Gary and Tucker's Grandma Aggie, finishes her long and distinguished run on the series, which started all the way back with Season 1's "The Tale of the Lonely Ghost." She is credited with seven appearances on the series, but since she doesn't really appear in "The Tale of the Silver Sight Part 2," it is more accurate to say she graces the series six times with her presence.

• Walter Massey, who plays Bob McGorrill, returns to the series after dealing with a strange, new tenant in Season 4's "The Tale of the Room for Rent."

• Director Mark Soulard does a fantastic job behind the camera for the trilogy, and will return to helm three more episodes in this final season, including the last episode, "The Tale of the Night Nurse," bookending his work.

EPISODE 82:

"The Tale of the Lunar Locust"

U.S. Airdate: April 9, 2000

Written by: Michael Koegel

Directed by: Jim Donovan

Guest Cast: Aaron Ashmore, Hamille Rustia,
Tara Lipinski, and Shawn Potter.

Favorite Line: "So, you're telling me you're like a lizard girl from outer space on a mission to destroy a band of intergalactic flesh-eating parasites that want to eat Earth, and then make this your home?"-Jake

Opening Campfire: The gang arrives after a massive downpour and finds the campfire area soaked. They decide to sit on the ground because their cushy seats are more bathtub than couch. Megan arrives last, kitted up with a fancy raincoat, and wonders why everyone is sitting on the ground. Don't they know what lives in the ground? She goes on to list a series of bugs, which Tucker reminds her are all pretty harmless. "I wouldn't be too sure about that," she replies, and lays out a blanket over the storyteller's chair so she can sit down on it. "My story's about that very thing. It's about what you can't see just under the ground. Who knows what you're stepping on?" This sobers the gang up real quick as she eases into her tale.

The Tale: Jake meets Ellen, who is truly out of this world, and needs his help to stop an invasion of alien parasites, but despite her seemingly good intentions, she may not be telling poor Jake the whole truth.

Closing Campfire: "Now I know why you didn't want to sit on the ground," Tucker says, after enjoying her story. "Well yeah, and I also don't like getting my bottom wet," she replies, and saunters off into the woods with a dry bottom. The gang realizes their backsides are muddy and moist, so the only thing they can do is bend over with their behinds to the campfire to let it dry them. "I really hope nobody else can see this," comments an embarrassed Quinn. "This is definitely the end," Tucker replies, putting the perfect button on the scene and the situation.

Review: Borrowing the opening from *The Blob* (1958), and pretty much everything else, this 1950s sci-fi throwback episode is a real blast. Writer Michael Koegel manages to turn in an homage to the sci-fi films of yesteryear and tick all the plot-point boxes along the way, while delivering modern twists and a satisfying conclusion in the tight runtime of the episode. There are even shades of H. P. Lovecraft here, which aids in the finale when the Lunar Locusts are partially revealed.

There are no real monsters, which some can consider a letdown, but the fact that the episode ends in failure for our heroes, who thought they had been triumphant, is such a rewarding ending when it comes to horror stories that I think we can ignore the fact that we don't actually get to see what the creatures look like. It isn't about the creatures; it's about the humans being tricked into helping the bad guys end the world. That's some great, potent stuff in my book.

It's fun to see a young Tara Lipinski playing an evil alien. They should have worked in some ice-skating, but maybe that would have been too much. So far Season 7 is firing on all cylinders, because this is one of the finest episodes in the entire series.

Series Mythology

- Aaron Ashmore, who plays Jake, returns to the series after dealing with toy wielding aliens in Season 2's "The Tale of the Thirteenth Floor."

- Tara Lipinski, who plays Ellen the alien, only appears this one time in the series, but at age fifteen she became the youngest figure skater to win the gold medal in the 1998 Olympics.

- Shawn Potter, who plays Pete, returns to the series after playing hockey in Season 6's "The Tale of Jake the Snake" and opening doors in Season 5's "The Tale of a Door Unlocked."

EPISODE 83:

"The Tale of the Stone Maiden"

U.S. Airdate: April 16, 2000

Written by: Mark David Perry

Directed by: Adam Weissman

Guest Cast: Jeff Saumier, Terra Vanessa, Maggie Castle, and Ryan Best.

Favorite Line: "That's like tearing up the
Mona Lisa for postcards!"-Vivian White

Opening Campfire: Quinn hates lugging the firewood and wants to make it a point that anyone who arrives late has to lug the firewood for a month. Megan arrives, a few seconds shy of being considered late, lugging a heavy chunk of marble. She has a story about artists and the amazing things they create. "That's pretty low on the amazing scale," Quinn comments in his jerky fashion.

"But it isn't.

To us this is just a chunk of marble, but to an artist there's a beautiful creation inside, waiting to be released." The gang agrees, passing the chunk around and admiring it. "It's the vision of the artist that turns a piece of nothing into something special. That's what my story's about," she softly intones, grabbing their full attention.

The Tale: Searching for her missing boyfriend, Julie discovers a strange stone statue in the woods with the help of a hobo, who claims that the water dripping from it turned her boyfriend into stone and the only way to bring him back is to find the Stone Maiden's missing boyfriend statue.

Closing Campfire: Megan ends her tale, but her struggle has only begun, because now she has to lug the heavy marble back home. No one is willing to help bare her burden, except for the kind-hearted Andy. Megan tosses the rock at him and flees into the woods, leaving the poor guy to lug the thing alone. "From now on, anyone who leaves early has to lug the firewood for a month. All right?" He shouts into the deaf ears of the woods, bookending the firewood discussion.

Review: This is an interesting episode because it isn't scary, and it isn't necessarily thrilling either, but it works in a fairy tale kind of way. There is no ticking clock or looming threat to worry about, just a bad situation that needs to be corrected, and there doesn't seem to be an easy way to correct it.

The character of Henry the hobo is a bit of an outlier here, because for a while I thought he was the ghost of the statue (stranger things have happened on this show) and was trying to return himself to his Stone Maiden, but he was just a guy who happened to have all the right answers. If he wasn't in the episode, our heroine Julie would have been more active, and I think would have fared better story wise.

The addition of Henry muddies the waters, because he gets in the way and really hurts the development of the rest of the characters. That being said, this is a good episode. Not a great one, but a good one about the power of love, which is something that isn't always dealt with on *AYAOTD?* beyond the excellent Season 3 episode, "The Tale of the Dream Girl."

Series Mythology

- Megan's last tale as a member of the Midnight Society.

- Martin Neufeld, who plays Henry, returns to the series after playing the ghostly prisoner One-Eyed Jack in Season 5's "The Tale of Prisoners Past."

- Linda Smith, who plays Diane Tyler, returns to the series after having appeared in the pilot episode that eventually became the fourth episode, "The Tale of the Twisted Claw."

- Terence Bowman, who plays Bob, returns to the series after riding the rails in Season 4's "The Tale of Train Magic."

EPISODE 84:

"The Tale of Highway 13"

U.S. Airdate: April 23, 2000

Written by: Ted Elrick

Directed by: Jim Donovan

Guest Cast: Matthew Lemche, Benjamin Plener, Adam MacDonald, and Adam Kenneth Wilson.

Favorite Line: "Hurt? No, we all died."-Bulldog

Opening Campfire: Megan complains (again) about the filthy condition the couch has taken, and Andy reminds her that part of the fun of being out there is not having to worry about cleaning, at which point a mouse crawls on his arm, sending him and Megan scurrying away. Vange grabs the mouse and Quinn introduces them to Jerry, her cute and harmless little pet.

Tucker arrives, dragging his bike, which busted its chain. It was a hand-me-down from Gary (guessing the BMX bike busted, too), and this becomes the first mention of events and characters from the opening trilogy of episodes. Quinn turns to Megan and explains hand-me-downs to the rich girl as "something you didn't get new." She knows what the word means, rolling her eyes at him with her voice. "Well, that's sort of what my story's about," Quinn says, sitting down in the stone chair for the evening's tale.

The Tale: Two friends restore a muscle car from the junkyard and find themselves reenacting a race that caused the untimely deaths of the previous owners.

Closing Campfire: "So, before you take a hand-me-down, make sure you know what you're really getting," Quinn says, concluding his tale. "I think I have a hand-me-down, too," says Megan. "I think my mother gave me her fear of mice. But, I want to deal with it." She stands and approaches Vange and her tiny, white pal, Jerry. She asks her to hold Jerry, and Vange agrees. "It's actually kind of cute, I'm ok," she says, as Jerry nuzzles in the palm of her hand. Vange is happy to hear that and decided to introduce her to her massive pet rat, which she dangles in front of Megan's face by its tail. This, of course, sends her running for her life. "That's one hand-me-down she's never getting rid of," Quinn comments as they gather around to pet the new, less cute and bigger pet.

Review: This is a great haunted car episode, that's more about the previous drivers than the wicked metal underneath the cherry red paintjob. The plot seems to veer one way, and then reveals itself to be about something else, and it's the sudden turn in the plot that really distinguishes this story from similar ghostly car tales. We get a fun montage sequence also and as far as my memory serves I believe it's the first-ever in the series.

Director Jim Donovan does a great job making this episode really stand out visually, and one-time writer Ted Elrick does a great job giving the boys believable dialog that allows the fantastical to become palatable. The one goof I noticed is that you can clearly see the stunt driver working the big wheel on the truck, instead of the bald-headed trucker character, in a few of the shots. That's a minor quibble for an episode that feels like another old-school *AYAOTD?* entry.

It's cool to see Benjamin Plener return to the series, much changed by the passing years from the tiny, big-eared boy we saw in Season 1, even if he did just play a supporting role.

Series Mythology

- Writer Ted Elrick's first and last script for the series.

- Benjamin Plener, who plays Justin, returns to the series after dealing with Irish fairy folk in Season 1's "The Tale of Jake and the Leprechaun."

- Adam MacDonald, who plays Bulldog, returns to the series after dealing with tricky Chinese food in Season 6's "The Tale of the Misfortune Cookie."

EPISODE 85:

"The Tale of the Reanimator"

U.S. Airdate: April 30, 2000

Written by: Kenny Davis

Directed by: Adam Weissman

Guest Cast: Emma Taylor-Isherwood, Philip Eddolls, Michael Yarmush, and Jean LeClerc.

Favorite Line: "I'm sorry! I'm sorry! I'm sorry!"-Vange

Opening Campfire: We open on Vange trying to knock down a hornet's nest, sending the rest of the gang running for the hills. She manages to knock the dried-looking thing down and approaches slowly, but a soft buzzing from inside sends her fleeing to the campfire where she meets her friends, weary of the fact that she might have dragged the nest back with her. Quinn is the most freaked out, but Tucker changes the subject by awkwardly asking him if he has a story. "Yeah, I got a story. It's about messing with things that shouldn't be messed with," Quinn intros, solemnly. "If you go looking for trouble, chances are you're going to find it."

The Tale: A young girl works for a botanist who has developed a serum that revives dead plants. Not believing her sister's claims, the jerky big brother pours some of the liquid onto a grave and manages to raise the dead man six feet under.

Closing Campfire: Tucker declares the meeting closed and douses the fire, the hiss of the smoke mixes with a strange buzzing sound, and everyone quickly realizes that the noise is the sound of angry bees. They dash off into the woods, every which way, looking for cover from the homeless bees that are looking for revenge.

Review: Again, the show writers allow the stories to shift gears and even jump genres, which is clearly evidenced here. It starts out about a mysterious botanist working on plant experiments and you think the show will deliver a monster plant episode, but it suddenly becomes a zombie show.

I expected a bit more from the zombie effects, which are pretty plain, but despite that small issue, I really enjoy this episode. The young leads do a great job of carrying the material, and the developing plot is unique and compelling. There is a bit at the end of the episode that makes no sense to me where Jake, Julie's brother, claims that once he saw the plant monster costume she's holding he thought he'd had it. She then proceeds to say that she got him, playing off of the April Fool's elements of the story. I'm not sure what this final conversation is in reference to, because she never wears the plant monster costume or "gets him" in any sense of the word. Come to think of it, this *should* have had a plant monster; that would have opened it up to some really great stuff.

Series Mythology

• Quinn's last tale as a member of the Midnight Society.

• This episode no doubt takes its inspiration from the H. P. Lovecraft story, "Herbert West-Reanimator," and the classic horror film based on that story, *Re-Animator* (1985).

• This is director Adam Weissman's last of three episodes for the series, having started in Season 6 with "The Tale of the Misfortune Cookie" and "The Tale of the Zombie Dice."

• This is writer Kenny Davis' first and last script for the series.

- Emma Taylor-Isherwood (credited as Emma Isherwood), who plays Julie, returns to the series after being banished to the titular place in Season 6's "The Tale of Oblivion."

- Michael Yarmush, who plays Peter, returns to the series after sort of dealing with Bigfoots in Season 5's "The Tale of the Manaha."

EPISODE 86:

"The Tale of the Time Trap"

U.S. Airdate: May 7, 2000

Written by: James Morris

Directed by: Jim Donovan

Guest Cast: Richard Dumont, Cas Anvar, Jay Baruchel, and Ajay Fry.

Favorite Line: "Doesn't chocolate give you pimples?"-Megan

Opening Campfire: Tucker busts out some chocolate cookies from Grandma Aggie, referencing a character from the "Silver Sight" saga for the second time this season, showing that the past events do influence the new batch. The gang digs in like pigs at a trough and are soon stuffed and sick to their stomachs. "I think I ate about six too many," Vange complains. "Wimps," Quinn replies, still chowing down. "Too much of a good thing, isn't always such a good thing," Tucker says, and guess what folks, he has a story that illustrates that very same statement.

The Tale: Sardo comes into possession of a strange, golden box he calls the Persian Victory Box, and sells it to Jason, a boy who needs a little help with life. He soon discovers that the box comes with a white-haired genie named Belle, who gets bored too easily and causes trouble for our young hero.

Closing Campfire: Tucker finishes his tale and digs out the exact replica of the Persian Victory Box. He asks if they want to let Belle out, but in fact they don't and they flee in panic, having recovered from the cookie woes they suffered earlier. Quinn remains, now suffering the torments of too much sweet chocolate crunch as he writhes on the couch. Tucker douses the fire and picks up the cookie tin to find it empty. "You finished all the cookies?"

Tucker asks his woebegone friend. "I had to, they were too good," Quinn replies weakly. "I hope they tastes as good on the way up as they did on the way down," Tucker says, helping his friend of up and carrying him away like a wounded soldier.

Review: Sardo's final episode was luckily a good one. It's the ultimate wish fulfillment episode, and even though Jay Baruchel has appeared twice before as a lead, he's really just the perfect actor for this type of role. The episode twists and turns, but predictably so. We know already that if something is too good in the world of *AYAOTD?*, then it probably is. Regardless of familiar ground being covered, this is a really fun episode to watch and Richard Dumont really gets to hit a home run with his swan song. It's sad to see Sardo go, and yes I know the entire show is ending, but saying farewell to him is harder than saying farewell to Dr. Vink, who by this time is only a fond, eccentric memory. It's not always that a supporting character in an anthology show can leave such an impact, but then again that's part of the magic of this wonderful series.

Series Mythology

- Farewell Sardo! This is the eighth and final time that the purveyor of the Magic Mansion will grace us with his presence, which began all the way back with Season 1's "The Tale of the Super Specs."

- Jay Baruchel, who plays Jason, returns yet again for his fourth and final time as a new character in a tale. His first go around was with a bit part in Season 5's "The Tale of the Dead Man's Float."

- Ajay Fry, who plays Brad, returns to the series after appearing in the first part of Season 4's "The Tale of Cutter's Treasure."

- Eleanor Noble, who plays Belle, returns to the series after dealing with teenage lust in Season 2's "The Tale of the Dark Dragon," another Sardo tale.

- Ian Beny Anderson, who plays the aptly named Kid #1, returns to the series after playing the Young Laing Candle in this season's "The Tale of the Silver Sight" trilogy.

- Penny Mancuso, who plays the simply titled Woman, returns to the series after dealing with the comic villain in Season 4's "The Tale of the Ghastly Grinner."

- This is writer James Morris' second and last script for the series, having also penned the Season 6 Sardo episode "The Tale of Oblivion."

- The character of Bobo is most likely a reference to the character briefly mentioned in Season 3's "The Tale of the Carved Stone".

EPISODE 87:

"The Tale of the Photo Finish"

U.S. Airdate: May 14, 2000

Written by: Alan Kingsberg

Directed by: Mark Soulard

Guest Cast: Robin Weekes, Patrick Thomas,
Sacha Cantor, and Robert Crooks.

Favorite Line: "Say cheese!"-Jasper Davis

Opening Campfire: Andy tried to join the Ring Club, a service club that Tucker belongs to, but they didn't let him in despite Tucker vouching for him. The others, especially Megan, think it's completely unfair, but Andy isn't fazed by it. In fact, he got a story out of it.

The Tale: To join the Lion's Society, an exclusive fraternity, Chandler steals an old portrait from the library and reveals a hidden image underneath that transports him to an alternate dimension, and only his pal Alex, who'd been kicked out of the fraternity, can save him.

Closing Campfire: Andy ends his tale and it turns out all the commiseration was for nothing because he reveals that the Ring Club let him in after all. "It's all 'cuz of Tucker, he really fought for me, and when they still said no, he quit," Andy explains. "Well, since you quit, there was an extra spot in the club so . . . ." Tucker stands, indignant, "So, you took my place?" Tucker grumbles and rushes off to give the Ring Club guys a piece of his mind. But there's no need, Andy was just pranking him, which seems like a cold-blooded thing to do after Tucker went to bat for him. "I just like seeing him go all snaky like that," Andy says, admiring his new club ring. "He's still in, and so am I." The gang giggles at Tucker's torment and Quinn quenches the fire.

Review: An episode that starts out as if it will be dealing with the terrors of hazing, turns into an alternate-dimension story about a soul-trapping camera and the twisted soul behind the lens. This is the kind of storytelling that I really wish had infused Season 6, where the rug is constantly being pulled out from under us, but the resolution isn't weak and incomprehensible. I also really liked the shift in leads from Chandler to Alex, adding to the organic nature of the story, which makes it all the more believable like Season 5's "The Tale of the Chameleons."

The most interesting element of this episode is that it's really the first episode in the series to deal with racism, and while it isn't called out as that, it becomes quite obvious in subtext because Alex is the only black character in the cast. Equality is a powerful dramatic tool, and here it is used to tell a very sad tale. I wish more had been developed from Jasper's perspective, but his brief appearance is enough to get the job done.

Series Mythology

- Patrick Thomas, who plays Chandler, returns to the series after dealing with probable cannibals in Season 6's "The Tale of the Gruesome Gourmets."

- Wild boar makes yet another appearance in the form of guts (aka cherry gelatin), perhaps a slight nod to the long gone Dr. Vink.

- Victor Knight, who plays Professor Felix Barish, returns to the series after dealing with antiques in Season 4's "The Tale of the Long Ago Locket."

EPISODE 88:

"The Tale of the Last Dance"

U.S. Airdate: May 21, 2000

Written by: Mark David Perry

Directed by: Jim Donovan

Guest Cast: Jennifer Finnigan, Jason McSkimming,
Audrey Gardiner, and Adam Frost.

Favorite Line: "You know, for a smart guy
you're kind of not very . . . smart."-Scot

Opening Campfire: Andy's up tonight again and he's got a special surprise for everyone: he plays the violin . . . sort of. He proceeds to murder the cat-guts, much to the dismay of the other Midnight Society members. "Maybe you should take up stamp collecting," Vange comments politely. "It's hard learning to play an instrument," Andy explains. "My story is about someone who plays really well. People love to hear her play. The trouble is one person likes it so much that they'd do anything to get her to play for them and them alone. Anything."

The Tale: Tara, a young violinist, finds herself the object of desire of a music-loving mystery man who hides behind the walls of her school, and anyone who stands in the way of his attaining her will regret it.

Closing Campfire: "That was beautiful," Megan says, moved by the tale. Andy reaches for his violin again, scattering his friends into the woods, except for Megan. "Go for it," she prompts and she prepares herself for pain, but Andy lets loose a masterful swiping of the strings. "I was just getting warmed up," he says, leaving Megan with her mouth opened. Is this the beginning of a Kristen-David/ Gary-Sam relationship? I bet if the new batch had gone one more season, we would have seen these two flourish into a couple.

Review: This is basically a modern-day riff on *Phantom of the Opera*, which isn't necessarily a bad thing, but it takes the creative teeth out of the episode, because it doesn't really explore new ground. There aren't any surprises in this episode if you know the tale, and by now most people are at least aware of what the Phantom does, making this episode less dynamic than some of the rug-pulling ones from this season. That being said, while it isn't groundbreaking, this is a very good episode. The sewer setting is fantastic.

Jennifer Finnigan's performance as the beleaguered Tara is wonderfully passionate, and the Paul Hopkins' Lurker scenes are quite moving, especially the last dance itself, which to me is a direct nod to the end of *AYAOTD?*

Series Mythology

- Andy's last tale as a member of the Midnight Society.

- Director Jim Donovan's last of five episodes for the series, which began with Season 6's "The Tale of Oblivion."

- Writer Mark David Perry's last of six scripts for the series, which began with Season 5's "The Tale of the Chameleons."

- Paul Hopkins, who plays the Lurker, returns to the series after playing the desperate soldier in Season 4's "The Tale of the Long Ago Locket."

- Quasimodo is mentioned, mixing references a bit.

- According to some sources, this is was the last episode that was filmed.

EPISODE 89:

"The Tale of the Laser Maze"

U.S. Airdate: May 28, 200

Written by: Peggy Sarlin

Directed by: Mark Soulard

Guest Cast: Kim Schraner, Laura Vandervoort, Russell Yuen, and Matt Holland.

Favorite Line: "Super!"-Drake

Opening Campfire: A staring contest between Vange and Quinn, which has been going on for ten minutes, ends in a win for Quinn when a loud sound out in the woods causes Vange to break eye contact. "No do-over, victory is mine," Quinn crows, pleased as punch. "But winning isn't always such a great thing, you know," Tucker says, and he has a story, his final one, to demonstrate that winning a game may not be the ideal situation.

The Tale: Competitive twin sisters, Kara and Ashley, take part in a strange laser tag game where losing the game means losing your freedom.

Closing Campfire: Quinn announces he's going to take Tae-Kwon-Do, but Vange wants a staring re-match first, and Quinn agrees. However, the party is over and they have to head out, so Tucker grabs Vange and Andy grabs Quinn to lead them out safely while their eyes remain glued to each other. "This is going to be a long walk back," Megan sighs as she douses the flames.

Review: There is some really good humor in this episode. I especially like the early scene with the Tae-Kwon-Do instructor.

The leads, Kim Schraner and Laura Vandervoort, as Kara and Ashley respectively, do a great job with the martial arts, and it shows that they actually did know how to throw a kick, which is usually painfully obvious when someone fakes it.

Matt Holland as Drake is a lot of fun, and if the series had gone one more season, I could have seen him as a returning character along the lines of Sardo or Vink. The laser maze setting is great and exciting, and provides the episode with some real visual oomph.

Again the folks behind the show demonstrate their love of a good, twisty story. The plot goes from warring sisters to laser tag of death, to alien clone-bots, and it keeps it consistently compelling. I also love the interplay with the new batch of Midnight Society members, too. They've really come into their own, and it's a shame their run is about to come to an end.

Series Mythology

- Tucker's final tale as a member of the Midnight Society.

- Writer Peggy Sarlin's first and last script for the series.

- Russell Yuen, who plays the Tae-Kwon-Do Instructor, returns to the series after dealing with Chinese food in Season 6's "The Tale of the Misfortune Cookie."

- Matt Holland, who played Drake, returns to the series after the Sardo-infused Season 6 episode "The Tale of Oblivion."

EPISODE 90:

"The Tale of Many Faces"

U.S. Airdate: June 4, 2000

Written by: Alan Kingsberg

Directed by: Lorette Leblanc

Guest Cast: Sarah Edmondson, Jessica Welch,
Martin Watier, and Mandy Schaffer.

Favorite Line: "Got any masks that will make you look taller?"-Tucker

Opening Campfire: Vange walks around the group, showing them how different masks can display different emotions for the wearer. "The thing about masks is that they let you be whatever you want to be," she states. "Underneath you are still you." I think we know where she is going with this. "My story is about the horror of losing what's behind the mask," she reveals, and it draws a confused grunt from Andy, who has to learn to look beyond the words. Vange clarifies and tosses in a handful of midnight dust to begin the second to last tale for the Midnight Society.

The Tale: Emma, a wannabe actor, runs into an eccentric woman named Madame Visage, who promises to make her a star, but steals her face with an ancient power and keeps her hostage alongside other faceless girls, until she can find a way to break the spell and restore the many faces that were taken by the witch.

Closing Campfire: "So, it doesn't matter what mask you wear, beneath it you're still you, and no one can take that away," Vange says, and realizes the gang has donned the masks she's passed out and are silently standing and creeping toward her. "Ok, now you're creeping me out," she manages to say, as they loom closer, threatening with their masked deafness. Suddenly, Tucker rips off his mask and breaks the tension by proclaiming, "Good story!"

Review: I feel like this type of episode has been recycled time and time again in the series. The elements are slightly different, but the eternal youth-craving witch and the luckless teen girls falling prey to them feels like real old-school *AYAOTD?*, and not in a particularly interesting or innovative way.

There are things I really did like about the episode, though. The old-lady face dissolve was well done, and I love the look of the no-face girls; there was some real genius behind that pucker-lipped design. Sarah Edmondson is also great, pulling double-duty as Emma and the Madame Visage-version of Emma. The overall episode feels like it's missing a few twists and turns to keep it really interesting, and while the ending makes sense in a fantastical world, it doesn't have the emotional impact it could have.

This was not the strongest story for the second-to-last episode, but it still works better than the similar, and nonsensical Season 5 episode "The Tale of the Mystical Mirror." We are in the home stretch now, folks. Prepare yourselves for the final night at the campfire with the next episode.

Series Mythology

- Director Lorette Leblanc's sixth and final episode, which began with Season 5's "The Tale of the Vacant Lot."

- Writer Alan Kingsberg's fifth and final episode for the series, which began with Season 5's "The Tale of Prisoners Past."

- Sara Edmondson, who plays Emma, returns to the series after dealing with a shadow demon in Season 6's "The Tale of Bigfoot Ridge."

- Martin Watier, who plays Jacques, returns to the series after dealing with our old friend Doctor Vink in Season 3's "The Tale of the Dangerous Soup."

- Irene Contogiorgis, who plays Girl 90, returns to the series after playing with vampires in Season 5's "The Tale of the Night Shift."

- Amanda Gay, who plays Lizzie, returns to the series after dealing with magic paintings in Season 4's "The Tale of the Unfinished Painting," which shares story similarities to this episode.

EPISODE 91:

"The Tale of the Night Nurse"

U.S. Airdate: June 11, 2000

Written by: Michael Koegel

Directed by: Mark Soulard

Guest Cast: Shadia Simmons, Charles Biddle Sr.,
Keenan Macwilliam, and Amanda Strawn.

Favorite Line: "All right, nobody breathe on anybody."-Tucker

Opening Campfire: It's a cold night for the final meeting of the Midnight Society, and the new batch huddles around the last campfire. Andy sneezes, complaining of allergies, and Vange wonders if Andy got his flu shot yet. He hasn't and it turns out none of them have either, because they are all averse to needles. "There's nothing worse than getting a shot," Quinn says, matter-of-factly. "I can think of something and that's exactly what my story's about," Vange says and takes her place in the storyteller's chair for the final time.

The Tale: Two sisters visiting their grandfather connect with the ghost of a sickly little girl. The creepy Night Nurse, who killed her decades ago, seems to have returned to take care of the sisters, too.

Closing Campfire: "And that's supposed to make me want to go out and get a flu shot? I don't think so," Megan comments, and I'm with her. Vange said she had a story that was about something worse than a shot, but then tells a story about how dangerous shots can actually be! Suddenly, they all start sneezing and it becomes obvious very quickly that Andy's bug has jumped ship and infested the lot of them.

The gang scatters into the woods, leaving the warmth of the campfire once and for all, heading back home to the warmth of their beds and ease of their cold medicines. Vange is left alone, laughing to herself, as she grabs the trusty red bucket and douses the Midnight Society campfire for the last time. As the smoke rises, she sneezes. She realizes that despite the flu shot, her friends have infected her with the dreaded cold. "Oh man, you guys got me sick!" She shouts to the dark woods that once housed many a scary tale, and disappears into the shadows to find her sick pals. We fade out and leave the Midnight Society meeting grounds once and for all.

Review: The show ends with an episode that feels like really old-school *AYAOTD?*, but in a good way. Kids coming to spend the summer somewhere is where most of the classic episodes begin. I love the idea of solving a ghostly mystery by traveling back in time to right the wrong, something that the show has done a lot in the past; most recently with this season's "The Tale of Highway 13."

The one flaw is that the Night Nurse plays her part like she's the devil incarnate, but in reality she just made a terrible mistake and wasn't out to murder anyone, so why would her "ghost" play Hannibal Lecter if that wasn't the actual disposition of the character? It's a cheap trick to fool the audience, and it never works, because it always plays false and ruins what could have been a really solid, simple episode. The twist is nice, and appreciated, but I wish they had asked Danette Mackay, who played the Night Nurse, to turn the menace way down. I wish they had given the Midnight Society a proper send off, too, like Gary and Sam got for the semi-finale of Season 5, so we must interpret our own ending.

In my opinion, the gang took some time off to get well, and came right back, we just weren't privy to their further tales. Maybe we didn't get an ending because in the alternate world where the Midnight Society does exist they just kept going and going. One can dream, and one should.

Series Mythology

- Vange's last tale as a member of the Midnight Society.

- Director Mark Soulard's sixth and final episode for the series, which began with Season 6's "The Tale of Jake the Snake."

- Writer Michael Koegel provides here his third and final script for the series, which began with the fun and twisty Season 6 episode, "The Tale of the Gruesome Gourmets."

- Amanda Strawn, who plays Emily's Mother, returns to the series after playing a mom in Season 5's "The Tale of the Chameleons," and a nurse, coincidentally, in Season 2's "The Tale of the Shiny Red Bicycle."

- Danette Mackay, who plays the titular Nurse, returns to the series after playing the blind and blond Keeper in Season 6's "The Tale of the Wisdom Glass."

- Kerry Duff and Shadia Simmons also played sisters in the *Goosebumps* episode "Night of the Living Dummy II."

- "Unfinished business" is once again given as the reason that ghosts come back, referencing Megan's thoughts in Season 6's "Tale of the Walking Shadow."

- This is the last episode of *AYAOTD?*

THE TALE OF THE WITNESSES:

JASON ALISHARAN

(Frank)

Jose: Was acting something you wanted to do as a child, or were you steered into it by your parents?

Jason: No, it was something that I very much wanted to do, and I don't think my parents were that excited about it initially. I was passionate about it.

Jose: *Are You Afraid of the Dark* was your first professional gig, so how did you come to land a role as a member of the Midnight Society?

Jason: They were casting the show and I think I might have been twelve at the time. I auditioned once and I was out on the road when I got this call that they wanted me to come in for a callback, but I couldn't come in, so I think I submitted a tape or something like that. Then I got a call later and they said, "Yeah, you're on the show. Fly up to Montreal." It felt great, it was a huge boost of confidence. *Are You Afraid of the Dark* was great not just because it was a great series, but because it was the only show really where you could be a series regular and still have a life. We only shot three months a year, so it wasn't like I left school and was working full time. I actually got to do both. I got to be on set and do that, and then got to be a normal kid. So, I feel very fortunate because there was no other show where you could really do that.

Jose: Did you get to meet the rest of the cast before getting to the set?

Jason: A bunch of them were locals. Raine was from Montreal. Jodie was from Montreal. Ross was from Montreal, but he was moving to Toronto or something like that. It was Rachel and Nathaniel, who were from Toronto, and I was from Vancouver. So, the hotel kids got to meet each other first, because we were staying in the same hotel. I think I might have met the rest of them at a costume fitting or something like that.

Jose: Let's talk about the campfire set. I'm guessing that was shot indoors so as the real, natural elements didn't become a hindrance.

Jason: The first season we shot at this studio, and yeah it was a set. They planted a bunch of trees and they fogged it up. Then for the second season, we were in a warehouse somewhere. I remember looking up and saying, "That looks like asbestos on the walls. Where the hell are we?" But it was fun, and it was basically like being in a Christmas tree emporium. By the end of the shoot, the trees were dying, though they did water them down. I think they even used to spray paint them near the end.

Jose: As the bookends of the episodes, were you guys given only your Midnight Society segments, or the whole script?

Jason: We were given the whole script. I didn't tell a lot of the stories, I just sort of talked during the campfires, but I think if you were telling the story you would probably read the episode. I mean, I think in the first season I read a lot of them, but also it would depend on how many scripts they'd finished. Over time I stopped reading them, but if you were telling the story then yeah you would read that script.

Jose: How would the shooting work in terms of breaking up the season?

Jason: They would shoot all the campfire stuff at once. They would shoot the whole season's worth of campfires over like a month, depending on how intricate each of those episodes were. It would just go in order, I think. Meaning, whatever that campfire episode was, they would try to knock that one out. So, it was possible that you might be finishing up the end of episode three in the morning, and be rolling into episode four in the afternoon.

Jose: I always wondered about how the Midnight Society segments were filmed, because there were times when a storyteller went twice in a row, so I wasn't sure if that was an airdate issue or just how it was filmed.

Jason: Now I'm very familiar with the other side of the camera, so I know that all filming is dictated by the production itself, and not the actors. The actors are just supposed to show up and hit their marks and do their lines. There would be times when let's say they were coming off of doing nights for the episode, and you might actually be shooting nights in the studio, which is unheard of really because you only shoot nights when you need actual nighttime. But they did that so you didn't have to turn the crew over and lose time, because if you turn them around you have to give them a day and a half off. I remember one time they said, "Oh, we might be ahead of schedule," and we we're supposed to shoot the next episode the following day, where I had this big chunk of dialog. The director came to me and said, "Jason, do you think you could prep all this stuff so we can jump ahead, so instead of doing it tomorrow, we can do it after lunch?" And I did. You learn it and you figure it out.

Jose: So, a whole season of campfires could be taken down in a month?

Jason: Yeah, a couple of months. It would be a month here and then another month somewhere else.

Jose: So it wouldn't be consecutive?

Jason: No, that's the reason that I left. The reason I only did four seasons was because it was my junior year of high school and it was a huge year for me academically and I was getting ready to go to college. You know, I had a pretty good relationship with D. J., so I called him and I said, "Hey man, I love the show, I love being a part of the show. It's been amazing for me. But just know that this is a big year for me in terms of school, so if there was a way for us to shoot this in or around spring break, or altogether in a certain off time that would be great. Please, don't think I'm asking for special treatment." I knew they were starting to schedule the next year, and I wanted them to know that I would have loved to do the show, but if the scheduling didn't work out I couldn't do it. At that point I had done four seasons. It was great, don't get me wrong, but in terms of the longer play of my life, me doing a fifth season of *Dark* versus getting into a good school, one was more important than the other thing.

Jose: How did D. J. take that?

Jason: D. J. was great. He said, "Yeah, I'll try to make this work." But they just couldn't, and it's completely understandable, because in production there are so many variables. You know, you're trying to juggle thirteen episodes and there is so much stuff going on. So, that's why I left the show.

Jose: I would imagine it was tricky in general to keep the Midnight Society together, because you lost Eric at the start of Season 2, and then Kristen and David leave at the start of Season 3.

Jason: Well, with Nathaniel I think he went to do the show *Kung Fu: The Legend Continues*, where he was the star of the show. That was a forty-some episode straight-to-syndication thing, and I think that's why he left. I'm pretty sure. Then Rachel, I think, took another show, and that's when they brought in Joanna. I honestly cannot remember what happened with Jacob Tierney.

Jose: Did you guys manage to bond off set?

Jason: You know, it's interesting, because in every show there are characters and relationships, but these are real people, so in real life people gravitate to others naturally, and gravitate away from others naturally. I was always friendly with everybody, but I think I was closest to Rachel, and Joanna. I hung out with those two more. I mean, obviously separately. We used to get meals together; I saw them in different cities when they'd travel. But I think that part of it was that we were staying in a hotel, and some of the other people were local and would go home on the weekends or whatever, so we bonded.

Jose: Did you watch the finished show when it aired?

Jason: Yeah, of course. I mean, when I was on yeah, totally. I was very excited. I remember the first time it aired and it was very exciting.

Jose: Did you watch it when you left or was it a case of cutting ties, for lack of a better word?

Jason: I'm sorry to say I did not. I loved the show and I loved being a part of the show. I didn't cut ties at all, and I saw a lot of those people after the fact, but to answer you truthfully I don't think I watched it.

Jose: Were you ever recognized in public?

Jason: It was a pretty popular show, and I was on there from when I was twelve to fifteen, so yeah, for sure.

Jose: What was your most memorable fan interaction?

Jason: Honestly, the ones when I was a kid I can't remember, but this one happened recently. I'm a producer now and I work with different screenwriters in Hollywood and they write scripts for me and I sell them. So,, there's a guy who's writing a script for me and when he and I were meeting for the first time to see if we wanted to work together I asked, "Did your agent tell you anything about me?" I meant my producing career, and he said, "Yes, and I actually know you from something else. I watched *Are you Afraid of the Dark?* as a kid." That was hysterical to me. Also, I remember one night, I think I might have been in college, I get a call and the person says, "Hey man, it's Gary." And I said, "Who?" He says, "Yeah man, it's Gary from *Are You Afraid of the Dark?*" I take a moment and then say, "Ross?" Then I'm asking him about his mom and stuff, and the guy pauses. I say, "This isn't Ross, is it?" I just hung up the phone. That was weird. I mean, who would call me and say the character's name? I mean I know Ross, but not as Gary.

Jose: It happens in the last season with Ross and Tucker, but was there ever any talk early on to have you guys become a part of the stories instead of the storytellers?

Jason: Yeah, I remember D. J. and I talked about it once. It was definitely an idea, and I know they played with it, but I guess they just never figured it out. I think even D. J. said to me, "Look, if you have an idea on how to do it, if you want to sketch it out, send it to me." I could never figure it out, but yeah it was definitely considered.

Jose: You were also part of the videogame, *The Tale of Orpheo's Curse*, what was that process like?

Jason: I believe after the first season they had a lot of ancillary products that they wanted to do, and that was one of them. I don't remember who made the game, but I have a copy of it somewhere at my parent's house. My brother and his friend played it once, but I never played. They shot cut scenes for it. They would shoot us doing stuff so you would get these little pop-ups in the game.

Jose: Did you have a favorite episode from the ones Frank told?

Jason: "The Tale of Cutter's Treasure." I thought that was cool, and I got to do it with Ross. It had a good energy.

Jose: Did you have favorite episode in general?

Jason: One of my favorite episodes is "Shiny Red Bicycle," where this guy's friend dies and he can't get over the loss of his friend, I mean that was an incredible episode of television, really.

Jose: Frank told all the memorable Doctor Vink stories, did you ever get to meet the man himself?

Jason: If I remember correctly, and this was twenty-some-odd years ago, he was a bit of a crank. He was a terrific actor, but actors are weird people, so what are you going to do?

Jose: While working on the show, did you ever imagine it would last as long as it had in the fond memories of those who watched it?

Jason: I don't know that I thought it would last as long, but I did think it was something special and I think that's a credit to D. J. and Ned, especially to D. J. At first they were going to pitch the show for tweens, for seven to eleven year olds, which is really a demographic they never went after. And what was really great about the show was that it was this *Twilight Zone* anthology series, but it didn't dumb it down; some of it was really terrifying, some of it was really scary, and some of it was really emotional. The show never pandered to kids. It treated them like adults. I think it was something new and different and people really responded to it. That's a complete credit to D. J.

Jose: Now you've switched into producing, but do you still act?

Jason: I do not act. I loved acting, but I couldn't do the lifestyle of acting. When I was in high school it was fine, because you split your time between the set and school. But the idea of being an actor, waiting tables, going to acting classes and auditions, and spending ten years on it only so that at the end of ten years you realize you're basically in the same place, is not for me. The truth is that, especially now that I'm on the other side, it doesn't matter how talented you are; it's somewhat predicated on luck. The lifestyle drove me crazy. I wasn't very happy. So, for me there were aspects of entertainment, specifically storytelling, which I could do without the acting part. I worked at Dreamworks for three years in live-action, I ran Tom Ford's company and

I produced his first film, and now I have my own company. This is a better fit for me than acting.

Jose: Do you have any last words for the fans of *AYAOTD?*

Jason: I love the fact that you guys out there enjoyed the show so much. You do get the occasional person who remembers you, but for me the biggest kick, the thing that touches me the most, is that you were such an important part of people's childhoods and that the show had such an impact on them, and that's a real honor. I thank the fans for everything.

RICHARD M. DUMONT

(Sardo)

Jose: Was the pronunciation of Sardo in the script, or was that your improv?

Richard: The pronunciation was always: "Sar-Dough", emphasis on the "dough." It was D. J. MacHale's brainchild. I just rode in on his coat tails.

Jose: Did you have a say in your colorful and eccentric wardrobe?

Richard: None whatsoever. The only thing that I did say regarding the costume was, "This is friggin' cool!"

Jose: Do you have any special memories from your first episode "The Tale of the Super Specs"?

Richard: Tons! Where to start? I remember that both Ron Oliver, the director, gave me loads of "free-roaming" space to explore "Sardo". He was, and is to this day as I have been fortunate to have worked with him on several films since our *AYAOTD?* days, always open to improving during filming as long as it was true to the story and to its characters, meaning that he would not, understandably, let my performance turn into a "stand-up" bit. Since that time I am proud to today call him my friend.

Jose: Do you have any memories of your second episode "The Tale of the Dark Dragon," which really solidified the mold for Sardo's continued participation in the series?

Richard: I believe that episode may have been the first where Sardo accepts less money for a potion than he was hoping for and therefore utters the phrase: "All right . . . but I'm losing on the deal!!"

Jose: What do you remember most from you third episode "The Tale of the Carved Stone," which had some really fun moments and great characters?

Richard: Are you kidding? Two words, one name: FRANK GORSHIN! He was INCREDIBLE to work with. I mean, come on, THE RIDDLER for gosh-sake? I loved every second of working with that incredible talent. He was a joy and a blast to work with on and off set!

Jose: You and Vink got to share the screen in your fourth and fifth appearances in the epic two-parter, "The Tale of Cutter's Treasure Pt.1-Pt.2," what do you remember most from making those episodes?

Richard: Squinting. It was hot, real hot, and very, very sunny on the day that we did most of the exteriors with Dr. Vink (Aron Tager), and the cameras were setup with the sun BEHIND them and therefore the actors were FACING the sun for the entire shooting of the exteriors. Re-watch those scenes and you will see us—especially me—squinting all the way through the action. Also, this was the first and only time that the characters of Dr. Vink and Sardo actually met and had scenes together!

Jose: Do you have a favorite episode?

Richard: "The Tale of the Super Specs." It was my first exposure to the whole *AYAOTD?* thing and I loved it! Working with Ron Oliver and D. J. MacHale . . . well, can you have better than that? The effects were very cool . . . and the ending! You realize, if you're a real fan of the series, that it was actually Sardo's LAST appearance—even though it was his first in the series—because he and the two young kids in the episode are cast off into oblivion at the very end. That means that ALL of the other Sardo appearances happened BEFORE this particular episode . . . time-wise, that is. Freaky, huh?

Jose: Was there ever any talk of Sardo becoming a regular, or did it just happen?

Richard: I think that it just "happened." I believe that D. J. really liked that particular character and because we had so much fun with the first episode that Sardo appears in, well, I guess D. J. simply decided to have him return.

Jose: Did you believe you'd return so many times to become such an integral part of the world of *AYAOTD?* and be remembered fondly by the fans?

Richard: At the time, not at all. I had a great time playing that character and he seemed to be liked by the fans so I was just lucky to have had the privilege to play him. Very lucky, and blessed that the fans liked him as much as they did, and still do, I am led to believe.

Jose: What are you up to currently and where can fans connect with you?

Richard: I voice-direct a lot these days and my voice is on many animated series and films. I voice-direct many games as well; *Splinter Cell, Prince of Persia, Assassin's Creed,* to name only a few. Fans can go to my website: www.richardmdumont.com. Good night everyone, and remember to check under the bed before you turn the lights out. I'm just sayin'.

#

(Editor/ Show runner)

Jose: You edited the pilot, which is now episode 4, "The Tale of the Twisted Claw." Was working on that piece different in any way from the editing of the rest of the series?

Paul: Because it was shot before Nickelodeon committed to the series, it was shot and edited in isolation, meaning that we weren't working on any other shows at the time. That gave us the opportunity for more back and forths between D. J., Ned, and myself.

Jose: You go on to edit every episode in the first five years, so how do you handle that workload?

Paul: It was a pretty consuming process. Rushes would come in from Montreal, the assistant editors would have two days to log and digitize the footage. Once the footage was in the edit system, I would have two days to edit an assembly. The assembly would be over-nighted to the director of that episode (no streaming in those days). I would have a day to respond to notes from the director and fashion a rough cut, a day to tweak further with a second batch of notes from the director along with D. J. MacHale's first notes to produce a fine cut, and then a day to lock picture. The schedule ramped up pretty quickly so that by the third week I would be editing four episodes in various stages of polish. Monday might be the locked picture for Episode 7, Tuesday the fine cut for Episode 8, Wednesday and Thursday the Assembly for Episode 10 and Friday the rough cut of Episode 9. The days were long and there wasn't any time to catch your breath, but it was exhilarating. Every day was a new challenge since each episode was so different. Sometimes the challenge was pulling out performances, other times building the right tension or creepiness would be the focus, and on a show that had special effects there was the exacting working of laying out the framework for the effect shots with Steve Kullback. The schedule and technology at the time meant that we were flying blind in the offline for those scenes, but even though Steve and I were in different locations he was able to direct me in such a way that I don't recall us ever having any big effects headaches.

Jose: Was there a lot of footage provided for you to work with, or were the shoots pretty lean, making it fairly easy to piece together, but with not much wiggle room in terms of coverage?

Paul: I don't know if I would call it wiggle room. There were choices available. The directors were pretty ambitious. I think that's one of the reasons the series was so good; every episode was shot like it was a movie. Given the tight shooting schedule, tough decisions were the order of the day both on set and in the edit room. Was the performance in a particular take solid? Do we shoot another take and perhaps risk forfeiting an additional angle that's really dramatic because of a time crunch? Then when we see it in the edit room we would have to massage performance, pacing, and mood out of however many takes and setups they were able to squeeze out. I don't recall many, if any, instances where I felt like I couldn't make a scene work in the manner intended because I didn't have enough coverage.

Jose: What's the toughest part about editing a show like this?

Paul: The schedule was pretty grueling. Once we got started it was pretty much three months at break neck speed. There was never any time to catch your breath and regroup. Working out the timing of special effect shots without the technology we have today was a little scary at times, but Steve always seemed to make it work. I never got a call from him saying, "Paul, you're killin' me."

Jose: What precipitated the move into show running when the show's sixth and seventh seasons rolled around?

Paul: If I remember correctly, the decision to come back for a sixth and seventh season came two years after we had wrapped the original run of sixty-five episodes (five seasons), and D. J. and Ned approached me to see if I was willing to take on the role of show runner. It was important that the new seasons had the same feel and were of the same quality as the original and there were only a small number of us who had worked on every episode and had the "institutional "knowledge to be able to safeguard against any drop off.

Jose: You had to recast the Midnight Society, so was that the most difficult element of reviving the show?

Paul: It was certainly one of them. The original cast was an iconic ensemble. They were the identity of the show to many of its fans. It was also tricky because I think the idea of replacing those members of the original cast weighed heavy on the actors we auditioned for the new roles. Many of them had grown up on the show and were replacing "legends" in their minds. But I think the new members of the Midnight Society did a great job of respecting what came before them while at the same time making the role their own and adding to the series. That was the biggest challenge for all of us, staying true to the show but bringing something fresh and unique to it.

Jose: How much input did Nickelodeon or the other TV networks have when it came to the final two seasons?

Paul: Nickelodeon and YTV were always very good with input. They were attentive, but not intrusive, and they were very respectful of the strains of the shooting and post-production schedules. I don't recall a lot of notes coming from either, but the notes that came showed an understanding of the series and were usually spot-on.

Jose: What's a typical production schedule like for an episode as the show runner?

Paul: You're never dealing with just one episode. My day—and they were long (14-16 hours)—would include visits to the set when we were beginning a show, starting at a new location, had a new actor debuting, or if there were any set-ups that were particularly tricky such as stunt work or special effects shots. I would be in the production office to deal with any of the business issues like hiring key staff, producing a weekly cost report, checking on wardrobe or artwork/props for upcoming shows, meeting with the director and assistant director for an upcoming show to go over their shot list to see if their intended shooting schedule looked manageable. I would also spend time on the road scouting new locations for upcoming shows, running over to the casting agency to sit through auditions and once post-production begins, there were music, mixes, special effects and color corrections to approve! I would also be on set to wrap each day to see where we stood. Then it was back to the production office or apartment to do notes on the cuts the new editor was churning out. Full and crazy every day, but a lot of fun!

Jose: How far into Season 7's filming were you made aware that it would be the show's final season?

Paul: I'm pretty sure we knew going in. I don't recall the specifics of when we "found out. "It wasn't like we were cancelled. My recollection was that the plan was to do two seasons. There wasn't anything special that needed to be done. We wrapped the production just as one would normally. For those of us who had worked on the show for a while, there may have been a few bittersweet moments the last week of shooting, or at the wrap party, but the truth is the process is so hard that you don't have the ability to reflect until you've had time to step away and recover.

Jose: What did you prefer, editing or producing?

Paul: Got to hedge on that. They are very different challenges with their own rewards, but I enjoyed both and the fact that I got to do both on the same show was a blessing; I am very lucky.

Jose: Do you have a favorite episode in the series as an editor and later as a producer?

Paul: That's hard. Especially for the shows I edited. They were all so different. Episodes like "Lonely Ghost" and "Shiny Red Bicycle" were understated, but very spooky. I also liked the episodes with Doctor Vink. Getting the mix of humor and scary with Doctor Vink was challenging, but great fun. If I had to choose one I would probably go with "Midnight Madness" and Nosferatu. "Dream Girl" also holds a special place in my heart; just great story telling and it was fun when M. Night Shyamalan said it inspired Sixth Sense. As for the episodes for which I was show runner, I'd probably go with "Forever Game" and "Vampire Town."

Jose: Why do you think *AYAOTD?* still has a rabid fan base and is remembered fondly to this day?

Paul: It was such a unique offering for kids. It wasn't a comedy or a music show. It was a series of shows that were different every week. The only thing that was consistent-and this was critical-was the fact that kids were empowered protagonists who faced challenges that were just real enough to be scary. And on top of that, the presence of the Midnight Society meant the viewer belonged to something and I think that's important to kids—all of us, really—and the fans never left the Midnight Society. I guess it's like being an alumni at a school, your school spirit never dies.

(Composer)

Jose: When did you discover music, Jeff?

Jeff: It was discovered that I had perfect pitch at three when I got a toy piano and started to pick out melodies. This was followed by a real upright piano on which I played chords and pretty much anything I heard. By the time I was eight, I was on TV improvising any song in the style of any composer I had heard, i.e. Chubby Checker in the style of Bach or Beatles in the style of Chopin. My piano teacher gave me twenty-five cents whenever I brought in something I picked up by ear, such as a very basic Gershwin Rhapsody in Blue.

Jose: That's amazing! You certainly have a heck of a track record, so how did composing for TV begin for you?

Jeff: I was arranging lots of jingles in the early 1980s, not actually composing them but doing musical direction, arranging and synthesis. This was before the computer music era. I would bring a bunch of synths to various twenty-four-track tape recording studios, lay down basic tracks with a small rhythm section or drum machine, maybe a few orchestral players, and lay down synth tracks direct to tape and direct vocals. The person I was doing this for picked up an animated series that I ghosted on in this manner. Then I got the call to be the composer. My first series was *Madeline*, and I would improvise my score live to forty-eight-track tape. Synchronization and rewinding those big tape reels took forever compared to today's computer-based sequencing. I guess I did a good job, because after that I kept on getting more children's series work. At one point I was scoring and writing library for three different series at once.

Jose: And how did you fall in with the twisted folks behind *Are You Afraid Of The Dark?*

Jeff: It was the aforementioned animation company, CINAR. The CEO, Ron Weinberg, approached me to score the pilot for a live-action campfire scary show. I believe the pilot was entitled "the Phantom Cab."

Jose: You went on to compose 48 out of 91 episodes. Was there a reason you didn't do all of them?

Jeff: Expediency. The episodes were scored 100% to picture. They were almost wall-to-wall music. There were three days to deliver the first draft, and two levels of re-write thereafter; often the picture would be re-cut in the interim. The production needed to get the shows out quickly. There were always two episodes being scored at the same time. So, they brought in my friend Ray Fabi to split up the workload. Also, I was composing for other projects and doing quite a bit of live TV in Montreal, and it would have been inhumanly possible for one composer to deliver quality in such a short time frame.

Jose: Your specific music was very distinctive to the series. How did you go about working on the show musically?

Jeff: There would be a conference call, which was the briefing. We'd sit down and brainstorm the style and placement of the music, and I'd run with it. The scores were dense and bigger than life. I had a lot of freedom with the score; it was fun to do! The scores were orchestral, plus electronic; usually both. Stravinsky meets Tangerine Dream. There were recurring character themes, tension and release, red herrings, always a musical or sonic hook.

Jose: In terms of character-specific themes, did you work on bits for the characters of Dr. Vink and Sardo?

Jeff: Yup, I was asked to create recurring themes for Vink and Sardo. I don't remember what I came up with for Vink, I'd need a copy of a show for that. I do remember being asked to create a warped carnival-ish ditty for Sardo; it was sort of a 1920s burlesque-y thing, but it never really harmonically resolved.

Jose: Did the producers give you many notes as to how to approach the music, or were you left pretty much alone to do your thing?

Jeff: Yes, usually many notes. You can't really talk about music, but you can know the power of it and be specific as to its placement and tone. Very important to the success of the score were the many levels of dynamics and intensity, always leaving room for the big punch, the culmination, and the subsequent resolve. Once, though, I got a two-word briefing: Unleash Jeff. Sometimes D. J. would be a bit hesitant about some element of the episode; perhaps the actors were not acting scared enough. The addition of music was the last chance to fix or enhance whatever wasn't quite working. I loved the respect that D. J. had for music in general, and I was grateful to be able to help in my small way.

Jose: You worked on the first episode and the final episode, so did the mood and tone of the show's music change for you between the beginning and the end in terms of how you approached it?

Jeff: Definitely! With experience I got better at all elements of composing, scoring, and mixing. When you work alone, the hardest thing can be to see the forest, when you have so many details to deal with. Plus, at that time, the software I used to automate my roomful of samplers and synths (Digital Performer) used to struggle to play 120 Midi tracks with automation. Getting an entire twelve-minute scene to play to DAT without hiccups, glitches or a crash was a struggle in patience. Not like the digital audio multicore Macs we have now. Anyways, there were things I did that just worked, other things were iffy, so with time I just got more efficient. Always in the spirit of keeping it fresh and giving each show its own sound, but learning with experience how to streamline and make things work under sound effects and dialogue. Learning when to bring out the Big Guns, and when to just coast.

Jose: Do you have a favorite episode of the show that you composed?

Jeff: I have a few favorites, but it's been too long for me to remember the titles!

Jose: That's understandable. Nowadays do you get recognized for the show? Do you have people coming up and asking you if you're THE Jeff Fisher?

Jeff: Yup, and it's both surprising and gratifying. I am used to visibility because of the hundreds of TV shows I have played keyboards on, live and on-camera on three TV networks in Québec. So, if I go to jam at my favorite Montreal blues bar, my friends know me. But one night there, I met some twenty-something musicians who grew up watching *AYAOTD?* and listening to the music. Apparently they actually had parties where they would crank up the sound and play the episodes to listen to the scores. Wow, who would have thought that the music would have such an impact? I get recognition from orchestral players in Las Vegas (I'm playing with Céline Dion these days) who listen to the shows with their kids and they are impressed. It's very cool.

Jose: Is there one memory you will always keep with you about your time on *AYAOTD?*

Jeff: I recall my daughters Ali and Emily sitting on the couch in my recording studio watching me score some of the tension scenes. I'd be layering stuff and there would typically be the classic high-string crescendo as the camera would pan towards inevitable doom (usually a red herring, but the audience is not supposed to know that). I must have done a good job because they would have their hands over their eyes, they couldn't actually watch the thing. A little imagination is a powerful thing.

ROSS HULL

(Gary)

Jose: So, how did you become a member of the Midnight Society?

Ross: I was an actor in Montreal, and there wasn't a lot going on at the time, and this project seemed pretty exciting, meaning that there was a U.S. opportunity and as Canadian actors, even though we wanted to do Canadian content, we knew the U.S. was a big market, so I auditioned for the pilot. I believe D. J. was in the first audition, if not the callback, and almost initially when I met D. J. I got a really good feeling; I felt a creative connection to him. So, I ended up getting cast in the pilot as David. I think that was only a one-day shoot, maybe two. The campfire set for the pilot, compared to what the show became, was pretty anemic. I think it went pretty well, but the pilot never aired the way it was shot. Anyway, I didn't hear anything for about a year almost, and then I got a call from my agent saying they wanted me to audition for *Dark* again, but as Gary, a different character. I think D. J. was there again when I went in and again I got a positive feeling from him. The rest of it is history and I went on to shoot sixty-five episodes of the show. It was pretty cool; it was my first major acting role on a show. I was nervous initially, but I was more nervous for the pilot than I was the series.

Jose: I didn't know about that hidden pilot where you played David. I wonder if that's floating around somewhere.

Ross: It was "The Twisted Claw," so, the actual story part aired, but they changed the campfire to the cast they eventually went with. They were smart enough not to completely can that episode.

Jose: Were you given any reason why they switched you to Gary?

Ross: Actually, that's a good question. He never really gave me the definite answer. It was kind of awkward too, because I was friends with some of the people who were in the original pilot, and they couldn't figure out why I was chosen. I still don't know to this day why I was. I mean, who knows, maybe when executives looked at all these things they thought I fit the Gary mold a little better. Maybe because I looked older than the other cast members they decided to go with, they thought they could throw me into that leader role.

Jose: Did any of the people from the original pilot guest star on the show afterwards, maybe as a consolation prize?

Ross: Yes, some of the other cast members, I believe, did appear in the actual story parts, which was nice.

Jose: You mentioned Gary being the leader. That's very evident when watching the show, but was the hierarchy ever discussed between you and D. J.?

Ross: I think it was set from the beginning. I remember it was mentioned in the script that he was the leader. So, there was never any doubt about that. And I think I kind of took on that role with some of the cast members, in terms of being that leader. Especially with Daniel DeSanto, as my little brother, we did develop a connection. He would do the annoying stuff that a big brother would get pissed off at and all those things.

Jose: Did you guys ever work out back-stories between yourselves in terms of how you all knew each other and what happened to the characters beyond the campfire?

Ross: Not really, nothing that serious. We would kind of joke around about some of the stuff that may have happened before or after. I mean I created a bit of a back-story for myself; what my character was about, what he was looking to do, his fears, and so on. But we all just played it in the moment. There was a lot of guidance from D. J., especially early on; he was very hands-on in those early episodes.

Jose: What was the easiest part of filming the show?

Ross: Hey, I was seventeen or eighteen when we were shooting the series so you had unlimited food, and you were getting paid pretty good money; that was pretty good for someone my age at the time. Also, I loved the cast.

Jose: There was a bit of shifting around when it came to the Midnight Society, so did you have a favorite iteration of the Midnight Society cast?

Ross: I enjoyed working with everyone, and there was never a time when someone wasn't liked or any of those things. We did build a bond with the cast, I know when we lost members we had to recast and rebuild that bond, but it was all a lot of fun. You know, there was some pressure on us at times. It's a production, so you have to make sure you know your lines and you have to hit your marks and all those things, but at the same time we were kids in the fake woods having a good time around a campfire. That was a good feeling.

Jose: Would you say then that the production machinery itself was the most difficult aspect of making the show?

Ross: What happened over the course of shooting *Are You Afraid of the Dark?* was that Montreal actually got quite busy with productions. We were initially in this pretty comfy, really large studio where they would put actual trees and create this forest and it would be big enough that you could actually almost get lost within it. It was really realistic. But then that studio was booked, so we had to go to some warehouse. I think some of the difficulties too was that we would oftentimes do block shoots, so you had to make sure you knew where you were within that episode, and sometimes the episodes hadn't been shot yet, so, we weren't made aware of some of the subtleties. Obviously when you're a kid, or you're in your teen years, you don't always want to be working eight-hour days or whatever, but it was overall a great experience.

Jose: The order of storytellers always confused me, because sometimes a teller would go twice in a row, so were you guys made aware of what the hosting order was, or was that something decided later?

Ross: It was a bit of a mystery to us, in a sense, because we didn't actually always shoot the episodes in the order that they were going to air on TV. So, it would make sense if someone told two stories in a row, because maybe they just had those two episodes ready. So, yeah, sometimes it would happen where we would shoot two episodes in a row and it would be the same cast member. Then we started to see the patterns as to which characters he was sort of gravitating towards to tell certain kinds of stories. I think it was pretty equal in terms of how it was broken up and which cast member told what stories. There was kind of a competitive edge to who told the most stories, though.

Jose: Gary told most of the Sardo stories, before Tucker took over in the final two seasons, so did you ever meet the estimable Richard Dumont?

Ross: I met him on "Super Specs," because in the beginning of that episode Gary's actually in the magic shop, and he had some scenes in that shop as well, so I met him there. It was a quick meeting; we didn't have a deep discussion. But he did a great job with that character. I felt he really brought that character to life, and to me that meant that he was likely going to be written in for more episodes, which meant my character was going to get to tell more stories.

Jose: Which cast member caused the biggest shakeup when they departed the Midnight Society?

Ross: Jason's character, Frank, was very particular and very streamlined about what he was about. I think there was a lot of stuff you could do with Frank. So, when we lost his character I think that was a pretty big change in terms of the dynamics of the cast. But I think every character had this thing that we lost when they left. On the other hand, I think it was interesting when we did get a new character, like when Sam came in. That was really cool because Gary sort of had an opportunity to build an interesting relationship with her.

Jose: Do you have a favorite episode as a storyteller?

Ross: I think "Super Specs" is an interesting one, and it was hard to do something like that; show different dimensions and all these things. I think they did a good job on it, and just the idea of what that episode was about was pretty interesting to me.

Jose: What about your favorite in general?

Ross: "Laughing In The Dark," that sort of stands out in my mind. "Lonely Ghost," as well. Ghosts and paranormal activity just always fascinated me as a kid.

Jose: Let's talk about your biggest adventure in the series, namely your appearance in "The Tale of the Silver Sight." I bet that was a blast to actually take part in the story.

Ross: Oh, totally! I was honored that they had me come back. I never expected it and I never even thought about it for a second when they brought the show back, partly because I went on to do another TV show, *Student Bodies*, which was kind of a *Saved by the Bell* type show. So, when I got the call I said, "Yeah, great! I'll definitely do it." It was great that Gary got to come back and you got to see a different side of him; there was definitely an arc there. I got to work with Daniel DeSanto again, and Elisha Cuthbert and the new cast members. All of them were great. I had no clue that that season was going to be the end, and I don't think the cast members knew either.

Jose: What did you see from your time at the new campfire that you wish had been incorporated into your run?

Ross: They changed things around a little bit, in a good way. They changed the kinds of things that the Midnight Society members sat on. I mean there was a couch, which we would have loved to have! It's too bad that they added that only then.

Jose: You and Daniel DeSanto were playing brothers, so how did you guys bond to make sure that relationship worked on screen?

Ross: Daniel and I actually worked together prior to *Dark* on a different show called *Eric's World*, which was sort of a sitcom designed for tweens. We got to know each other quite well on that show. I don't know how old he was when I first met him, maybe seven or eight, but he had the attitude of a thirty-year-old. I mean the character he played on that show was kind of like a little man, so I think some of that came out in his personality when I hung out with him. I only found out he was cast on *Dark* the first day we all kind of got together and arrived in Montreal. I thought it was great. I think the fact that we knew each other already and had that chemistry together helped. He wasn't afraid to throw anything at me, literally, so that helped that he didn't have that fear and I think that helped the interaction between the two characters because everyone else seemed to have some sort of respect for Gary, but Tucker didn't show it as much as some of the others.

Jose: To speak to that point, I really appreciated, and I know the other fans did as well, that the Midnight Society had its own internal logic and on-going storylines, whether it was Kristen and David's romance, or Gary trying to work up the guts to tell Sam how he felt.

Ross: I think that's some of the genius that D. J. brought to the whole thing. He certainly had these arcs and these little things that he could tweak for the characters in mind, and it was genius because he threw in just enough that it didn't overwhelm the introduction of the story, and it also managed to get people attached to characters and it got them to tune in the following week. I think Rachel and Nathaniel did a great job with that, initially, and I set the pattern that there be some character traits that people could pick up on.

Jose: Playing off of the character traits, the more you watch the show, the more you realize that each storyteller had a certain story they always told. Kiki always told the stories with the diversity casts, Frank almost always told a Doctor Vink story, and Gary's would be magic. Was that ever consciously discussed or did it just turn out that way?

Ross: I think D. J. had that in mind and he set that out initially when he was writing these campfire kids. He kind of handpicked an area of interest or a passion that each one of these kids would have, and maybe that was sort of the catapult for him to write some of the stories as well. It was certainly something set from the get-go that that was the way it was going to be.

Jose: Currently you've turned your attention to the weather?

Ross: Yeah, I'm a meteorologist now, and I think some folks who aren't used to watching television in Canada are shocked as to how I got on that path. After *Dark,* I continued to work as an actor for another five or six years, and I was in my mid-twenties and hadn't gone to university then, so I went to a university here in Toronto which was well known for communications, journalism, and production and so on. In my last year of the university I got a job at the Weather Network, which is Canada's version of the Weather Channel, and I fell in love with weather and meteorology. It is a passion of mine, but I still audition for things here and there.

Jose: It's been twenty-five years, as of this book's release, since the airing of the pilot. What are your thoughts on the longevity of this show?

Ross: I really am shocked by it. I live in Toronto, so if I walk out on the street right now, people will still recognize me from that show, which to me is unbelievable. It obviously left a mark on people, and it's an honor to be a part of something like that. In Canada we weren't really exposed to the success of the show as early as perhaps in the U.S. It was more of a gradual progression in Canada, but I think it hit a crescendo at one point because the show was on all the time on YTV, which was like our Nickelodeon, and I think it was just the right timing. I think people, especially those that are now in their twenties and thirties, remember those experiences and those Halloween marathons. I did the show twenty-five years ago, so I've kind of moved on, and I am extremely grateful that I got a chance to do it, but over the last few years I have looked back at the show a little more just because of its continued interest.

Jose: Since you're being recognized to this day, what are your thoughts on the show's fandom?

Ross: I think the show became more than just a show for some of these kids. Some of these kids were going through major stuff in their lives, and the show in some way got them through that. To me, I don't understand how a TV show that wasn't even dealing with some of those issues got you through, but I guess it was some form of escape. Also, I know Nickelodeon shows presented a reality in terms of kids, it wasn't like the *90210* type of situation where everyone seemed perfect. These characters had some flaws and weren't perfect, so I guess some of those kids saw themselves in that. There are worse things to be remembered for.

(Producer)

Jose: What impressed you the most about working with D. J. on the *Encyclopedia Brown* series?

Ned: D. J.'s ability to take complicated information and present it clearly and simply. I had seen D. J.'s Afterschool Special about religious freedom and Christmas. He had taken an involved case, synthesized and simplified the story, and presented it with passion, emotion and clarity.

Jose: Were you worried that scary stories for kids would be a hard sell to a TV studio?

Ned: Not really. After *Encyclopedia Brown,* we knew we could tell dramatic stories for kids in a twenty-two minute format. And campfire stories are perfect for that. Nick was looking for new genres for kids. *Scary Tales* (what *Dark* was pitched as) drew a great response from Nick immediately. I should mention that it still took four years for a series go-ahead.

Jose: Where did you guys decide to draw the line between what was acceptable and what was too scary?

Ned: The sales line was "so scary that you can't watch the next episode." Of course, every episode empowered the protagonist and concluded with complete success for him or her, as scary as we could.

Jose: Was there a specific age range in mind when you were crafting the episodes for air?

Ned: SNICK was set up for eight to twelve-year-olds, so that's what we aimed for.

Jose: I'm sure there are a ton of things that are extremely tricky about putting a show like this together, but what would you say were the toughest elements in regard to quality?

Ned: Three things: 1) Good story, 2) Correct scariness, 3) Could be done well for the budget we had. Each of the episodes was hard because of at least one of these elements.

Jose: How important is the casting for a show like this?

Ned: Better actors made for better episodes, but *Dark* was written well enough to handle not so great actors. To me though, diversity was the key. Because of that we were nominated for an NAACP award.

Jose: When the show got popular, were you mostly left to your own devices, or was more control imposed?

Ned: Nick read and commented on every script and certainly looked at the cuts. Having said that, we were completely in control of story ideas and execution. By year three, Nick pretty much left us alone and trusted our judgment.

Jose: Hindsight is twenty/twenty as they say, so is there anything you would go back and do different with the series?

Ned: I know we should have fought for a higher budget to do more ambitious shows. And though not a realistic option, it would have been better if we could have done the shows in the US. We wouldn't have had so many actor/writer/director limitations. But, we still solved the constraints.

Jose: I'm sure it's a hard choice, but do you have a favorite episode in the series?

Ned: "Lonely Ghost." Sweetest episode; scary, but a nice emotional impact.

Jose: Why do you think *AYAOTD?* still has a rabid fan base and is remembered fondly to this day?

Ned: Because it was a fun premise that was beautifully executed. Good is good. More than anything, audiences respond to good.

D. J. MACHALE

(Series Creator/Writer/Director)

Jose: How did *AYAOTD?* come about?

D. J.: I was hired by Ned Kandel to write the TV version of *Encyclopedia Brown, Boy Detective* for HBO. Ned and I had a great experience working together so we decided to try and create a show of our own. Our initial idea was to make a direct-to-video project that was all about bedtime stories for lazy parents. We planned on getting some familiar, old-time actor to sit in a big old chair in front of a warm fireplace reading fairy tales. The idea was that when parents didn't feel like reading bedtime stories to their kids, they could just pop the tape in. Great idea, until we tried to figure out what kind of fairy tales to tell. Most of the public domain stuff seemed kind of dull. So, Ned asked me, "What kind of stories did you like when YOU were a kid?" I replied, "Scary stories." That made the light bulb go on over both of our heads. So, *Fairy Tales* became *Scary Tales* and that was the name of the show. But having an old-time actor reading scary stories to kids seemed a bit too creepy. We didn't want the storyteller to be scary, like the Crypt Keeper. So, the idea came up that the best people to tell scary stories were kids sitting around the campfire. It was a natural. The idea grew from there and we realized it would be more fun to actually SEE the scary story play out rather than hear it. But that increased the budget and we realized this wasn't going to work as direct-to-video, it would need to be a TV show. So, we pitched it to Nickelodeon. They turned it down at first. They thought it would be too scary. But a year later a fellow by the name of Jay Mulvaney who was hired to be in development at Nickelodeon found my original three-page pitch for the show in a file drawer. He pulled it out and asked, "Why aren't we doing this show?" If not for him, the show would not have been made.

Jose: Were you ever given any mandate to make sure the episodes weren't too scary?

D. J.: Never. They trusted us to use our judgment. Though they did have a concern at Nickelodeon that parents might protest that we were freaking kids out. So, I was asked to try and base some of the stories on literary antecedents. Their thinking was if parents called to complain, they'd reply, "What are you talking about? We're just re-imagining classic literature!" But we never got any complaints from parents. Not a single one (at least not that I heard of). It seemed to me that everybody got what we were doing, and loved going along for the spooky ride.

Jose: What was the casting process like? Were you looking to cast certain types, or just the best kids for the job?

D. J.: Nickelodeon had more input on casting than on any other aspect of the show. They prided themselves on putting "real" kids in their shows, rather than showbiz kids. A fellow by the name of Michael Koegel ran the casting department at Nick and was right with me at every casting session. Casting was a challenge since it was an anthology show. We needed dozens of kids every season, not to mention adults. Add to that, that Nickelodeon wanted us to cast as many minority actors as possible, and they threw out any kid who seemed like a typical "Disney kid," we really had a Herculean task. Not all the kids were great actors but we were desperate. And it wasn't like we could run a crawl at the bottom of every episode saying, "Cut us some slack on the performance here. We ran out of decent kids!"

Jose: Would you have the entire season written out before you filmed anything?

D. J.: Not entirely, but since we shot the campfire scenes together toward the beginning of each season, I needed to know what each of the stories were so I could write the campfire scenes.

Jose: So, the Midnight Society portions were shot first?

D. J.: We usually shot those scenes a few weeks into the shooting schedule. It gave me more time to figure out what all the stories would be, and also gave the crew a chance to catch up on their sleep by coming back into the studio to shoot the campfires. Remember, the title of the show is *"Are You Afraid of the DARK?"* which meant we had many, many night shoots. The campfire week was a relative vacation. But we couldn't hold off on shooting those scenes for too long because we needed the footage to start editing the shows.

Jose: What was a typical shooting schedule for a tale, excluding the campfire bit?

D. J.: Every episode took exactly five days to shoot (Campfires were a half-day each). So, in all an episode took 5.5 days to shoot. That's a pretty luxurious schedule by today's standards. You don't see shows for kids being shot like that anymore. But they were like shooting small movies so we needed the time. It was a real challenge because each episode had different sets and different locations. Usually we'd shoot the daytime exterior scenes first, followed by the interiors. If we had night shooting, which happened a lot, we gradually moved into night as the week progressed. We spent many a morning eating breakfast in a cemetery as the sun rose. The only episode that took more than 5.5 days was from the first season; "The Tale of the Pinball Wizard." That show was way too ambitious for the normal schedule, especially since we shot the entire episode in a shopping mall and had to do it overnight when the mall was closed. We ended up shooting an extra day on that one.

Jose: I would imagine show running a series is a remarkably stressful endeavor, how did you manage writing, directing, and producing on multiple episodes with different casts?

D. J.: The first season nearly killed me, and it was only twelve episodes since we'd already shot the pilot the year before. I didn't get a whole lot of sleep and lost a lot of weight. On one scouting trip I actually passed out from exhaustion and probably malnutrition. The toughest part of any season happened somewhere in the middle when everything was going on at once from writing the final episodes to working on post-production sound of the first few. That first season I directed most of the episodes, as well as all the campfire scenes. As the seasons wore on, I directed less and less. That made things a bit more sane for me. The norm became that I'd direct the first episode, one somewhere in the middle, and then the final episode. With the final twenty-six, I didn't direct at all and didn't even set foot in Montreal, where we shot, but I still developed all the scripts and made notes on every aspect of the show. By then I had delegated much of the boots-on-the-ground work to Paul Doyle. Paul was the editor on the first sixty-five episodes, and Ned and I gave him the nod to run the final twenty-six.

Jose: I like that the Midnight Society had a through line for their characters. They weren't just narrators, they were real kids, like one of us. They had birthdays and anniversaries and when they left the show they usually left an impression. Was that always intended or did that just develop from becoming a family during filming?

D. J.: It was totally intended. It's tough to get viewers to buy into an anthology series because there are no continuing characters. Besides being the storytellers, The Midnight Society became the recognizable cast the viewers came to know. They each had their own type of stories that they would tell (i.e. Gary told the Sardo stories, Frank told the Vink tales, sweet Betty Ann always told macabre stories, while Kristen told tales of romance). Though The Midnight Society played a very small part in each episode, they became the familiar characters that viewers cared about. One of my favorite moments in the series was the very end of episode #65, "The Tale of the Night Shift." I had written a mini-romance between Gary (Ross Hull) and Samantha (Joanna Garcia) that played throughout the season. Gary had a crush on her, but didn't have the guts to tell her. In that final episode, Gary finally tells her how he feels, and she replies that she likes him too. Aww, how sweet. But the best part was that they didn't leave the campfire with the other kids. They stayed and sat by the fire. At the time, I thought this was going to be the final episode of the series so the idea of keeping the fire burning was intentional. Little did I know that we'd be coming back two years later to make two more seasons. Oops. But at the time, I thought it was a fitting way to end the series.

Jose: You re-use a lot of actors for the tales, and I'm curious if it was just because there was a lack of actors available like you mentioned previously, or you figured that they were different stories so they were different universes?

D. J.: Originally I didn't want to re-use any actor, or at least in a recognizable way. There were plenty who had multiple roles, but were usually under so much make-up that you couldn't tell. The reason I didn't want to re-use actors was because in my mind I wanted each of the stories to be unique tales that were supposedly imagined by the storytellers. I felt that if you recognized an actor, it would take you out of the illusion of the tale and make it feel more like a TV show. It was a lofty ideal because I soon realized that there were just so many actors available, especially in Montreal where English isn't the first language. So, I eventually gave up on that idea and we re-cast actors many times. In hindsight, I'm glad it worked out that way because it was like we had our own troupe of actors and if you're a fan of the show, you'll recognize them from different episodes. It also freed us up to bring back some terrific actors.

Jose: Was it accidental that Zeebo, Vink and Sardo became recurring elements and characters? What distinguished them from the other colorful rogues' gallery of characters on the show?

D. J.: Vink and Sardo weren't originally intended to be recurring, but once Aron Tager (Vink) and Richard Dumont (Sardo) created such amazing, colorful characters, I simply thought, *Why not?* It was fun to think of the various incarnations that Dr. Vink would take. He was a chef, a barber, a filmmaker and a scientist. The "Wild Boar" was one of his continuing signatures. He experimented with the brain of a wild boar in "Phantom Cab." He cut hair at his "Wild Boar" salon in "Cutter's Treasure." The restaurant that served the "Dangerous Soup" was called The Wild Boar. It's fun to come up with recurring touchstones like that. The name "Sardo" came from a bath oil product. I remember the commercials on TV when I was a kid. I don't remember how it was spelled, but it was pronounced Sar-DOH, accent on the DOH. Richard Dumont created the style of Sardo along with the director of "The Tale of the Super Specs," Ron Oliver. His flamboyant style was all Richard. It was a joy to come up with bits of business and dialog for both of those characters. It was especially fun to have them together for the one and only time in "The Tale of Cutter's Treasure." I have a picture of the two of them in their one scene together hanging in my office. Zeebo, on the other hand, as memorable as he is, was only in one episode. Though in "The Tale of Train Magic" we had a character playing a video game called "Zeebo's Funhouse." That was just done for fun. If you watch the episode and freeze it on the shot of the video game, you'll see an image of Zeebo on it.

Jose: For all intents and purposes, the show ends in Season 5, only to be resurrected a few years later under semi-new management. Were you actively trying to get the show back on the air during that period, or was it something that just sprung up in terms of possibility for Nickelodeon?

D. J.: Actually, Nickelodeon had very little to do with bringing it back. They had their sixty-five episodes and that's all they wanted. It was the Canadian producer, Cinar Films, that wanted more. They had the rights to license the show internationally. Licenses normally lasted about five years. By 1998, the five-year licenses that were originally sold were running out, and Cinar wanted foreign broadcasters to re-up the series. They thought that if they had new episodes to sweeten the deal, these broadcasters would be more inclined to license them all. So, they approached me to see if I'd do more.

I'd been working on other projects in the two years since we'd finished so all the old wounds had healed and I thought it might be fun to go back. Nickelodeon came on board, but only as a licensee of the show. They wouldn't put up the same amount of money as they had previously so our budgets were cut drastically, but as for production, it was very much the same as the first sixty-five. Most of the crew was back. I still developed all of the scripts and guided postproduction. The quality of these shows was every bit as good as the first sixty-five. Some of my favorite episodes came out of that last twenty-six!

Jose: The Silver Sight trilogy is a great mini-movie for the series. Does its appearance in Season 7 mean that you knew that was going to be the last season? It would have been a perfect ending, so was there ever talk of making that the final episode?

D. J.: It was more out of my desire to do something unique. The Midnight Society had never played a role in the tale, and after eighty-some-odd episodes I thought it was time. I loved writing that movie. It had to work both as a movie, as well as be cut up into individual episodes, which was a challenge. I'm very proud of the way the multiple stories overlap and play off of each other. Also, exploring the original roots of The Midnight Society was a blast, not to mention bringing back Gary. It's one of my favorite episodes.

Jose: I know asking you if you have a favorite iteration of the Midnight Society is like asking you which of your kids you like better, but do you have a favorite overall season, in terms of everything gelling together and working as closely to what you initially envisioned?

D. J.: I do! Of course I have many favorite moments and episodes and experiences from all seven seasons, but I'd have to say that my favorite season as a whole was Season 2. The reason was that with Season 1, we were just finding our way. Our crew was wonderful. I know this is cliché, but we were like a family that came together and really cared about the show. Each and every person went above and beyond to make the show special. Many crewmembers stayed with the show for all seven seasons. Without their talent and concern, the show would never have been as good. But in that first season, most everybody was looking at me like I was crazy. I had this vision of not only the show, but each episode in my head and I think most of the crew thought I was nuts, but they went along with me and the results were great. When we came back for Season 2, everybody was now on the same page. It all became so much easier. Rather than have to explain what was in my head, all I'd have to say was something like, "This has to have the creepy feel like the bedroom in "Lonely Ghost," and everybody would know immediately what I was talking about. Rather than trying to figure out what was in my head, everybody took what was on the page and pushed it further. Everybody. Make-up, hair, wardrobe, production design, locations, lighting, music, sound effects; everybody. It was fantastic. Simply put, we were all with the program and we started doing some incredibly great work in Season 2. We certainly did some fabulous work in future seasons as well, but it was in Season 2 that it got fun.

Jose: You wrote quite a bit of the episodes yourself, but did you have a permanent writing staff or did freelancers write the other episodes?

D. J.: We had a writing staff of one. Me. Everybody else was a freelancer. I wouldn't hire writers, I bought script ideas. At the beginning of each season writers would pitch me ideas. If I liked the idea, the writer would be hired to write it. I think they hated working with me because I'd really make them work hard. I had them pound out outlines over and over again until the story was perfect. Then I'd have them write the script, which at that point was fairly easy because we had worked the story out so thoroughly. I was all over every script because I needed the episodes to feel as if they were all part of the same series. I probably wrote or re-wrote every line of dialog from every script, but I could never have done it on my own. Ninety-one episodes is a lot of stories. I worked with some incredibly talented, imaginative writers who thought up some really twisted tales.

Jose: As protection against the rampaging parent, I know a few of your tales were inspired by famous horror stories, like *Dr. Jekyll and Mister Hyde*, but where else did your inspirations come from?

D. J.: Here are a few that I remember: The pilot episode "The Tale of the Twisted Claw" was a re-telling of *The Monkey's Paw*. "The Phantom Cab" was based on some old story I dug up. I think it was called *The Phantom Coach*. "The Tale of Laughing in the Dark" was inspired by an old folk tale, *The Golden Arm*. We did a take off of *The Legend of Sleepy Hollow* called "The Tale of the Midnight Ride." "The Tale of the Captured Souls" is a spinoff from *The Portrait of Dorian Gray*. I tried to do a re-telling of some Poe tails, but they were just too gruesome. I couldn't figure out how to do Frankenstein either. Those are the ones that jump to mind. However, most of the episodes were wholly original ideas that either came from me, or the freelance writers.

Jose: I'm curious about the ancillary products like the video game and the novels; how involved were you with all of that?

D. J.: I was always consulted and was able to give my input. With the board game, I made sure the spots on the game board coincided with places from episodes of the shows. I helped with the writing of the Midnight Society scenes with the CD-Rom game. I also had input and gave notes on many of the books. I even wrote one with my sister. It was *The Tale of the Nightly Neighbors*. The first half was a novelization of the episode, but in the book we continued the story as vampires took over the town. So, if you were a fan of that episode, find the book to learn what happened to Emma and DayDay Toll, and Lex Braun, after the episode ended.

Jose: Do you have a favorite moment from the making of the series that you could share with us?

D. J.: There were hundreds, but one springs to mind. During the first season, there was a lot of pressure. I was in way over my head and working twenty-two hour days. I wasn't entirely sure if the show was going to work, but I had to keep pushing forward. There was one moment where I was totally stressed and exhausted so I left the office and walked downstairs to the soundstage where we were building sets for some of the very first episodes. I was all alone. The construction crew had gone home. The giant soundstage was quiet. I walked to the center and stood there, surrounded by the sets of shows that hadn't been shot yet. They stood there, for real, having sprung from the pages of the scripts and from my imagination. In one corner was the exterior and the interior of Dr. Vinks's cottage. Across from it was the colorful, circular room of doors from Zeebo's funhouse. Next to that was the empty bedroom from "The Lonely Ghost" with the mirror and "EMPLEH" written hundreds of times on the walls. I stood there staring at these sets and thought, "Wow, this all right. I'm a lucky guy." From that moment on, whenever I got stressed and caught up in the drama of TV production, I'd go down to that soundstage and sit on whatever set it was that was being made for an upcoming episode and just enjoy the fact that I was privileged to be able to make that show.

Jose: Talk to us about that final day on Season 5 when the campfire roared for the last time; I would imagine it was a very bittersweet moment.

D. J.: The day when we DIDN'T extinguish the campfire for episode sixty-five, the episode we thought would be the last episode. That was tough. I wasn't directing the campfires anymore at that point, but I came back to direct that one—and to say good-bye to The Midnight Society. That was very emotional.

Jose: I personally think there is, but do you think there is a place for *AYAOTD?* in today's world with today's audiences?

D. J.: I'd like to think so, but the reason I'm not doing kid's TV anymore and writing books instead is testament to the fact that kid's TV has changed. Simply put, dramas aren't being produced anymore and I think that's a shame.

Kid's programmers are all going for the lowest common denominator, and that means comedy. I love comedies, but I think kids should be exposed to more. *Are You Afraid of the Dark?* Was, of course, a spooky show, but it was also a show about real kids dealing with real, relatable issues that had nothing to do with ghosts. That's one of the things that I believe made the show so popular. The kids were real. They weren't cartoons. They didn't constantly snark at each other to get three jokes out on a page with a laugh track.

Jose: If you could go back and tweak any one episode, or a handful of them, which ones do you wish you had a chance to remake?

D. J.: All of them.

Jose: Do you have an all-time favorite episode (or three)?

D. J.: My favorite was "The Tale of the Midnight Madness." It goes back to the fact that in Season 2, we really hit our stride. Was it the best episode? I don't know. But it was the one I look back on fondly because it showed what we were capable of doing. Some other favorites are The Tale of: "The Dead Man's Float," "Train Magic," "Silver Sight," "Laughing In The Dark," "The Water Demons," "The Time Trap," and oh so many more. There are some I'd like to forget, but we won't go into that.

Jose: What did you learn from your time on *AYAOTD?* that you will always treasure?

D. J.: Whenever there's a conflict, there is always the right course to take. When people disagree on something, it usually has to do with their own egos or prejudices or selfishness. But if you take a step back and look at any conflict, there is always the obvious route to take that's hard to argue with. When making that show, there were thousands of conflicts and challenges. Every day. There were arguments all the time. Often, they'd end up in my lap. What I would always say to those involved was, "What's best for the show?" Suddenly, the argument would stop because it was always clear what was best for the show. I try to apply that same reasoning all the time. I take a step back from a conflict, get my ego out of the way, and suddenly the way to go comes clear. If there's anything I learned from making that show, it's that you have to remember what's important.

Jose: To me the show wasn't just to scare kids, but to show them that you don't have to be scared of the dark, and you can triumph if you persevere, was this an intended goal, or am I inferring?

D. J.: I tried to create stories about kids who were going through conflicts that were real and relatable and had nothing to do with the boogieman. That not only makes for characters you care about and root for, but it shows kids growing up and taking control. If there's one common thread that goes through all of my writing, it's that concept of self-empowerment. I take kids, put them into difficult situations and then take away the people who would normally help them, usually that means their parents. With no parents to help them, the kids have to rely on themselves. That pretty much applies to every episode of *Are You Afraid of the Dark?* and every story I've written since.

Jose: If you could revitalize the show today, reboot it, would you do anything different?

D. J.: I'd shoot it digitally and do a lot more hand-held work. There's no way I'd get 5.5 days to shoot an episode anymore.

Jose: So, in closing here, I have to ask: are you afraid of the dark?

D. J.: No. I'm afraid of clowns.

RON OLIVER

(Director/Writer)

Jose: Next to creator D. J. MacHale, you are the most prolific of the series directors for the show, is that a distinction you wear with pride?

Ron: OF COURSE! I loved doing the series, and as it was the first television series I wrote and directed, it was very important to me as a writer/director to develop new ways of telling stories.

Jose: You've worked on some very memorable and important episodes, but let's talk about "Phantom Cab," which became the first episode, but wasn't the pilot. How were you first hired?

Ron: D. J. and the Nickelodeon executive, Jay Mulvaney, had seen my movie *Prom Night 3: The Last Kiss* (1990), which I wrote and directed, and decided I had the right sensibility for what they were trying to do with their series.

Jose: You always seemed to land the unforgettable monsters, so tell me about "Laughing in the Dark," which is considered an early series high point, and how you stealthily handled the Zeebo character.

Ron: Zeebo the Clown was creepy for sure. D. J. has this clown thing; he's really freaked out by them, so when he gave me the script I knew it was something important to him. I decided I didn't want to ever actually *see* Zeebo moving or coming to life; I just thought it was scarier if we only ever saw the after-effects of Zeebo. So, you were never really sure if it was actually happening or if it was the Carny guy making it all just in our hero's mind until the physical manifestations started happening.

Jose: "Super Specs" introduces us to Sardo, so tell me about not only the making of the episode, but also how you worked with Richard Dumont to hone Sardo into perfection.

Ron: Sardo was a great character! And Richard Dumont and I had a blast with him; he had to be a bit of an over the top guy, but you still had to believe he was just a normal fellow caught up in weird circumstances. I remember there's a scene during the final séance and Richard was supposed to hide under the séance table while the dry ice machine was pumping smoke clouds out. He held his breath and endured the dry ice smoke, which is pretty horrible after a few moments, and when I yelled "cut" he came out from under the table with his face red and covered in moisture and exhaled with a gasp! He was a real trouper, and I've been proud to have Richard in two other movies: *A Dennis The Menace Christmas* (2007) and *Beethoven's Treasure Tale* (2014), where he plays a variation of the same kind of guy. He's a terrific actor and should be a much bigger star in my opinion.

Jose: You directed my favorite episode, "Dark Music," which is simple and almost low budget, but it's creepy as heck and has one of the darkest endings in the series. How did you approach that one?

Ron: As you said, it is simple and almost low budget. I wanted to keep the focus on the creepy fear inherent in the idea and not on the special effects. So, we did most of the stuff "in camera" and didn't use a lot of visual effects. I remember the last shot of that episode, with the boy's little smile as he realizes that The Thing In The Cupboard might just be the answer to his sister problems. I asked the actor to think of his favorite dessert when he looked at the camera, and that's why he smiled. I love that episode too, and besides "Full Moon," I think it's my favorite!

Jose: Next you work on "Frozen Ghost" with Melissa Joan Hart. It's an old-school ghost story, so was there any movies you held up as a visual template for it?

Ron: Actually, the movie that came to mind when I read the original script was an obscure thing called *Let's Scare Jessica To Death* (1971). I liked the idea of seeing/not seeing the ghost, and we did a lot of exterior work on that one. The "footsteps in the mud" was accomplished very simply; we just locked the camera in position and had the actor step in the mud, and then retrace his steps back out, and then we did an old fashioned camera dissolve to make the footsteps seem to appear.

Jose: You become a writer/director for "Full Moon," which has an interesting twist and goes from eerie to comical. Was this all your idea, or were you given the concept?

Ron: D. J. asked if I wanted to write an episode for Season 2, and I jumped at the chance. I started as a writer on *Hello Mary Lou: Prom Night Two* (1987) and it's always my preferred route to making a movie or TV show; writing and then directing your own script is really a marvelous feeling. So, I came up with the idea of a kid private eye, but since it was for Nickelodeon we couldn't have missing kids, so I decided on missing pets! (And then about a year or two later, they made a movie called *Ace Ventura: Pet Detective* (1994), so I guess I had the right idea!) I always loved the idea of a kid version of *Rear Window* (1954), which is kind of where the original thought came from. What would happen if you saw the guy across the street turn into a werewolf? And then it sort of grew from there. Also, I love jazz, so it made sense that the werewolf guy would be a jazz musician. I asked the composer of the music for the show to do a "big band" sort of sound for the episode, and he did a great job, I think! I remember I got into a lot of trouble for "Tale of the Full Moon" because it was so peculiar and funny and campy. The network didn't want something that outlandish. They wanted the "real world" of the stories to seem real, and they felt all the characters were too over the top. But I loved doing it and it's my favorite episode of all that I made for the series.

Jose: "Magician's Assistant" finds us with another character who would live on in the series in name only, but I would imagine an episode about a very theatrical magician would be fun to shoot.

Ron: Well, I was a magician when I was a kid, and kept doing it into my late teens. I used to do birthday parties and stage shows and nightclubs with my act. I used to float ladies, cut people in three, that kind of thing. So, "Magician's Assistant" was right in my wheelhouse!

Jose: "Old Man Corcoran" has a great twist and some fantastic set pieces. What was the trickiest element in that episode when it came to shooting to make sure you preserved the final shock as long as you could, but that it didn't hinder your sense of believability?

Ron: It's funny, I remember when I first read "Old Man Corcoran" I didn't like the script very much, because I didn't think there was much story there. But as we started to design the episode, I realized I was wrong and the simplicity of the story was its strength. I could therefore have fun with all the visuals and make something pretty scary. As to saving the final twist surprise, I kept the point of view of the story firmly in the kids' hands, so we were always with them; that kept us from suspecting anything was wrong, I hope!

Jose: "Carved Stone" makes Sardo a part of the action again, so you get his manic energy, but it's mostly confined to one location like you had with "Dark Music." Were you given these types of episodes because they knew you had a knack for them?

Ron: I don't know exactly. D. J. had some kind of mysterious alchemy formula for assigning scripts to the directors, and he was usually always right!

Jose: How were directors chosen for the episodes?

Ron: I think that was D. J. and possibly a bit of the network too, but I imagine D. J. did the selections based on his understanding of each director's strengths and weaknesses.

Jose: Did you have any input story-wise, and did you hope to write more episodes?

Ron: I didn't have much story input beyond our first script meeting where we'd discuss the tone of the episode, and we could add ideas. D. J. was great at taking suggestions and very collaborative. Working with him as producer spoiled me for other TV shows, as he was incredibly gracious about letting us all be part of the creative process. At the same time as I was directing episodes of *Dark*, I was also working on a sci-fi series in London, England, as well as a kid series for Showtime in Nottingham, England and producing/directing and co-writing a pilot of another Nick series, as well as writing a feature film, so it was a crazy hectic time. I'm not sure how much writing I could have done for the *Dark* series anyway! I'm just glad I got to make a couple of them from scratch.

Jose: "Curious Camera" seems like it would be a very difficult episode to make work, because the villain is a picture of a gremlin, so how did you approach this one?

Ron: The story of "Curious Camera" has been told quite a few times in various ways, originally as a *Twilight Zone* episode and then later as an episode of *Goosebumps* (starring Ryan Gosling!), but I have to be honest, I don't really remember much about the "Curious Camera" episode other than it was freezing cold when we were shooting in some suburb in Montreal, and all I could think about was that when we wrapped we were going on a three week hiatus and I was going to Martinique for Christmas!

Jose: The titular character in "Crimson Clown" is hands down the scariest clown in the series, in my opinion, because he actually goes face to face with his victim, as opposed to Zeebo's sneaky ways. Was it fun to go full tilt on a creepy clown story?

Ron: Are you kidding??? It was a blast! I loved that episode, and to this day I have adults who tell me that they were terrified as kids by the Crimson Clown. One young friend told me her parents used to tease her as a child and tell her if she didn't behave, the Crimson Clown was going to get her. She's never forgiven me!

Jose: In a related topic, did you believe that Zeebo was a real clown, or was it the sideshow Carny trying to freak the kid out in "Laughing in the Dark"?

Ron: Oh, Zeebo was a real clown, definitely. And he's still out there someplace, waiting for you.

Jose: "Renegade Virus" gives us another great villain. It was a fun episode, so I assume it was a heck of a lot of fun to shoot.

Ron: Actually that was a lot of fun. I loved the idea of doing as much of the visual effects in-camera as possible; reversing the film, slow motion/fast motion etc. And the guy who played the virus was a pretty well-known character around some of the local Montreal bars, so he was hilarious on set.

Jose: "Water Demons" gives us some great water zombies; were you visually inspired by Carpenter's *The Fog* (1980)?

Ron: Well, of course John Carpenter is a brilliant filmmaker and anytime you have fog and zombies together, you're going to look to *The Fog* as inspiration! I think that episode is one of my scariest, and when that kid wakes up in the hammock and sees the zombies around him, even I jumped!

Jose: It seems like you were earmarked for the great villains of the series, did you take D. J. aside and get your pick of scripts before anyone else had a crack at them?

Ron: Nah, D. J. just gave me the good villains because he knew I loved doing those episodes. And because D. J. is a great guy!

Jose: You take matters into your own hands again by writing and directing one more time on the unforgettable "Ghastly Grinner," another series benchmark. What inspired this episode?

Ron: I always loved the idea of a comic book character coming to life, and especially an evil one. The name of the Ghastly Grinner just kind of came to me one day, and then our production designer brought in a comic book artist to bring him to life, and then wardrobe and makeup went beyond the call of duty to really make that character shine, I think! He was pretty scary. And of course we couldn't kill the parents or anything, so having them become giggling, drooling zombies worked instead. The character of Hooper Picalarro in that episode, with her eraser, is based on a girl I knew when I was in first grade up in Canada; she had the glasses, the sweater with the button clasp, everything. And a couple years ago, I discovered that there is/was an indie rock band called Hooper Picalarro playing in the Pacific Northwest. I emailed them a thank you and they were delightful, and very kind to say the "Ghastly Grinner" episode made such an impact on them they wanted to name their band after the heroine!

Jose: "Station 109.1" sees you working with Gilbert Gottfried and Ryan Gosling, who's gone on to superstardom. What do you recall about working with these two?

Ron: Gilbert made us laugh every day on set, but he was a total pro and I found out later that he was a big *Fangoria* magazine fan; Fango's past editor Tony Timpone told me that Gilbert used to come to the office in New York and go through all the back issues. Ryan Gosling and I became fast friends on that show, and we're still close friends to this day. In fact, he lived in the guest suite of my condo in Los Angeles when he first made the move to Hollywood, and I am proud to say I drove him to his first audition for *Young Hercules*, which helped launch him into the stratosphere. He's a great guy and I'm very proud of what he's accomplished, and what a fine man and husband and father he's grown into.

Jose: "Prisoners Past" is a very interesting episode in terms of locations and plotting, how did you approach your work on this one?

Ron: I remember thinking I wanted to see the environment of the prison, and how it dwarfed the kids, so I used a lot of wide-angle lenses, and impressionistic camera angles to get a sense of claustrophobia. The directors of photography on the series were all incredibly talented, and they taught me a great deal about filmmaking during my time with them.

Jose: Your final episode for the series is "Door Unlocked," featuring Sardo again. Did you all know the series was going to be "cancelled" when shooting, and if so did you approach this episode any differently?

Ron: To be honest, I don't really remember if we knew it was over or not, but it was near the end of five seasons and I think we all knew we had been part of something wonderful so if it ended, well, fair enough. We did it! I remember often saying to the crew and cast that these shows were going to be part of the childhood of the next generation to come, so we needed to be aware of our responsibility to the audience, and to their future, and I'm happy to say that I'm often told how much *Dark* meant to people. They remember it fondly and want to share it with their own kids today through Netflix or DVD or whatever.

Jose: Even though you didn't work on the two-season revival afterwards, were you happy to see it come back to life?

Ron: I was very happy to see D. J.'s terrific idea revived. I think it would do well again now, in fact! But I was also happy to see other hands take the reins and guide the Midnight Society for a new generation. My stories for that series had been told, I think, so it was time for fresh blood.

Jose: Do you have a favorite episode that you directed?

Ron: "Tale of the Full Moon," hands down, followed by "Ghastly Grinner" and then "Tale of the Dark Music." And of course "Station 109.1" because it introduced me to my wonderful friend Ryan.

Jose: Lastly, you worked with Vink and Sardo, did you have a favorite character to work with?

Ron: I loved both of those characters, but I have to admit I had a soft spot for Sardo. He always seemed to try so very hard and nothing ever worked. He was a bit like Wile E. Coyote really, and I always root for the underdog.

DAVID WINNING

(Director)

Jose: How did you get hired on to direct for *AYAOTD*?

David: This is way back when, when I had just started directing and I was working on a Vancouver police series with Carl Weathers for Cannell called *Street Justice* (1991). I had also just finished an episode of *Neon Rider* (1989) that won some awards. I remember I was sitting in a diner somewhere in BC on a road trip in 1992 or early 1993 and I got a call from D. J. asking what my credits were, and if I'd be interested in a new scary series for kids being shot in Montreal. I love travelling so it's always the location that peaks my interest first. Jumped at the chance. I also shot the ABC series *Dinotopia* in 2002 almost solely on the fact that it was being produced in Budapest, Hungary; a place I had never been. Travel points are good in this job.

Jose: Was the idea of a *Twilight Zone* for children appealing to you?

David: I remember being terrified by the follow-up show to *Twilight Zone*, which was called *Night Gallery*. Really freaked me out, especially the Roddy McDowell pilot episode. I was way too young to watch, and I remember calling my Mom in from the other room to shut off the TV. Ha. Just too freaked out. So, with *Dark* I got to return the favor to millions of kids. You're welcome.

Jose: Do you have fond memories of your first episode, the time-traveling high school thriller "The Tale of Locker 22"?

David: I came in late; second season. My first episode, I remember the production team was amazing at building great sets and we had an unusual back hidden hallway wing where Candy's locker was set way in the back under a stairwell or something. The other school stuff was shot at one of the many high schools in Montreal, but Candy's locker portion was a studio build just because so much happened around it.

Jose: Your second episode was particularly fun, "The Tale of the Dream Machine."

David: "Tale of the Dream Machine" had one of my favorite set pieces; the hidden stairwell that the boys fall thru to find the typewriter. It was built as kind of a half-set with cutaway stairs, and the dark cobweb-covered secret hideaway. One of the photos of the old author on the wall was series director of photography Karol Ike. Look for the beard.

Jose: Your third episode for the series, "The Tale of the Shiny Red Bicycle," is considered by most fans, and Jason Alisharan, one of the best episodes in the series.

David: So proud that this episode on one online survey got voted the scariest of the sixty-five original episodes. Had a great time shooting this show in the loch system outside of Montreal. Amazing the power of the rushing water down the canals, actually even more powerful and noisy than it appears on film in this episode. Just felt like this one had all the right elements to make a great episode; a troubled hero, nightmares, and a creepy ghost. Plus one of my favorite shots ever: the slow-motion shot of the bike falling away from the camera toward the thundering water. I'm very proud that I still own the original shiny red bicycle; D. J. and the crew gave it to me as a present when we wrapped. It's safely tucked away in Mom's garage.

Jose: "The Tale of Watcher's Woods," your fourth episode for the series, has some really great pop scare moments. What was it like shooting that one in what appeared to be the deep forest?

David: I just remember the entire show seemed to be a night shoot and we froze in pouring rain, and then got eaten by mosquitoes at a real camp for kids outside Montreal. Larry Lynn was the guest director of photography on this episode. He also shot "Dream Girl." And we went on to work together on *Breaker High* (1997). This was definitely one of the more physically challenging episodes. It was the first of two times (second was "Unfinished Painting") I got to work with then eleven-year-old Jewel Staite, who went on to *Serenity* (2005) and *Firefly* fame as Kaylee. I remember Tom Rack who played the tree monster was also then a contestant on Jeopardy and I think his episode aired while we were shooting so he was anxious to shed his tree suit and rush home to watch TV. The devil and head and tree bursting out from the ground was a challenging physical effect with the guys having to build a pit in the middle of the woods at night so the monster could rise out of it. Green-colored painted rats in a bucket was another fun memory. The three older ladies were sweethearts. I worked with Sheena Larkin again on *Black Swarm* (2007) years later. Two *Dark* stars appear in that. The bowling alley manager from "Dream Girl," Montreal actor Michel Perron, played the mayor of the doomed town.

Jose: Gordon Masten, who appeared in Season 6's "The Tale of the Gruesome Gourmets," was also in that one, but let's talk dolls, specifically your fifth episode, "The Tale of the Dollmaker"?

David: "Tale of the Dollmaker" was such a blast to make. What excited me about shooting the shows, aside from trying to make them as scary as possible, was the seamless combination between real locations and sets built in studios. Hopefully if we did our jobs right, it's hard to tell when we make the transition. Obviously the attic and hallways in the house were all built sets. And the transition thru the magic doorway to the outside was handled with green screen, intercut with actual location stuff. A bit scary because we really had the little girl and uncle that high up. The construction crew had to carefully remove the actual window at location and cameras were on cranes. Pretty dizzying view from the second floor, but the great old houses off the waterfront in Montreal were incredible to film. This is one of the episodes that I constantly hear about really freaking out viewers; especially little girls who found the dollhouse model quite creepy. Later-celebrated VJ, Amanda Walsh from Much Music, played the friend who turns into a doll.

Jose: "The Tale of the Dream Girl," your sixth time in the director's chair, is such a powerful episode, and it almost feels too good for what some might dismiss as a kid's show, but it's an example of the wonderful things that *AYAOTD?* did.

David: Probably my favorite episode, and legend has it that M. Night Shyamalan liked it too, and used it as the inspiration for *The Sixth Sense.* Great script by David Preston. I had fun shooting in the back secret areas with the pin machines at the bowling alley, the place no one gets to see. Fab Filippo and Andrea Nemeth had amazing chemistry. Fab is still acting, but sadly Andrea gave it up and now teaches criminology in Vancouver. Andrea's heart-breaking performance in the cemetery at the end always gets the tears flowing; incredible actress and she was fourteen at the time!

Jose: You got to switch gears and go full-creep with your seventh episode, "The Tale of the Quiet Librarian."

David: "Quiet Librarian" was shot in the Atwater Library, one of the oldest buildings in Montreal, which was about as creepy and dusty as it looks in the show. Leni Parker guest starred in a small part as the lady cop investigating the kids in the ending. She went on to play one of the lead Taelons, Da'an, in five seasons of Gene Roddenberry's *Earth: Final Conflict.*

Jose: You deal with time-traveling necklaces again with your eighth episode, "The Tale of Long Ago Locket."

David: "Long Ago Locket" was shot in a beautiful wooded area outside of Montreal. Exciting stuff. Got to work with galloping horses and charging minutemen armies firing real vintage muskets. We hired one of the local re-enactment groups to play the general's army. Will Friedle was lots of fun to work with, fresh off *Boy Meets World.* It was also my second outing with great Montreal actor Joel Gordon, who also played in "The Dream Machine" as the guy's friend who gets pushed into Blind Paul's gravesite.

Jose: Your tenth episode was "The tale of C7," which turned out to be your swansong.

David: My final episode of *Dark*. Best thing about this episode was I met my real-life girlfriend and a lifelong partner who plays the ghost Iris, Ontario actress Stephanie Bauder, who went on to star in *Night of the Demons III* (1997) and *No Surrender* (2011) opposite Mena Suvari. Stephanie today is a proud mom of three kids. We had a ton of fun shooting this episode at a bed and breakfast in the country estate in Quebec and it had a real old dock with a rowboat. Lots of use of tracking cameras in this to create the POV of the ghost approaching the house. Loved the wet footprints on the deck and all the false scares bumping into Mom. Colin Ferguson who played long-lost Tommy went on to a busy career in Hollywood. Real life brother and sister, Jesse and Tegan Moss, also had busy careers acting; Tegan just had a baby. Time flies.

Jose: My three favorite episodes of yours are "Shiny Red Bicycle," "Dream Girl," and "Dream Machine." Do you have a favorite episode?

David: I was really proud of "Shiny Red Bicycle." I thought it turned out to be quite frightening and creepy and it seems to be the episode I get asked about the most; especially the scene in the nurse's office, where Ricky suddenly appears in place of the nurse. I think that was made up on the day as an afterthought. Happy accidents. "Dream Girl" was just a magic combination of great actors and a really cool script, a beautiful cemetery set (check out all the names on tombstones) and an okay director; it all came together. And we were especially proud with it being able to influence Shyamalan to make one of my favorite suspense films ever with *The Sixth Sense*. I remember watching it and thinking in the theatre, while hiding behind popcorn, *Why does this movie seem so familiar?* I am very proud of *Dark's* connection to that movie. M. Night was apparently a huge *Dark* fan. My other favorite episode, largely for personal reasons, was "C7." I thought it had some incredible Hitchcock and John Carpenter elements in the way we shot it, and a beautiful ghost!

Jose: Did you have your choice of scripts or were they handed to you?

David: The myth of picking scripts when you're a workhorse director always amuses me. We never pick; we're assigned scripts. And I was very happy with the scripts given to me.

Jose: Did you ever direct any of the campfire sequences?

David: No. The campfire scenes were all shot independent of the series and all in one block because filling the stage with that many trees was too time-consuming to do every week and we needed that space and those stages for other swing sets throughout the season. The campfire scenes were all directed by D. J., Jacque Laberge (my first assistant), and Lorette LeBlanc (series script supervisor). They did an amazing job. *Dark* was shot in the same Montreal studio as *300* (2006) would be decades later.

Jose: Was there a style imposed upon you when it came to directorial choices, or were you left alone to make it the way you saw it?

David: I think D. J. and Ned Kandel and Bill Bonecutter trusted us to use our own imagination to come up with the scariest way to tell the stories. I was a big John Carpenter fan, so you can see some of *Halloween* (1978) in almost every episode I directed.

Jose: Does anyone, besides myself, bring up your history with *AYAOTD?* in your current work as a director?

David: I get asked about *Dark* almost every week. I've directed twenty-three movies and episodes for twenty-seven series, and *Dark* comes up all the time! Everybody has a favorite episode. Apparently we scared an entire generation of kids. The other one they almost always mention for some reason is *Sweet Valley High,* I directed four seasons in L.A., and *Breaker High* with Ryan Gosling. I directed the pilot episode and the first seven episodes in twenty-one days in 1996!

Jose: Now that *AYAOTD?* is the stuff of legends, what are you up to currently, and where can fans connect with you?

David: You name it, I've directed the genre. In 1996, I moved to Los Angeles and directed the Power Ranger sequel for 20th Century Fox. In Canada, you kind of had to do a bit of everything, so I've directed horror movies, tons of science fiction, *Stargate Atlantis* (2004), *Andromeda* (2002), tons of kids series—I think seven series for Nickelodeon—multi-cam live audience kids shows like *Mr. Young,* and most recently *Stanley Dynamic* and *Max & Shred.* I directed three monster movies for the SYFY Channel. I recently directed the SYFY Channel post-apocalyptic *Mutant World* (2014) with Kim Coates and Ashanti. Lately it's been mostly romantic comedies and Christmas movies for Lifetime and Hallmark. My most recent movie is *Unleashing Mr. Darcy* (2016), a modern take on *Pride & Prejudice* with dog shows, which got 3 million viewers, and generated over 47 million hits on Twitter; that was fun. I'm on YouTube, too. Follow me on Twitter @DirectedByDW and director's reels, videos and photos are on my website at www.DavidWinning.com.

Jose: Any last words to the legion of *Dark* followers with phobias that you helped shape?

David: Thanks to all the fans for being so loyal to *Dark.* We thought it was just a tiny little, low budget after-school special made with lots of love in the early 1990s. Never realized it would have such a dedicated following.

CLOSING CAMPFIRE: READYING THE RED BUCKET

Now, it's time for me to say "the end," and douse the campfire. I've got the familiar red bucket of water sitting next to me, waiting to pour out and bathe the fire into steam. But before I do that, before we stand and wander off to our normal lives back somewhere on the other side of the woods, let's do a bit of imagining.

Let's be the storytellers now, you and I.

Let's assume the world of *AYAOTD?* went on without us so we can end it like a tale, shall we? Are you with me?

Okay here goes: Gary graduated college with a Master's Degree in English and went on to become a famous horror novelist, who to this day competes with Stephen King for the top spot. His head is kept from swelling by his lovely wife of many years, Sam, who became a successful children's book author. They have two kids and a dog named Sardo.

Tucker went on to run a successful haunted house business with his pals Andy and Stig; they named their clown-themed haunt "Laughing in the Dark," as suggested by their friend, Betty Ann. Most of their rooms are patterned after the creepy critters from the Midnight Society tales of old. Besides being the man in charge of the gore for the sets, Stig is their most dedicated and gung-ho scare-actor.

Betty Ann went on to become a teacher, and her favorite time of the year is Halloween, where she initiates her entire class into the Midnight Society by having them each write their own spooky tale. She keeps the actual red water bucket by her desk as a tiny trashcan, and every time she looks at she smiles.

Frank went on to open a bar and grill and he named it "The Campfire." The most popular drink on the menu is the Vink, and the least popular food item is the wild boar sandwich. One time, a man that resembled Doctor Vink walked in to the establishment, gave a dazed Frank a handshake, and walked back out into the night. Coincidentally, Frank's wife's maiden name was Vink, that's what brought them together initially.

David and Kristen, having reconnected after their families moved away, married and now have three boys; Kristen is a photographer, in the vein of Ansel Adams, and David is an architect, who was responsible for designing the floor plans for the "Laughing in the Dark" haunted attraction.

Kiki went on to play pro basketball, until she damaged her left knee, which ruined her career. She met a sick little girl in the hospital where she was convalescing that helped her get over her depression, and she decided to become a doctor and help kids just like her. To this day, Kiki has helped hundreds of kids, and every Halloween her friend Betty Ann comes to the hospital to help her lead a big Midnight Society meeting for the kids too sick to go trick or treating.

Eric never forgot his brief time in the Midnight Society, or his friends, and has kept in touch throughout the years. He became a playwright, and his most popular play is called "Jake and the Leprechaun," which he dedicated to his pop pop.

Quinn was a semi-pro boxer for a while, until he met and married his wife, and she convinced him to take a less-damaging career path. He became the owner and operator of her family's movie theater. During October the theater shows horror movies exclusively, which culminates in a 24-hour marathon on Halloween. Throughout the rest of the year it shows old films, but every Saturday at midnight there is a new horror movie on display. It's called "Midnight Madness," and Frank hosts it.

Vange went on to a successful career as a stand-up comedienne, and starred in her own sitcom about the ups and downs of her life called, "It's Vange." The fan favorite episode is "The Tale of the Tale," where her movie-star pal Megan guest stars as a long-lost friend who helps Vange come up with a really scary story to freak out her apartment roommates on Halloween.

Megan went to Hollywood and got famous, but she hated being away from her friends and that brought her back home, where she reconnected with Andy. They were married, had twin girls, and are currently working on a screenplay for a Midnight Society movie that the entire gang hopes to fund out of their own pockets.

To this day, the entire gang gets together at least once a year for dinner, drinks, and to share a few stories, of course.

Let's imagine further, shall we? Let's go one level deeper into the world, beyond the Midnight Society, and on into the palpitating aliveness of their tales and the various odd characters that populate them. What happened to them, you ask?

Sardo managed to break out of the alternate-dimension void he found himself in during the end of "Super Specs," and brought with him knowledge of the universe that was unparalleled. It allowed him to foresee the future, and with that gift he played the stock market and was able to open Magic Mansion franchises that stretched from North America to Europe. He has become an icon now and has a one-man show in Vegas called, "Sardo, Accent on the Magic."

Belinda the bookish babysitter, who is one of my favorites, went on to found a library where to this day she is able to physically show hundreds of kids the power imagination has in the hands of the right words.

Zeebo the clown continues to spook kids in that dark midway in the middle of nowhere. The Carny is the only one who knows Zeebo is more than just a pneumatic prop. The events that occurred to Josh long ago have become the stuff of legends, and no one has dared mess with Zeebo's nose again.

The Crimson Clown sits in an antique store, possibly the one nearest to you, waiting for some bratty kid to teach a lesson to.

The Ghastly Grinner continues to plan his escape into the real world, but Ethan's comics, which have continued in popularity, are keeping the blue and yellow demon jester safely at bay. Ethan and Hooper got married, but she kept the Picalarro so as not to lose her feminine identity.

The Chameleons were close to world domination, until one of them caught a human cold and once it spread through the group, they were stopped dead in their tracks, literally.

The Lurker doesn't hide in the sewers anymore. Thanks to Tara's friendship, he was able to come out into the open and get the surgery he needed to fix his deformed hands. He is always her guest of honor whenever she performs at a concert.

Andy Carr used his Dark Music powers to not only teach his bratty sister a good, solid lesson, but it got him out of chores. He went on to teach every bully in his school a lesson, until he realized the darkness would consume him, and he stopped venturing into the basement. A few years later, he returned and the music conjured nothing; the dark thing in the basement had left, or died of loneliness.

Mr. Olsen still owns the toy store and the pinball machine, which only he plays, and only after business hours, to watch poor Ross go through the same challenges over and over again to rescue the princess.

The Silent Servant scarecrow has helped renovate five farms, and is currently enjoying the place of honor inside a fancy pantsy barn. He has not killed anyone. And Vink? Dear, sweet, bearded curmudgeonly Vink? After he and Sardo departed that day when the Cutter's Treasure business had been dealt with, he set sail for parts unknown. No one has heard from him in years. They say Vink lurks in the woods, approaching campfires and asking for dangerous soup or wild boar anything. They say he's making more living movies or cooking up devilish riddles or cutting hair somewhere out in the deepest reaches of Romania. Or was it Timbuktu? They say these things, but no one knows. He has vanished, and maybe that's the best way for a man like Vink to depart.

Ok, I'm ready now.

It's getting late. The chill is creeping in despite the warmth of our campfire. I suppose it's time to say goodbye and return to the normal world. Before you go, turn to the last page and you'll find that special surprise I mentioned at the beginning. Odds are you peeked already, but if you haven't then it's doubly earned. You are now an official member of the Midnight Society, my friend. You'll notice D. J. MacHale, the Chairman of the Campfire, has signed the certificate. It has also been countersigned by Ross Hull, who played Gary one last time, to make it extra-official for you. Feel free to tear that out and frame it, it's as good as gold.

Welcome to the club.

You can go on without me, I'm going to sit here and watch the campfire smoke away into nothing. I'm going to sit here and listen to the wind whisper through the brittle branches as the night stretches its bones. There are red zombies and silver sights and dark music running through my head still. I'll go home when it gets too cold, and return to the regular world, but not for a while.

Not yet.

I now declare this meeting of the Midnight Society . . . closed.

-Jose Prendes, February 13, 2016

Long live the Midnight Society! Photo courtesy of Paul Doyle, Jr.

APPENDIX A

Storyteller Tally

Tucker (13)

Season Three:

1) "The Tale of the Midnight Ride"

2) "The Tale of the Phone Police"

3) "The Tale of the Guardian's Curse"

Season Four:

4) "The Tale of the Water Demons"

5) "The Tale of the Fire Ghost"

Season Five:

6) "The Tale of Prisoners Past"

7) "The Tale of the Manaha"

Season Six:

8) "The Tale of the Forever Game"

9) "The Tale of Jake the Snake"

10) "The Tale of Oblivion"

11) "The Tale of Bigfoot Ridge"

Season Seven:

12) "The Tale of the Time Trap"

13) "The Tale of the Laser Maze"

Gary (12)

Season One:

1) "The Tale of the Super Specs"

2) "The Tale of the Pinball Wizard"

Season Two:

3) "The Tale of the Magician's Assistant"

Season Three:

4) "The Tale of the Carved Stone"

5) "The Tale of the Crimson Clown"

Season Four:

6) "The Tale of Cutter's Treasure Part 1"

7) "The Tale of Cutter's Treasure Part 2"

8) "The Tale of the Renegade Virus"

9) "The Tale of the Unfinished Painting"

Season Five:

10) "The Tale of a Door Unlocked"

11) "The Tale of Badge"

Season Seven:

12) "The Tale of the Silver Sight" (technically)

Betty Ann (12)

Season One:

1) "The Tale of Laughing in the Dark"

2) "The Tale of the Nightly Neighbors"

3) "The Tale of the Sorcerer's Apprentice"

Season Two:

4) "The Tale of the Thirteenth Floor"

5) "The Tale of the Whispering Walls"

Season Three:

6) "The Tale of the Dollmaker"

7) "The Tale of the Bookish Babysitter"

8) "The Tale of the Curious Camera"

Season Four:

9) "The Tale of the Silent Servant"

10) "The Tale of the Ghastly Grinner"

Season Five:

11) "The Tale of the Mystical Mirror"

12) "The Tale of the Chameleons"

Kiki (10)

Season One:
1) "The Tale of the Captured Souls"

Season Two:
2) "The Tale of the Dream Machine" (as told by Gary, due to laryngitis)

3) "The Tale of Old Man Corcoran"

Season Three:
4) "The Tale of Apartment 214"

5) "The Tale of the Quicksilver"

Season Four:
6) "The Tale of the Quiet Librarian"

7) "The Tale of the Closet Keepers"

Season Five:
8) "The Tale of the Jagged Sign"

9) "The Tale of the Unexpected Visitor"

10) "The Tale of the Vacant Lot

Frank (7)

Season One:
1) "The Tale of the Phantom Cab"

Season Two:

2) "The Tale of the Midnight Madness"

3) "The Tale of the Full Moon"

Season Three:

4) "The Tale of the Dangerous Soup"

Season Four:

5) "The Tale of Cutter's Treasure Pt.1"

6) "The Tale of Cutter's Treasure Pt.2"

7) "The Tale of Train Magic"

Kristen (5)

Season One:

1) "The Tale of the Hungry Hound"

2) "The Tale of the Prom Queen"

Season Two:

3) "The Tale of the Final Wish"

4) "The Tale of Locker 22"

5) "The Tale of the Frozen Ghost"

David (5)

Season One:

1) "The Tale of the Lonely Ghost"

2) "The Tale of the Twisted Claw"

Season Two:

3) "The Tale of the Dark Dragon"

4) "The Tale of the Shiny Red Bicycle"

5) "The Tale of the Hatching"

Megan (5)

Season Six:

1) "The Tale of the Gruesome Gourmets"

2) "The Tale of the Walking Shadow"

3) "The Tale of the Secret Admirer"

Season Seven:

4) "The Tale of the Lunar Locusts"

5) The Tale of the Stone Maiden"

Andy (4)

Season Six:

1) "The Tale of the Misfortune Cookie"

2) "The Tale of the Hunted"

Season Seven:

3) "The Tale of the Photo Finish"

4) "The Tale of the Last Dance"

Vange (4)

Season Six:

1) "The Tale of the Zombie Dice"

2) "The Tale of the Virtual Pets"

Season Seven:

3) "The Tale of Many Faces"

4) "The Tale of the Night Nurse"

Quinn (4)

Season Six:

1) "The Tale of Vampire Town"

2) "The Tale of the Wisdom Glass"

Season Seven:

3) "The Tale of Highway 13"

4) "The Tale of Reanimator"

Eric (2)

Season One:

1) "The Tale of Jake and the Leprechaun"

2) "The Tale of the Dark Music"

Stig (2)

Season Five:

1) "The Tale of the Dead Man's Float"

2) "The Tale of Station 109.1"

Doctor Vink Appearances (5)

Season One:

1) "The Tale of the Phantom Cab"

Season Two:

2) "The Tale of the Midnight Madness"

Season Three:

3) The Tale of the Dangerous Soup

Season Four:

4) The Tale of Cutter's Treasure Part 1

5) The Tale of Cutter's Treasure Part 2

Sardo Appearances (8)

Season One:

1) "The Tale of the Super Specs"

Season Two:

2) "The Tale of the Dark Dragon"

Season Three:

3) "The Tale of the Carved Stone"

Season Four:

4) "The Tale of Cutter's Treasure Part 1"

5) "The Tale of Cutter's Treasure Part 2"

Season Five:

6) "The Tale of a Door Unlocked"

Season Six:

7) "The Tale of Oblivion"

Season Seven:

8) "The Tale of the Time Trap"

APPENDIX B

The Novels

- *The Tale of the Sinister Statues* by John Peel

- *The Tale of Cutter's Treasure* adaptation by David L. Seidman

- *The Tale of the Restless House* by John Peel

- *The Tale of the Nightly Neighbors* adaptation by Kathleen Derby & D. J. MacHale

- *The Tale of the Secret Mirror* by Brad and Barbara Strickland

- *The Tale of the Phantom School Bus* by Brad Strickland

- *The Tale of the Ghost Riders* by John Vornholt

- *The Tale of the Deadly Diary* by Brad and Barbara Strickland

- *The Tale of the Virtual Nightmare* by Ted Pedersen

- *The Tale of the Curious Cat* by Diana G. Gallagher

- *The Tale of the Zero Hero* by John Peel

- *The Tale of the Shimmering Shell* by David Cody Weiss & Bobbi J.G Weiss

- *The Tale of the Three Wishes* by John Peel

- *The Tale of the Campfire Vampires* by Clayton Emery

- *The Tale of the Bad-Tempered Ghost* by V.E. Mitchell

- *The Tale of the Souvenir Shop* by Alice Eve Cohen

- *The Tale of the Ghost Cruise* by David Cody Weiss & Bobbi J.G Weiss

- *The Tale of the Pulsating Gate* by Diana G. Gallagher

- *The Tale of the Stalking Shadow* by David Cody Weiss & Bobbi J.G Weiss

- *The Tale of the Egyptian Mummies* by Mark Mitchell

- *The Tale of the Terrible Toys* by Richard Lee Byers

- *The Tale of the Mogul Monster* by David Cody Weiss & Bobbi J.G Weiss

- *The Tale of the Horrifying Hockey Team* by K.S. Rodriguez

The Games

- *Are You Afraid of the Dark? The Game:* a board game by Cardinal Industries. Ages 8 and up. 2-4 players. From the description on the back: "Are you ready to be initiated into the Midnight Society? You and your friends will be sent on a journey through the scariest places ever imagined. If you can overcome all of the obstacles, gain points in categories such as knowledge, strength, courage, (and of course luck!) and be the first one back to the campfire you too will be a member of the Midnight Society. Beware: you'll have to take some chances, go through secret passages, and most of all, avoid The Pit. Good luck! You're going to need it!"

- *The Tale of Orpheo's Curse*: a video game by Viacom New Media that places you in the shoes of an initiate member into the Midnight Society. Gary has kicked off a story, and it's your job to finish "telling" it by playing the game. This game lets you interact, somewhat, with the cast of *Are You Afraid of the Dark?*, and according to the timing and the cast present

I would put this somewhere between the Season 3 or Season 4 eras. The prize at the end is the gang deliberates and inducts you into the Midnight Society by a show of thumbs up!

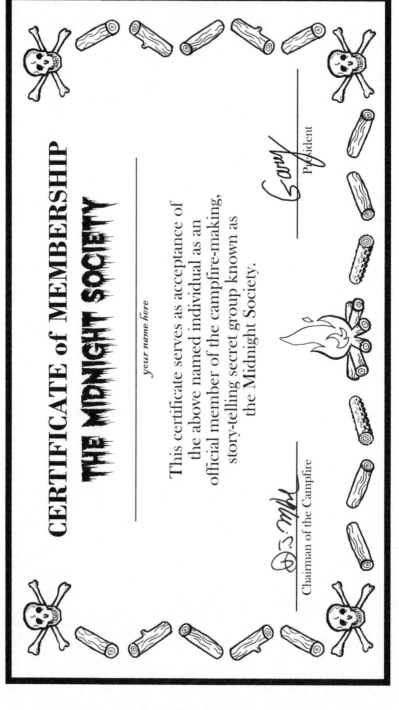

CERTIFICATE of MEMBERSHIP
THE MIDNIGHT SOCIETY

your name here

This certificate serves as acceptance of the above named individual as an official member of the campfire-making, story-telling secret group known as the Midnight Society.

President

Chairman of the Campfire

Printed in Great Britain
by Amazon

45367458R10185